DROVE ROADS
OF
NORTHUMBERLAND

Drove Roads of Northumberland

Ian Roberts, Richard Carlton & Alan Rushworth

The History Press

First published 2010

The History Press
The Mill, Brimscombe Port
Stroud, Gloucestershire, GL5 2QG
www.thehistorypress.co.uk

British Library Cataloguing in Publication Data.
A catalogue record for this book is available from the British Library.

ISBN 978 0 7524 4230 3

Typesetting and origination by The History Press
Printed and bound in Great Britain by
Marston Book Services Limited, Didcot

Contents

	Acknowledgements	6
	Illustrations	7
1	Introduction	9
2	Sources of Evidence	12
3	Pastoralism and Droving Before 1700	20
4	Droving in Northumberland from the Eighteenth to the Twentieth Century	53
5	Droving in the Twentieth Century: Local Events and Personal Recollections	81
6	What to See and Do: Remains of Droving	89
7	Conclusions and Topics for Further Research	131
	Appendix 1: Inquisitions Post Mortem relating to the Redesdale Liberty	135
	Appendix 2: The Newminster Charters relating to Kidland	142
	Appendix 3: Northumberland Fairs	145
	Appendix 4: Selected Stock Returns for Five Northumberland Parishes	149
	Appendix 5: The Oral History Project – Background Information	151
	Appendix 6: Source Material in the Northumberland County Record Office	152
	Bibliography	154

Acknowledgements

This publication grew out of a report completed by the authors for Northumberland National Park Authority in 2005 as part of its Drover's Project. The text has been substantially enhanced by the authors for the present publication, particularly through the use of oral testimony and fieldwork along many of the droveways mentioned in the text. Special thanks are offered to all those individuals who provided oral testimony for Chapter Four, notably Laurence Dagg, James Johnson, W. (Bill) Robson and W.A. (Willie) Robson. The following also kindly provided noteworthy oral information: Mrs D. Bell, W. Bolton, W. Brown, A. Cowen, G. Fenton, L.I. Hedley, A.D. McCracken, H. Robinson and Mrs M. Walton.

Mr G.W.M. Sewell provided helpful information regarding the use of the railways for the movement of livestock, whilst Tim Gates supplied information concerning the possible prehistoric origins of some of the cross-dykes in the Cheviots and Peter Ryder contributed a description of buildings at Elsdon. The assistance of the staff at Northumberland Record Office, in particular Keith Gilroy, in identifying and securing permission to reproduce cartographic sources and other illustrative material, is gratefully acknowledged.

Except where stated, the photographs used here were taken by Richard Carlton, who also prepared the illustrations, assisted by Marc Johnstone, who provided the base map for the map of Northumberland National Park on page 10, and Claire MacRae, who prepared the maps of settlement patterns in Upper North Tynedale on pages 31 and 44 and the Nent Valley drove routes on page 48, and also tried to ensure that the illustrations were correctly placed in the text.

Illustrations

The frontispiece and illustrations on page 54 are reproduced by kind permission of the Regional Resource Centre, Beamish. The illustration on page 10, a plan of drove roads and cross-dykes in the Otterburn training area, is re-drawn from *Fifty Centuries of Peace and War: An Archaeological Survey of the Otterburn Training Area* (Charlton, 1996), by kind permission of the author, Beryl Charlton, and the Defence Estates Otterburn Training Area.

The illustrations on pages 15, 16, 17, 53, 57 (top), 58, 59, 60 (top) and 74 (left), (county maps by Speed, Armstrong, Horsley & Kay, Fryer and Greenwood, the Bellingham Fairground Plan, Haltwhistle Fair Notice, East and West Woodburn Inclosure maps and Elsdon Tithe and Ordnance Survey plans), are reproduced from originals with the kind permission of Northumberland Record Office.

The illustrations on pages 31 and 44 (re-drawn maps showing settlement in North Tyndale in the late thirteenth century and the sixteenth century), were published in their original form in *Archaeologia Aeliana* (Harbottle & Newman, 1973), and are included here courtesy of the author, Barbara Harbottle, and the Society of Antiquaries of Newcastle upon Tyne.

Sir Edmund Swinburne's sketch of the old bridge at East Woodburn (front cover and reproduced on page 124) is also produced courtesy of the Society of Antiquaries of Newcastle upon Tyne.

The illustration on page 33 (a plan of shielings at White Kielder) first appeared in *Upper North Tynedale: A Northumbrian Valley and its People* (Charlton, 1987), and is included here courtesy of the author, Beryl Charlton, and Northumbrian Water.

The illustrations on page 58 (left), an Elsdon Inclosure Plan of 1731, pages 14 and 61 (Alnham Estate maps from 1619 and 1775) are reproduced courtesy of the collection of the Duke of Northumberland. The illustrations on pages 79 and 99 (top) appear courtesy of Joan Forster of Stannersburn.

The illustration on page 74 (right), *The Last Mart at Bellingham* (© Simon Fraser), a view of the last lamb sale at Bellingham Mart in September 2004, is reproduced by kind permission of the Tarset Archive Group (TAG).

Bellingham Heritage Centre kindly granted permission to reproduce Collier's photographs of sheep droving in and around Bellingham on page 77.

The illustration on page 160, a reproduction of a watercolour by Constance Mangone, is used by permission of Mr Walter Brown of Langleeford.

Other illustrations were supplied by the authors and by The Archaeological Practice Ltd, Newcastle upon Tyne.

Illustration of cattle and drover from Knight's Pictorial Museum of Animated Nature.

ONE
INTRODUCTION

This book began life as a study of the historical and archaeological background to cattle-droving activities in the area that is now the Northumberland National Park. The Archaeological Practice Ltd was commissioned to undertake this study by the National Park Authority as part of a wider project – The Drover's Project – funded by the Heritage Lottery Fund, English Nature, the Countryside Agency and the National Trust, to highlight the value of native breeds of cattle in the management of conservation sites and to research the culture and traditions associated with such cattle. Further research since the completion of the National Park project has permitted the authors to expand the study into a book detailing droving activities throughout the whole of the county, as well as to expand aspects of the study dealing with the twentieth century.

The term 'droving', in its most specific and commonly accepted sense, denotes the practice of moving cattle over very great distances, from the Scottish Highlands and Islands or Galloway and even Ireland, to the growing towns of England as far south as London and adjoining counties. This movement reached its zenith between the late seventeenth and mid-nineteenth century. More generally, however, droving might be defined as any practice which involved the driving of livestock over significant distances. Droving of this kind has been integral to pastoralist activity in the Northumbrian uplands for at least a millennium, and probably much longer. It was, for example, an integral component of various kinds of seasonal transhumance and other agricultural customs pursued by communities in the Northumbrian uplands during the medieval and early modern periods.

Several different ways of organising pastoralist activity are recorded in the Northumbrian uplands during the medieval period. The best known of these is the type of seasonal transhumance known as 'shieling' or 'summering', whereby entire communities moved up onto the high pastures in April and returned to their wintersteeds in the valleys during August. Less well investigated, in Northumberland at any rate, are the demesne farming systems that were adopted by both feudal lords and monastic institutions on their upland estates, which involved the establishment of directly managed cattle farms (vaccaries) and sheep farms (bercaries). The heyday of this kind of demesne farming lasted up until the mid-fourteenth century.

Thereafter, the fall in population levels and other socio-economic changes resulting from the Black Death rendered such direct seigniorial stock management less and less economic. Instead, landowners predominantly rented out the upland pastures to their manorial tenants for use as summering grounds during the late medieval and early modern periods. Hence, seasonal transhumance was even more prevalent during these centuries, and only finally ceased in the mid- to late seventeenth century as permanent settlement extended throughout the upper dales. Cattle were the most important livestock for farmers residing in upland dales such as Redesdale and North Tynedale during the sixteenth and seventeenth centuries. Although the role of sheep was not negligible, cattle were distributed more widely, the overall picture being one of numerous small herds, typically under twenty head of cattle.

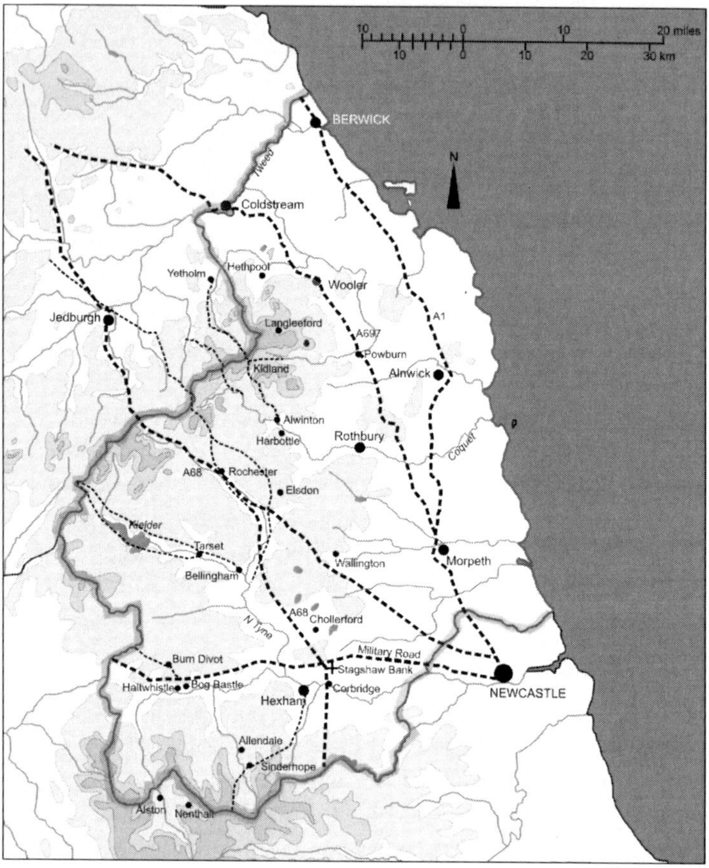

Left: Map of Northumberlan National Park, some of its principal settlements and reli features.

Right: Plan showing drove roads and cross-dykes in the Otterburn training area (reproduced from Charlton 1996, 122, Map 26). Sites particularly relevant to this study are identified in the text.

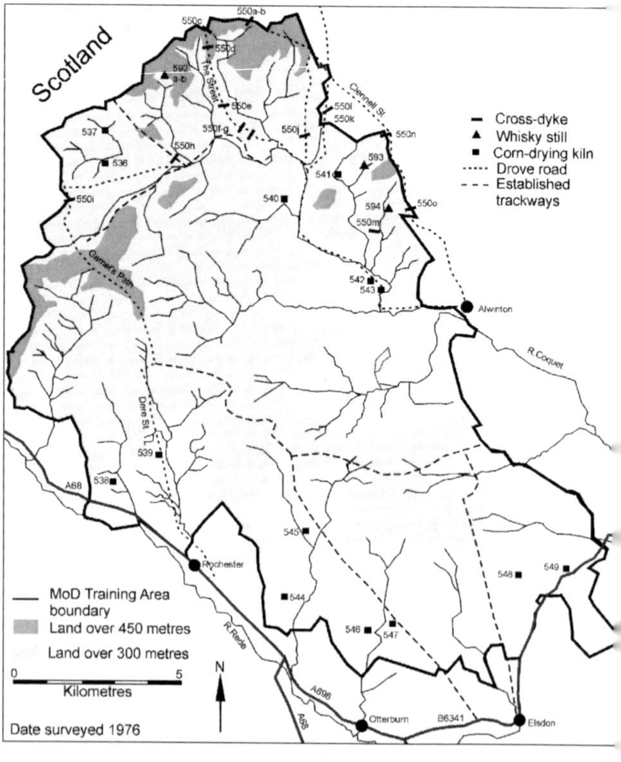

Records suggest the origins of the long-distance cattle droving trade from Scotland to England stretch back to the late medieval period, if not earlier. However, it was only after Anglo-Scottish economic relations had been placed on a permanently stable and peaceful footing, at the beginning of the eighteenth century, that the droving trade could fully develop to meet the growing demand for meat from the expanding urban centres of England, most notably London itself. As a result of this growth, by the end of the eighteenth century, 100,000 cattle were being driven south across the Border each year.

Considerable work has been focussed on the history of this long-distance droving in England, Scotland and Wales, notably by Bonser (1970), Haldane (1971) and Moore-Collyer (2002), but in contrast, relatively little research into the droving of cattle and other livestock in Northumberland has hitherto been undertaken. The research for this book has encompassed all aspects of droving in order to provide a broad overview of the part played by this distinctive practice in the development of traditional farming systems within Northumberland. The authors are only too well aware that many aspects have only been briefly touched upon, and that many more should be pursued further. There is a wealth of available data, and much distinguished scholarship in this – and related – fields, which can be drawn upon. A list of possible research topics is included in Chapter Six.

A multiplicity of routes through the Northumbrian hills was accessible as droveways for this traffic. The pattern of usage probably shifted significantly over time as the progress of turnpiking and enclosure restricted movement and access to pasture and increased the costs of droving along some of the routes. Particularly important were the routes down the North Tyne Valley and the Great Drift Road, which ran along the Coquet/Rede watershed from the border at Brownhart Law, via Featherwood and Dudlees to Elsdon, whence it headed south to Stagshaw Bank. The crucial hubs in the network were annual fairs held at places like Elsdon, Haltwhistle, Newcastle and, most important of all, Stagshaw Bank north of Corbridge, where all manner of livestock exchange might have taken place. From the end of the eighteenth century, sheep assumed greater prominence in the droving trade. This was also reflected in changes in the local economy, as landowners amalgamated several holdings to form larger, more viable tenancies, resulting in the creation of huge sheep farms in Redesdale, North Tynedale and Upper Coquetdale.

By the mid-nineteenth century, long-distance cross-border droving was being supplanted by the growth of the railways, which provided a more economic service and delivered livestock to their destination in better condition, whilst the historic fairs were gradually replaced by auction marts located beside railway stations. The drovers now became intermediaries between railhead, auction mart and fair, little diminished in numbers but employed in very different patterns of work, and, increasingly, in an urban rather than a rural setting. Droving still occurred in the countryside, mainly from farm to railhead, but this was carried out by the farmers, their families and employees, not by professional drovers.

From the 1920s or 1930s, road haulage gradually began to replace rail transport, although the latter remained important right up until the closure of Northumberland's rural branch lines to freight traffic in the 1950s and 1960s. The motor lorry, with its great flexibility, finally put an end to droving over all but the very shortest distances, and even this aspect of stock movement has been abandoned in the face of new Department for the Environment, Food and Rural Affairs (Defra) regulations introduced since the last outbreak of foot-and-mouth disease in 2001.

TWO
Sources of Evidence

A wide range of source material can be used in studying the history and development of droving. Relevant modern, early modern and medieval documentation includes farm account books, auction mart records, turnpike trust records, regional newspaper archives, parish burial records, records of the Northumberland Quarter Sessions, sixteenth- and seventeenth-century Border surveys and other contemporary official correspondence, ecclesiastical chartularies and Inquisitions Post Mortem. Several categories of cartographic and pictorial material – maps, sketches and photographs – can also prove highly informative. The surviving physical remains of droving – tracks and holloways, inns, water troughs, fairgrounds and the like – shed further light, whether examined on the ground or in aerial photographs, and this tangible evidence can be supplemented by the oral testimonies of the last individuals to actually engage in the practice during the mid-twentieth century.

Documentary Archives

Accessible regional archives, libraries and record offices were consulted for documentary material relevant to droving, including the following:

- Northumberland County Record Office (NCRO)
- Museum of Antiquities Record Room, University of Newcastle upon Tyne (MA)
- Local newspaper archives
- Newcastle Central Library Local Studies Section (NCL)
- Palace Green Library, University of Durham

In particular, the authors liaised with the staff of Northumberland Record Office to provide an assessment of the full range of data relating to droving held there.

Pictorial representations

The study also focussed on potential sources of pictorial representations – prints, sketches and paintings, and early photographs – notably those held at Northumberland Record Collections at Woodhorn, near Ashington, and at the Heritage Centre in Bellingham.

Published Syntheses and Published Collections of Sources

Very little detailed research has been devoted specifically to the subject of droving in Northumberland – essentially just a single short article by Cowper (1970) – although more extensive work has been conducted in Scotland and Wales which may provide relevant comparative data (see, for example, Haldane, 1971, and Moore-Colyer, 2002). Some information regarding droveways, fairs, inns and other ancillary features which played a part in the practice of droving may be gleaned from the relevant volumes of the *Northumberland County History* (XI, XIV and XV), John Hodgson's *History of Northumberland* (1827; 1840), and from David Dippie Dixon's studies of Whittingham Vale and Upper Coquetdale (1895; 1903).

Charlton and Day have studied some of the drove roads and associated cross-dykes and waymarker crosses in Upper Coquetdale and Redesdale as part of an archaeological survey of the Otterburn Training Area (Charlton & Day, 1979; Charlton, 1996). The detailed documentary surveys of High Rochester (Rushworth, 1994) and Harbottle (Rushworth & Carlton, 1998), completed for Northumberland National Park Authority (NNPA) in recent years contain analysis of, respectively, the role of Dere Street/Gamelspath as a drove road and Newminster Abbey's acquisition of the extensive Kidland pastures in Upper Coquetdale, which must have involved seasonal droving from lowland grange to upland pasture. The NNPA Historic Village Atlas Project also includes some discussion of the impact of droving traffic on individual villages in the National Park, for example Elsdon and Great Tosson.

In addition, of use, particularly with regard to the earlier forms of droving such as shielding, agistment and monastic droving, are the important published collections of medieval and early modern documentary sources. These have appeared either in collections, such as the Calendarium Inquistionum Post Mortem produced by the Public Record Office and the volumes of the Surtees Society, or incorporated in works such as Hodgson's *History of Northumberland* (II.I and III.I–III) and the *Northumberland County History*. The following were considered to merit particular scrutiny:

- Chartulary of Newminster Abbey (Surtees Society)
- Calendars of Inquisitions Post Mortem (PRO)
- 1604 Border Survey
- 1618 Redesdale Survey

The 1604 and 1618 surveys, for example, in combination provide very detailed information on contemporary settlement patterns in the upland valleys, with the names of the individual customary Border tenants, plus – in the case of Redesdale – the names of the tenants occupying each of the moorland summering grounds.

Archaeological Site Data

The Northumberland County Historic Environment Record was consulted for information relating to archaeological sites associated with droving such as droveways, cross-dykes and cross-socket stones. The most useful and comprehensive discussion of these structures currently available is contained in the reports on the archaeological survey work in the Otterburn Training Area, directed by Beryl Charlton and John Day (Charlton & Day, 1979, 225–9; Charlton, 1996, 122, 125–30).

The cross-dykes in particular are intriguing and, although catalogued as a single group, may have served several different functions. Some may have been intended to channel and guide herds of droving cattle on the Cheviot ridges, whilst others appear to have been designed to hinder the passage of livestock and may have been intended to impede the retreat of Scottish reivers with cattle they had driven off farms in Coquetdale or Redesdale. Two dykes on Windy Gyle (at NT 850153 and NT 851152; Charlton, 1996, nos 550a–b) may be interpreted in this way. Other sites of this type may have served yet another function,

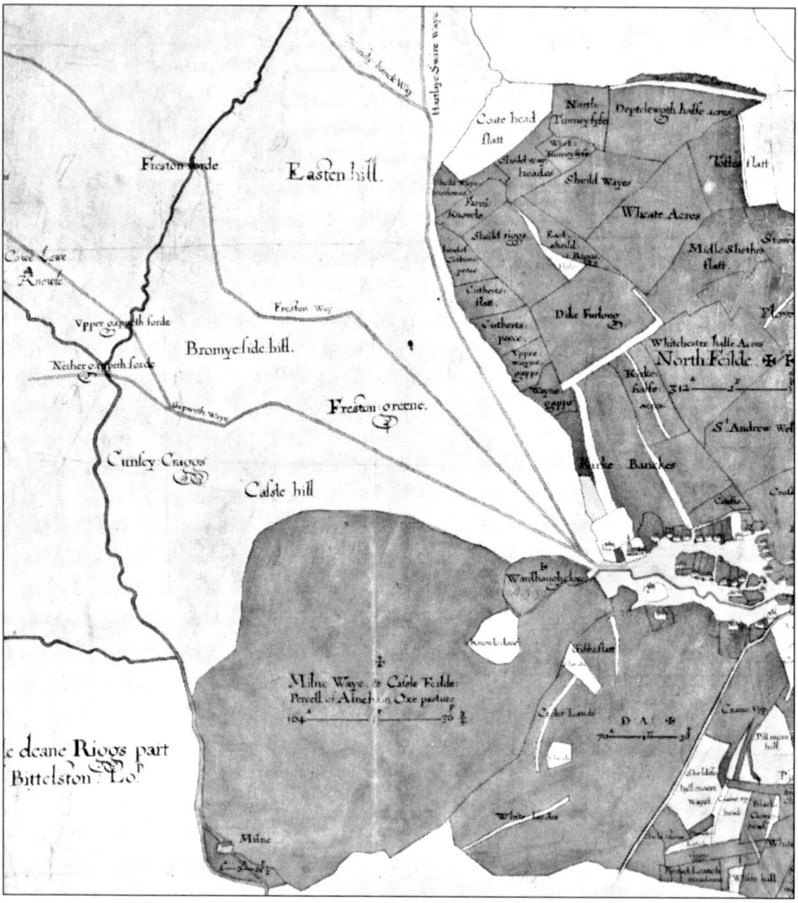

Trackways shown diverging out onto the common waste at the west end of Alnham Village, on Robert Norton's map of the manor of Alnham, 1619 (Aln Cas O.II.I.I NE).

as boundary-dykes. Thus, the large linear earthwork located beside Clennell Street on Wholehope (NT 903094; Charlton, 1996, no.5500), is probably to be identified with the *fossatum* which the monks of Newminster made as a boundary between themselves and Thomas de Clenill.

The cross-socket stones, known as the Golden Pots (NT 805072, NT 812063; Charlton 1996, 129–30, nos 551–2), are probably also medieval in date, and most likely originally belonged to waymarking crosses distributed along the ill-defined moorland course of Gamelspeth (cf. Honeyman, 1927).

Aerial Photographic Coverage

A sample of the locally accessible air photographic coverage of known droveways has also been examined in conjunction with the historic map evidence. This includes photographs held by Northumberland National Park Authority, the Northumberland County Historic Environment Record and the Museum of Antiquities at the University of Newcastle upon Tyne.

Oral History

A number of individuals who participated in droving livestock to railheads in the 1930s are still living in the National Park. A small oral history project to record their recollections of this final phase in droving history was undertaken and forms part of Chapter Five.

Historic Maps

Relevant historic maps and plans, including the successive county maps produced from the mid-eighteenth century onwards (e.g. Horsley & Cay, 1753; Armstrong, 1769; Fryer, 1820 and Greenwood, 1828), Tithe and Inclosure maps, the Ordnance Survey series plus detailed privately commissioned estate maps of the seventeenth to nineteenth centuries, have all proved useful in researching droveways. The Tithe and Inclosure maps, for example, generally provide a clear indication of the limit of enclosed ground (as does Greenwood's county map of 1827/28 more extensively), both pre- and post-commons enclosure, which was an important constraint on the possible routes which the Highland drovers could take.

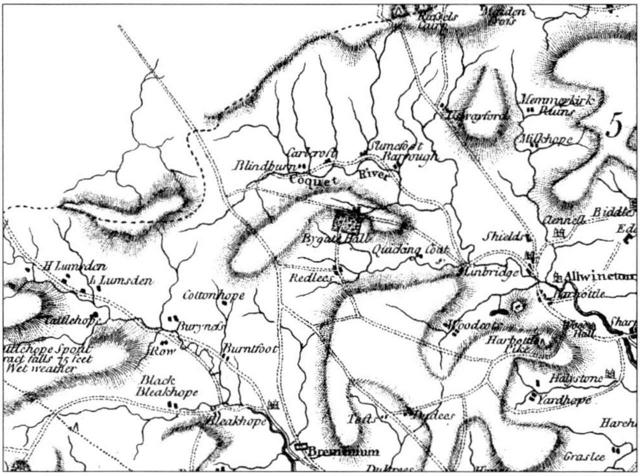

Left: The cross-border routes around the headwaters of the Rede and Coquet as shown on Cary's Map of Northumberland, 1789.

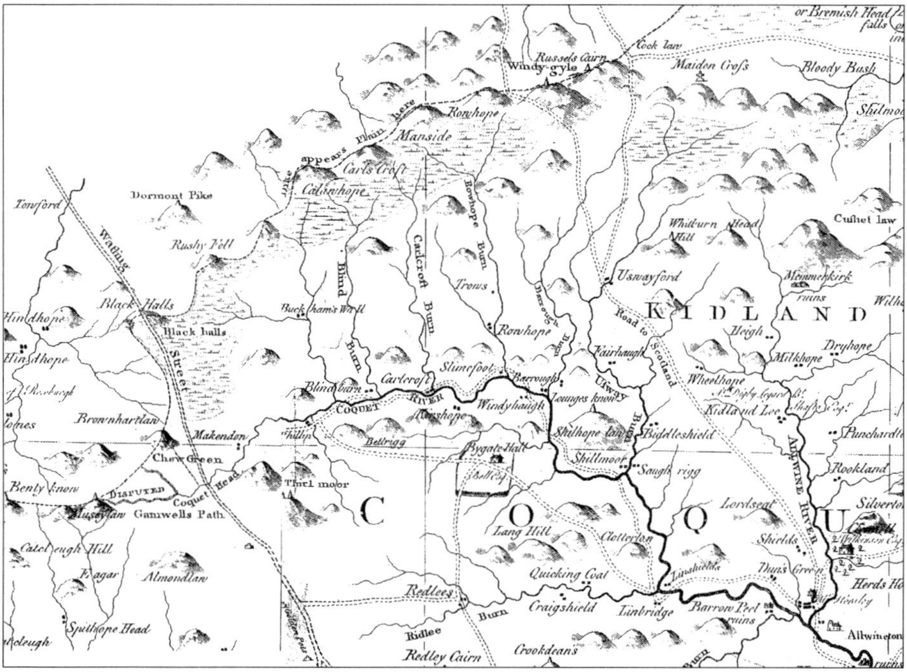

Below: An extract from Armstrong's county map of 1769 showing the border crossings of Clennel Street ('Road to Scotland') and Dere Street (labelled 'Watling Street', the name given to it by antiquaries at this time).

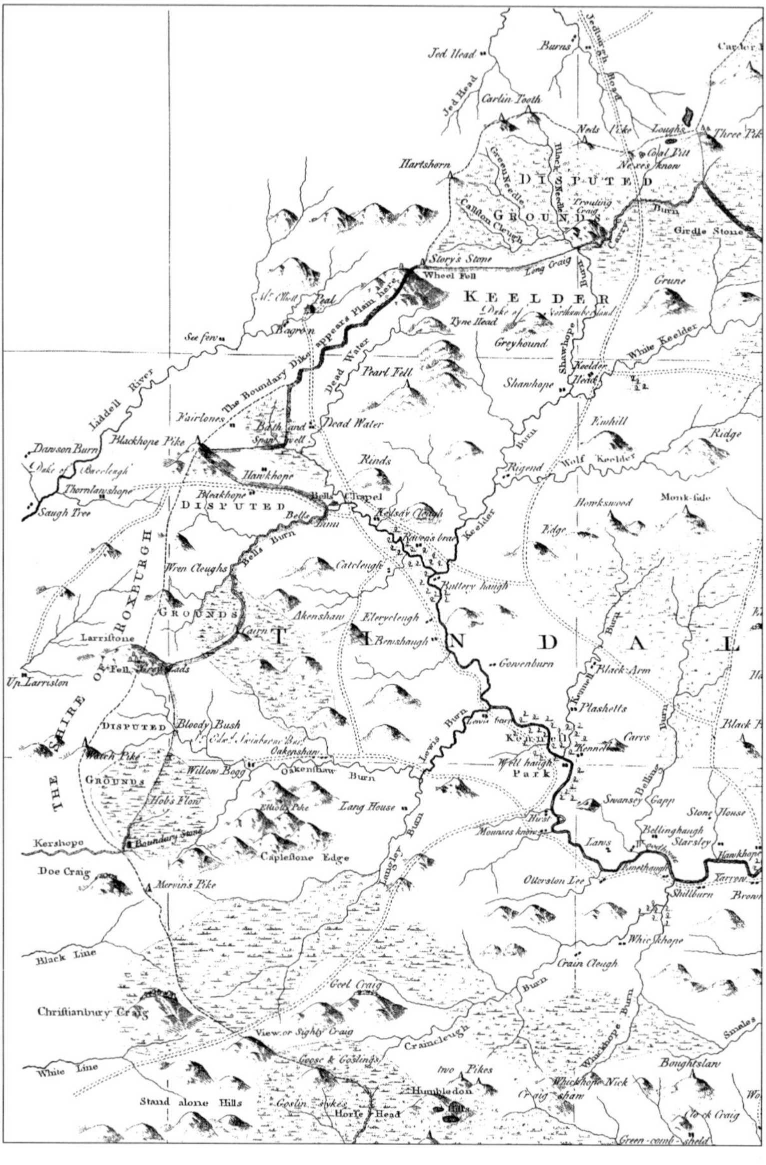

The routeways crossing the Border around Deadwater, at the head of the North Tyne, and the 'Jedburgh Road' heading north, as depicted on Armstrong's 1769 county map.

County Maps

Although none of the county maps produced from the late sixteenth century – mostly derivations of Saxton – depict any road courses, they do show some of the Border settlements and other features which suggest the existence of roads, such as Kemblespeth Hill (i.e. the course of Dere Street south of Chew Green), the Wheel or Whele (Whele Kirk on Saxton; Whele Fell on Blau, i.e. the position of a route, or series of routes, from North Tynedale to Roxburgh and Kelso), and Reedswire (Reedsqiur on Saxton, Reedsquire on Speede, and Jansson and Reeds Square on Armstrong) – known as a meeting place for wardens of the opposite Marches during the sixteenth century.

The first depiction of roads on the county maps occur from the later seventeenth century and show the east coast (present A1) route from Berwick to Newcastle, via Belford, linking with an east–west route from Tweedmouth to Jedburgh, via Cornhill, Wark and Carham. Warburton's survey of 1716 shows the east coast route from Berwick

Another extract from Armstrong's map of 1769 including part of South Tynedale, the central sector of Hadrian's Wall and the wastes to the north.

to Newcastle, and marks the old Roman road of Dere Street, labelled 'Watling Street' (an erroneous term which survived well into the nineteenth century), as well as a road running along the border line itself. Warburton also marks a number of routes joining the border road at Cairn Hill and the Hanging Stone on the southern edge of Cheviot.

Kitchin's (1749/50) plan offers little additional detail, but shows the two main Roman roads – Dere Street and the Devil's Causeway – as well as a route north and south of Wooler, the south part of which appears to follow the trajectory of the present A697 (partly along the Devil's Causeway), minor modifications notwithstanding. The east-west road is also shown, running south of the Tweed from Howden, through Wark, to Cornhill and beyond. Horsley's plan of 1753 is more obscure, and does not show the A697 route north of Wooler, or the Tweed route west of Carham.

General Roy's *Military Survey of Scotland*, which included the Border region in the period 1752–55, provides the earliest detailed depictions of roads such as Clennel Street over long stretches. Clennel Street is marked as a 'road from Morpeth to Kelso', while The Street, which joins Clennel Street near Mowhaugh on the Bowmont Water, is named 'Clattering Path', presumably an evocative reference to the sound made by large numbers of cattle being driven along it. North of Clennel Street, Roy's map shows a road from Yetholm to Sourhope via Whitelaw, and three crossings around Kirk Mains (Scotland) and Shotten (England), while still further north, several roads across the Border cross Wark Common or follow the Tweed Valley. Roy's survey shows Dere Street running up to and over the Border from the south side, also marking an off-shoot from Dere Street running north from the Border at Raeshaw Fell or 'Reshy Fell', bordered on the west by a large series of what appear to be enclosures, perhaps for cattle. His depiction of the 'Road from Jedburgh', west of Woden Law into Scotland is, however, difficult to trace accurately.

Armstrong's map of 1769 is the first map for the south side of the Border to include reliable detail almost on a par with Roy's plan of two decades earlier. Armstrong shows the Redeswire ('Reeds Square') Road along the Rede Valley (presumably in its unimproved state), Dere Street (as 'Watling Street'), including the section south of Chew Green known as 'Gamwells Path'. Clennel Street is also shown as the 'Road to Scotland', including the alternative routes between Uswayford and Mowshaugh on the Bowmont – perhaps these are to be associated with the current Cock Law and Windy Gyle Border crossings, (although neither of these now passes through the present Uswayford). The Street is not shown on Armstrong's plan, nor on Cary's little-changed plan twenty years later. No further crossings are shown by Armstrong until north-east of Yetholm, from which roads travel across the border along both sides of the River Bowmont. Roads to the north cross the Border between Haselaw and Mindrum, across Wark Common near Whitelaw and along the south side of the Tweed from west of Carham. No crossings of the Tweed are shown other than the (by now) bridged crossing at Coldstream and the old bridge at Berwick.

Fryer (1820) and Greenwood (1828) show progressively more detail, with additional tracks extending from both sides of Kilham Hill to the Border and a more extensive road network in the Lowlands between the River Tweed and the River Bowmont. Further south, particularly notable is the appearance of 'Clattering Path', shown as the north-westwards branch of what is now called Clennel Street at Uswayford, with the eastern branch continuing north to Cocklaw, where it is joined by the Salter's Road (unnamed) from the east. A separate road is shown running west of – and parallel to – the western branch of Clennel Street (i.e. that labelled 'Clattering Path'), but on a different course to that charted on modern maps as The Street; this suggests that 'The Street' was originally a generic name for numerous tracks running across the Border between Dere Street and Clennel Street. By the time of the first edition Ordnance Survey plan of the area was completed in the mid-nineteenth century the major tracks noted above, including The Street, all seem to have become well enough established for the surveyors to identify them.

Estate Maps and Plans

Prior to the commencement of the Ordnance Survey Series in the 1850s, the most detailed reliable maps of the Borders region, including Northumberland, were those produced for administrative purposes by the owners of large estates. Such maps include Tithe and Inclosure maps (not used systematically in compiling the present survey), but it is the detailed, privately commissioned estate maps of the seventeenth to nineteenth centuries which, although varying considerably in accuracy, provide the most detail. In this regard, Plackett (2007, 48) highlights the value of a map of *Moors and Waste Lands belonging to Sir Edward Swinburne*, by John Leadbitter (1792), which shows a number of drift roads. The following are examples of the sort of information that is available from such records:

A useful series of maps for a micro-region within upland Northumberland is provided by the Duke of Northumberland's Map of Alnham, 1619, which shows the roads system emanating from Alnham Village before it was cleared of its tenants in the eighteenth century. At the west end of the village, where deeply incised holloways can now be seen in the hillside, the village street divides into three roads, named as 'Gapweth Way', 'Freston Waye' and 'Hartleye Swyre Waye',[1] two of which further divide within a mile of the village. Another road leads south-west from the east end of the village (towards Scrainwood). A century and a half later, a map of 1775 shows the village following the removal of most of the houses depicted on earlier plans. The road running north from the village is now shown a 'a drift road into Scotland' (probably the Salter's Road) and crosses another, east-west route labelled 'drift road to Wooler' close to 'The Dodd' (now Little Dod). The prevalence of drift or drove roads on the 1775 map arguably reflects the dominant economic activity of the period, whereas the number of roads leaving the village is reduced, perhaps reflecting the smaller population working on the land.

Another series of maps that enable us to comment on local changes before and after the period of Inclosure and turnpikes is provided for Elsdon, where the Inclosure Map of 1731 shows the village and parts of its surrounding township, including east and west fairgrounds, prior to the Acts establishing turnpikes to the east and west; probably also before the main period of droving, which saw thousands of cattle passing through the village on their way down the Great Drift Road to Stagshaw and Morpeth. The Elsdon Tithe Map, 1839, shows Elsdon and district at the peak of the droving trade following road improvements due to Acts of turnpiking. Prominent on this map is a 'drove road from Scotland' (the Great Drift Road) entering from the north-west towards a toll bar west of the village, which drovers attempted to avoid using embanked tracks to the north and east. The two fairgrounds shown on the 1731 Inclosure map are not indicated, suggesting that they may have been made obsolete by Stagshaw, Morpeth and other stock markets in lowland Northumberland and beyond. The subsequent mid-nineteenth-century first edition Ordnance Survey plan shows a number of remnants of droving, including two smithies, several public houses, a pinfold and a building named Gatecheck.

In the north-east part of the Cheviots, a plan of Thompson's Walls, Kilham, dated 1800, shows a 'Road from Yetholm', or 'Staw Road', leading to Kilham and, via 'back staw road(s)' to Kirk- and West-Newton, from where the A697 route can be reached along Glendale via Akeld.

Modern Maps

Current Ordnance Survey maps show a proliferation of roads and tracks crossing the Border from Scotland into Northumberland and converging on markets such as Morpeth and Stagshaw. The study of these tracks and roads using both historic and modern maps is instructive in revealing modern roads and track which are based upon earlier drove roads, as well as suggesting locations where it might be fruitful to search for other features associated with droving, such as roadside banks, enclosures and watering troughs.

NOTES

1 The word 'swyre', or 'swire', 'squire' etc., from the Old English Germanic *sweora* – 'a hollow between two hills or peaks, especially with a road running through it' – is one of the few words specifically associated with a border crossing. Mercator's Map of Northumberland, 1595, includes 'Read Squire' at the head of Redesdale, while Speed (1610) includes 'Whit Squire' (adjacent to The Cheviot on the Scottish side of the border) as well as 'Red Squire' to the south-west.

THREE
Pastoralism and Droving Before 1700

Environment and Topography

The historic county of Northumberland provides a distinct contrast between a fertile coastal plain – broad in the south-east but narrower to the north and all eminently suitable for arable cultivation – and the extensive but varied tracts of hill country which prevail further inland. These upland landscapes range from the ancient volcanic mass of the Cheviots in the north, through the distinctive heather-clad profiles of the fell sandstone ridge and the more rounded forms of the North Pennine moorlands framing North and South Tynedale. The last dale is further distinguished by the series of escarpments which appear to roll across the landscape around Hadrian's Wall, to the north of the valley, like a succession of ocean breakers, the most prominent of all being the great basaltic crags of the Whin Sill.

The uplands all constitute a marginal environment in terms of arable cultivation as a result of a combination of elevation, a short growing season and, particularly in the case of Tynedale and Redesdale, relatively poor soils. However, the extensive moors and fell-sides provide abundant grazing, which can be integrated with the exploitation of valley bottom meadows (the latter providing either winter pasture or a crop of hay fodder) to sustain relatively large numbers of cattle and sheep throughout the year. At present, the sparsely populated hills tend to be viewed as a barrier to movement, the Cheviot watershed marking the line of a long-contested Border. Only one major cross-Border route, the A68, traverses this upland massif today, following the course of the Rede, which makes a deep incision through the hills, and crossing the Border at Carter Bar. In addition, the A69 makes use of the natural east-west corridor provided by the valley of the South Tyne to connect the county with the west side of the country, whilst a number of lesser A routes weave their way through the North Pennines. By contrast, at certain times in the past the very absence of extensive cultivation, dense habitation and metalled highways made this upland zone a favoured corridor for the large-scale movement of livestock, and many important routes then crossed the high Border.

Pastoralism and Droving in Prehistory

As a consequence of the environmental constraints described above, it is likely that pastoralism – the rearing and exploitation of livestock – was a crucial subsistence activity in upland Northumberland from the Neolithic period onwards, when cattle and sheep were first domesticated. It is possible that the cultivation of crops played a more significant role during the initial expansion of permanent settlement into the uplands in the Neolithic and especially the early Bronze Age, taking advantage of the nutrient-rich soils opened up by forest clearance. However, the rapid exhaustion of these virgin soils, coupled with peat growth on the now exposed moorlands following climatic deterioration in the Middle Bronze Age, led to a contraction in the extent of cultivation. Thereafter, despite periodic fluctuations in the balance between cultivation and stock rearing in response to climatic variation, population growth and economic demand for cereals, it is likely that the principal resources of Northumberland's upland communities were always their herds and flocks and their extensive grazing lands.

Although it is difficult to reconstruct precisely the rhythms of prehistoric pastoralist activity, it is inherently likely that some form of seasonal movement of stock played an integral role in order to effectively exploit the summer pastures on the high moorlands. Moreover, the origins of such activity might well lie in the detailed understanding of the seasonal availability of different grazing resources gained by earlier Mesolithic hunter-gatherer populations whilst following the periodic migration of deer through the landscape.

Pastoralism in the Late Iron Age and Romano-British Period

Certainly by the late Iron Age and the Romano-British period, the morphology of their settlements demonstrates that pastoralism was a key element in the subsistence economy of upland communities in Northumberland. The settlements of this time take a variety of forms: rectilinear enclosed settlements in Tynedale and southern Redesdale; oval and scooped enclosures on the steeper slopes of Cheviots and the upper limits of North Tynedale and Redesdale; and 'unenclosed forecourt settlements' in north-east Redesdale, the southern Scottish uplands and the Cheviots. However, common elements include one or more round houses within or attached to some form of walled or embanked and ditched compound, with stockyards towards the front of this enclosure.

Particularly well-defined are the rectilinear enclosed sites, which were a characteristic form of settlement in Tynedale and lower Redesdale during this period (see Jobey, 1960). These settlements typically comprised a roughly squarish, rectangular or slightly trapezoidal enclosure, defined by a stone wall or a ditch and bank, pierced by a single causewayed entrance in the middle of the front wall. Just inside the enclosure, on either side of the entrance, a couple of yards or pens (probably intended to hold livestock) can generally be found. Several round houses usually lay towards the rear of the enclosure.

Examples include the type-site at Riding Wood, near Bellingham, settlements at Sidwood and Boggle Hill in the national park, and a string of sites now drowned beneath Kielder Water, at Tower Knowe (next to the Northumbria Water visitor centre near the dam), Belling Law, Kennel Hall Knowe near Plashetts, and Gowanburn Camp. Excavation of this last group, directed by George Jobey in the 1970s in advance of the flooding of the valley, revealed that this type of settlement first appeared in a timber-built form during the late Iron Age (Jobey, 1973; 1977; 1978; 1983, 199ff; Higham 1986, 122–3, 134–7, 193–5). Radiocarbon dates for the earlier phases cluster in the last two centuries BC and first century AD, with a rebuilding in stone following no earlier than the mid-second century AD.

The location of these sites within the wider landscape is instructive. They generally occupied the valley bottom or lower slopes, being distributed relatively evenly to form a dispersed settlement pattern of farmsteads not dissimilar to that prevailing in more recent periods (cf. Jobey, 1960, fig. 9; 1982, 21, fig. 8). A vast expanse of higher moorland lies outside this distribution. It seems likely that the settlement sites were positioned to exploit the meadows and cultivable land, but the prominence given to stockyards at the front of the enclosures suggests that stock rearing was such an important element of the overall economy that it is unlikely that the grazing resources of the higher moorland were ignored. This in turn must have necessitated considerable movement of stock from lower to higher ground and vice versa, probably on a seasonal basis.

A similar pattern emerges in Redesdale, where numerous settlements of the period were identified by a programme of fieldwork in the valley and in the Otterburn Training Area to the north, undertaken in the mid to late 1970s by the Field Research Group of the Society of Antiquaries of Newcastle upon Tyne under the direction of Beryl Charlton and John Day (cf. Charlton & Day, 1978). The rectilinear settlements of the North Tynedale type, such as Woolaw, Woolaw East, Rattenraw and Blakehope, were largely restricted to the south or west side of the river in Redesdale, in marked contrast to their almost universal distribution in North Tynedale itself (op. cit., 77, 85 fig. 17).

On the north side of the river, above Otterburn, the form of these enclosed settlements changes from rectilinear to oval or circular in plan, a form more characteristic of settlements in the Cheviot Hills of north Northumberland, and in the Scottish uplands. Another type was also found on the north side of the valley, the unenclosed forecourt settlements, which placed the round houses around the outside of the enclosure, transforming the latter into a large stone-walled forecourt onto which the houses opened.

Nevertheless, despite their morphological variations, there is no reason to believe that the different architectural traditions marked the territories of distinct cultural groups, or possess any chronological significance. More probably, they should simply be considered as equivalent to the variations in vernacular building tradition familiar from more recent periods. The basic components of all these settlements remain the same, i.e. walled enclosures, stockyards and roundhouses, and the adoption of the different settlement forms was perhaps, in part, a response to topographical constraints.

The distribution of all these settlement types, taken together, parallels that found in North Tynedale and other upland areas of Northumberland, being focussed on the valley floor and the adjacent slopes. None of the sites were located above the 300m contour, and only a couple were situated above 250m (op. cit., 85 fig. 17). Furthermore, it is intriguing to note that none of these settlements, whatever their typological form, extended much higher up the valley than their later counterparts, the bastle farmsteads and small hamlets of the sixteenth and early seventeenth centuries, a time when transhumance, or summering as it was known, was very definitely practised. Thus, Woolaw and Birdhope figured amongst the sites highest up the valley in both these dispersed settlement patterns.

So, it is likely there was a strong emphasis on pastoralism, based on the exploitation of the extensive moorland grazing which was available to these upland communities, enabling them to rear substantial herds of cattle and flocks of sheep.[1] Upper Redesdale may have been exploited by some form of seasonal transhumance involving the migration of all or part of the community along regular pathways, as it was in the early modern period. The same may have been true of other parts of the Northumbrian uplands. It might be possible to reconstruct potential grazing territories attached to the various settlements using geographic information system (GIS) applications, supported by the comparative evidence of seventeenth-century documents relating to transhumance summering grounds, but in all likelihood any such pattern is likely to have been complex and subject to continual change and adaption over time.

Anthropological research into pastoralist societies in the developing world today might give some impression of the attitudes and mentalities of the family groups which would have inhabited each of those settlement compounds, and the way such groups might have fitted into a wider, segmentary, tribal society of lineages, clans and tribes defined by both real and notional bonds of kinship.

Cattle may have been more important than sheep to these Iron Age/Romano-British communities, as was apparently also the case in the medieval and early modern periods, with the sheep being vulnerable to foot rot and liver fluke and less suited to the poorly drained pastures prevalent before the agricultural improvements of the later eighteenth and nineteenth centuries. However, sheep would still have been essential for their wool. Above all, in a largely unmonetarised economy, livestock would have been the principal form of transferable wealth, and represented a family's savings to be drawn on in times of crisis, as is the case in similar societies in the developing world today – essentially a deposit account on the hoof.

The Early Medieval Period

The overall pattern of pastoralist activity in the Northumbrian uplands during the early medieval period is much less clear. Some major sites have been identified on the edge of the uplands, notably the royal estate centre of Ad Gefrin at the foot of Yeavering Bell. This was doubtless the centre of a multiple estate or shire which embraced much of the Cheviot massif, as well as the rich agricultural district of Glendale and the Millfield plain. Centres like Falstone in North Tynedale, where eighth- to ninth-century carved stonework has been discovered, are likely to have been important as small monastic complexes or estate centres, as are the later parochial centres, like Elsdon and Simonburn for example. Further south, contemporary upland settlements have been identified, for example the shieling (small stone-built huts) or farmstead complex at Simy Folds in Upper Teesdale (Coggins et al. 1983) and the Anglo-Scandinavian farmstead at Gauber High Pasture near Ribblehead in the Yorkshire Dales (King, 1978).

However, we have no clear understanding of precisely how such elements – the lowland estate centres, secular or ecclesiastical, and the upland farmsteads and shielings – were integrated together, even if theories can be put forward. Certainly the growth of some form of transhumance seems likely, as implied by the emergence of scale placenames in areas of significant Scandinavian settlement, even if the date of the equivalent Old English form 'scela', from which derive the shield placenames common in Northumberland, is rather less certain (McDonnell 1988, 4).

The Medieval Period: Patterns of Pastoralist Land Use

It is not until the high medieval period that the role droving played in the pastoralist exploitation of the Northumbrian uplands comes more firmly into focus. Several distinctive ways of organising the use of such hill country are recorded in documentary sources of the period. These practices have been analysed by McDonnell (e.g., 1988; 1990) and most recently by Winchester (2000, 84–99), whose work forms the basis of much of what follows.

Commons

The most straightforward means available to medieval communities was the use of moorland common surrounding a township's enclosed arable land and meadows. The short flush of grass growth on such commons would provide grazing during late spring and summer, and its exploitation would generally involve relatively short-distance movement of stock from the valley bottom up onto the adjacent hillsides and moors. Various mechanisms were used to regulate the use of these common pastures and prevent overgrazing, these being enforced through the proceedings of the manor court (op. cit., 78–84).

Seasonal Transhumance: Shielings and Summering

More peculiar to the northern uplands were the different forms of longer distance seasonal transhumance, variously labelled shielding or summering on the one hand, or agistment on the other. Summering or sheilding generally entailed at least a substantial part of the community moving with their herds and flocks from their winter dwellings to the summer hill pastures, known as shieling grounds.[2] The classic contemporary description of summering is that provided by Camden after visiting Cumberland and the region of Hadrian's Wall in 1599:

> Here every way round about in the wasts as they tearme them, as also in Giliesland, you mey see as it were the ancient Nomades, a martiall kinde of men, who from the moneth of Aprill unto August, lye out scattering and summering (as they tearme it) with their cattell in little cottages here and there which they call Sheales and Shealings.[3]

Thus, shielings were erected in the shieling grounds, to provide accommodation for the summering population. The seminal study of such shielings is still that compiled by the Royal Commission on Historic Monuments of England (Ramm et al. 1970, 9–43). There are also indications that hay may have been cut in the shieling grounds in some cases to supplement the winter fodder gathered on the home farms (Winchester, 2000, 93). This in turn would imply the construction of some form of walled or fenced enclosure to keep the stock out of the hayfield. In these circumstances it is easy to appreciate how somewhere like Greenhaugh in Tarsetdale, which was recorded as a shieling ground in the early fourteenth century, could have become a permanent settlement by the fifteenth or sixteenth century, perhaps evolving simply as a result of an intensification of existing activities.

Agistment, on the other hand, involved driving the livestock up to the summer pastures where they were left, perhaps in the care of local herdsmen. Agistment was suitable for animals which did not require milking, such as horses, geld cattle and flocks of wethers or hoggs, but was clearly not appropriate for cows or ewes, which required milking to sustain cheese production. The latter required the milkers to go with their milking stock, and is another example of the greater intensity of exploitation represented by the shieling ground vis-à-vis the agistment ground.

Whatever its precise form, such transhumant movement typically entailed the use of hill pasture well beyond a community's own moorland common, either within a neighbouring community's common or perhaps in the lord's forest or other demesne pasture. The transhumant community would thus either rent a specific shieling ground, which would contain a suitable site for a group of shielings along with sufficient surrounding pasture, or alternatively they would pay an agistment fee per head of stock to the relevant lord.

Vaccaries, Bercaries and Granges

In marked contrast, cattle farms (vaccaries – vaccariae) or sheep farms (bercaries – bercariae) might be established by the manorial lords in the upper reaches of some of the dales and their tributary side valleys or hopes. Monasteries had their own equivalent of such demesne farms, known as granges. Relatively little is known regarding the operations of vaccaries and bercaries in Northumberland, although it is clear that they did exist in the upland lordships, notably the liberty of Redesdale (see below). Instead, their workings have to be restored from known examples in other upland areas of northern England which have been studied in more detail, for example Swaledale in North Yorkshire, Calderdale in West Yorkshire or the Forests of Bowland and Rossendale (cf. McDonnell, 1990; 1988, 8–9; Faull & Moorhouse, 1981, iii, 758–61; Hey, 1986, 73–4; Winchester, 2000, 10–5).

McDonnell suggests a typical farm of this kind would comprise a fairly large foldyard for harbouring stock surrounded by byres, hay barns, a domus or aula for the farm bailiff or granger and any other administrative staff and bothies for the herdsmen (1990, 27). A milking shed and a cheese house would also be essential, particularly for bercaries. The number of beasts ran on such farms typically ranged between twenty and eighty cattle, or 200 to 300 sheep, on each farm (McDonnell, 1990, 28; Hanson, 1949, 50–55).

It is important to recognise that these vaccary or bercary systems could involve significant transhumance. The vast manor of Wakefield, held by the Warennes, embraced both low-lying meadows alongside the River Calder and upland summer pastures on the moors of Sowerby graveship (roughly equivalent to the present-day local government district of Calderdale), with livestock being moved on a seasonal basis to exploit these complementary resources. Several upland hamlets in Calderdale have place names ending in '–stall' (OE: cattle shed) which betray their origin as vaccaries, e.g. Heptonstall, Saltonstall and Wainstalls.

In general, seigniorial vaccaries and berceries or monastic upland granges were a feature of the earlier part of the period – the twelfth, thirteenth and early fourteenth centuries. From the mid-fourteenth century these establishments seem to have lost out to an increased use of agistment and shieling grounds. This formed part of a wider trend, as landlords everywhere abandoned direct management of their demesne in favour of leasing the lands out for rents in cash, confronted as they were by a declining population (due principally to repeated outbreaks of the Black Death) and consequent rising wages and falling prices, which undermined the earlier profitability of demesne farming (Lomas, 1996, 82–3; Bailey, 2002, 17).

Even in the earlier period, whereas the great monasteries tended to favour direct management using lay brothers (*conversi*) to staff the key administrative posts, some lay landowners leased their cattle and sheep farms out to individuals as in the de Gant lordship of Healaugh in Swaledale (McDonnell, 1990, 23–7). A system of sharecropping was apparently employed in the Warenne vaccaries in Calderdale and by the Lacys in the Forests of Bowland and Rossendale, with each cow-keeper or boothman provided with up to eighty head of cattle by the lord's instaurator, to whom annual accounts were rendered (McDonnell, 1988, 8–9; Faull & Moorhouse, 1981, iii, 759).

Forests and Lordships

Just as the way in which land was exploited in the hills differed greatly from the pattern of land use prevalent in the lowlands, so too did the tenural framework of lordship in the two zones. Indeed, the different structure of lordship in the northern uplands was a crucial factor influencing the development of practices such as summering and agistment transhumance, and the emergence of vaccary systems. Following the Norman Conquest, much of the uplands were designated as either royal or palatine forest or as baronial free chase, i.e. extensive tracts of land which were subject to the terms of forest law designed to ensure the maintenance of cover for game (Winchester, 2000, 10–13).[4] Thus, in 1199 Richard de Umfraville was granted a charter by King John stipulating that no one should pasture livestock or hunt or cut wood in Richard's forests of Redesdale and Coquetdale under penalty of £10 unless he had common rights in the forest (Hodgson, 1827, 14). In practice, however, this did not mean that forest areas were permanently restricted as hunting reserves. Certainly by the thirteenth and fourteenth centuries, if not earlier, their lords were actively seeking to generate income from grazing these upland tracts.

What the establishment of the forests effectively did do was to convert much of the upland pastures into seigniorial demesne, giving the landlord very direct control over the different patterns of exploitation which developed there. In some areas this resulted in the growth of demesne vaccary systems. Elsewhere, lords preferred to lease out grazing rights for particular tracts to transhumant tenants (op. cit., 10, 98). Other possible courses of action were to grant land to favoured monastic houses, as the Umfravilles did with the Kidland pastures, Newminster being the beneficiary in that case, or to open the upland dales to permanent settlement by their tenantry, although progress was often slow in this regard. Winchester highlights the distinction between the closed vaccary forests and chases on the one hand, and the open forests where tenant colonisation was permitted and perhaps even encouraged on the other.

It is significant in this context that designated forests or free chases were particularly characteristic of the large but territorially compact baronies to be found in the uplands of northern England. Forests form one of the most strikingly common features of the Cumbrian baronies examined by Winchester (1987, 3–5, 16–22), for instance. Moreover, the forest zones correspond to areas where the practice of transhumance can be documented either directly in historical records, or indirectly through scale/shield place name evidence, or can be attested archaeologically in the form of the shieling cottages and associated remains. Further, the baronies may themselves be based to a considerable extent on pre-Conquest units of lordship or multiple estates, as suggested by successive scholars (Jolliffe, 1926; Barrow, 1973, 7–68; Jones, 1976; Kapelle, 1979, 51–85).

The forests thus, in part, represent a device for drawing profit from the longstanding seasonal pastoralism prevalent in the northern region, a profit derived through agistment charges on the use of pasture and woodland by the peasantry of the dependent manors. Whether this method of exploiting the subsistence practices of northern communities was entirely a Norman innovation or was based – at least to a limited degree – on the customs of pre-existing multiple estates is a matter for debate.

A second and related factor, which is particularly noteworthy, was the very extensive nature of the individual lordships within the northern hill country. In particular, from Kidland and the Coquet southward a series of very large lordships furnished with what was essentially viceregal or palatine authority were established in upland Northumberland. These comprised the Umfraville liberty of Redesdale (which also embraced Kidland and the south side of Upper Coquetdale – 150,000 acres), the liberty of Tynedale (both the north and south dales encompassing more than 200,000 acres) where the Scottish Crown was the feudal tenant in chief, and Hexhamshire (80,000 acres) where the Archbishop of York held sway (cf. Lomas, 1996, 150–61). Here the baron was responsible for performing the administrative and judicial tasks undertaken elsewhere by the sheriff and other royal officials.

The great size of these baronial territories, however, was not a characteristic restricted to the border districts, where it might be assumed that the establishment of large powerful lordships reflected a desire to impose firm control over these areas. As noted above, for example, the manor of Wakefield, held by the powerful Warenne baronial lineage, embraced much of what is now West Yorkshire, from the lower Calder valley around Wakefield itself to the Pennine watershed.

Nor was it simply the palatine lordships in chief, the liberties or regalities which were so vast. The constituent manors which made up these lordships, particularly those in the upper dales, such as the manor of Tarset held by the Comyns in North Tynedale or the Umfraville demesne manors of Harbottle and Otterburn in the Redesdale liberty, were also often very extensive indeed (see below). Indeed, such large manors seem to have been the preferred means by which great lords or their immediate vassals exploited the upland dales. Such large manorial territories encompassed the full range of complementary resources required by the upland pastoralist economy, enabling landlords to exploit the upper valleys and their adjacent moorlands as integrated units, with full control of the transhumant and other pastoralist cycles operating therein.

The Medieval Period – Case Studies

The preceding discussion has summarised the various ways in which the grazing of livestock in the uplands was organised in the medieval period. To determine exactly what role the droving of stock over longer or shorter distances played in the upland economy in this period, we must now turn to a series of case studies showing how pastoralism was actually undertaken in different parts of what is now the Northumberland National Park.

Upper North Tynedale

North Tynedale formed part of the great liberty of Tynedale, the largest of the Northumbrian regalities, which was held by the Scottish Crown up until the end of the thirteenth century when it was confiscated by the English Crown following the outbreak of the Edwardian Anglo–Scottish wars (Moore, 1915, 21–6; Lomas, 1996, 155–8). The upper part of the valley seems to have been divided between three principal manors during the thirteenth century: Bellingham embraced the middle part of the valley around its confluence with the Rede and was the site of a chapel and later a market, higher up still lay the manors of Tarset and Chirdon, both of which displayed very distinctive upland characteristics.

The manor of Chirdon encompassed the entire valley of the Chirdon Burn, one of the main tributaries of the North Tyne on the south side of the dale above Bellingham (NCH XV, (1940), 273–80). As the Chirdon Burn and Tarset Burn flow into the North Tyne at virtually the same point, the core holdings of Chirdon and Tarset manors lay opposite one another – however, Chirdon manor was nowhere near as extensive as its neighbour. The manor was granted to the Justiciar of Scotland, David de Lindsay, in 1233, and held by his descendents until the outbreak of the Anglo–Scottish wars whereupon it was confiscated. The manorial centre, or 'capital messuage', was represented by Dally Castle, where the ruins of a small thirteenth-century hall-house can still be seen, esconced on a natural mound beside the Chirdon Burn. The estate contained a mill (probably situated near the castle), two parks, a dependent hamlet with five bondage tenants at Snabdaugh beside the river, and twenty-two shielings probably located along the upper reaches and side tributaries of the burn. In many respects Chirdon manor resembled a scaled down version of Tarset, which dwarfed both the other two principal manorial estates in the upper valley and merits the most detailed attention here.

Tarset – An Upland Manor

The manor of Tarset comprised all the land in the upper valley from the limits of Bellingham manor right up to the head of the valley, with the exception of the Chirdon Burn on the south side. It included Charlton, Sundaysight (Sundayheigh), Greenhaugh and Cariteth (le Caryte), Shitlington in Wark Parish, the modern parish of Thorneyburn, including Emblehope, Thorneyburn and Donkleywood, and the modern parish of Falstone, including Kielder, Belling (le Belles), Hawkhope (Haucop), Bewshaugh (i.e. Bowhous), and Greenside (Greenstead). The centre (or caput) of the manor lay at Tarset Hall or Castle, beside the confluence of the North Tyne and the Tarset Burn. In the thirteenth century the manor was held by the Comyns, one of the principal Scottish baronial lineages. The manor owed suit (i.e. the obligation to attend and support proceedings there) to the court of Wark.

The most detailed inventory of the manor and all its components is provided by the Inquisitions Post Mortem held in 1326 and 1329 to value the holdings of John Comyn of Badenagh, who had died in 1315[5]:

> (NCH XV, (1940), 244–5; Cal. Doc. Scot. III, no.886; Cal. IPM VI, no.697 – AD 1326)
> John Comyn held of the king in chief the manor of Tyrset in Tyndale by the service of one and a half knights' fees and doing suit at the court of Wark in Tyndale every three weeks: The manor and orchard used to be worth in time of peace 2*s* yearly, and now nothing lying waste and destroyed by the Scots.
>
> There are 38 acres of demesne land each worth in time of peace 12*d*, of which there are in occupation 10 acres which are farmed out at 3*s* 4*d* to be paid at the feasts of Pentecost and St Martin, the price of an acre 4*d* and the rest lies waste from want of tenants.
>
> There is a park which was worth yearly in herbage £10, and now 3*s* 4*d*.
>
> There is a hope called Tyresthope formerly worth yearly in herbage £26 13*s* 4*d*, and now 13*s* 4*d* to be paid at the said terms.
>
> There is another hope called Emelhope, formerly worth yearly in herbage £6 13*s* 4*d*, and now nothing because of want of tenants.
>
> There is a shieling called le Grenehalgh, formerly worth yearly in herbage £8 and now 2*s* 6*d*; also hope called le Caryte formerly worth yearly in herbage 106*s* 8*d* and now 4*s* 6*d*.
>
> And a hope called Kielder formerly worth in herbage £26 13*s* 4*d* yearly, and now nothing because it lies waste for want of tenants.
>
> And a shieling called Kielderheys formerly worth in herbage £4 yearly and now worth nothing for the same cause.
>
> And a hope called Thorneybourne with le Brendis formerly worth in herbage £12 10*s* yearly and now 13*s* 4*d*.

And there are 14 bondages in Charleton pertaining to the said manor, each containing one toft and 20 acres of land and each being formerly worth 20*s* yearly, of which there are in occupation 20 acres which are farmed out at 6*s* 8*d* to be paid at the said terms. The rest lies waste and uncultivated.

And a pasture called Byrchenshop formerly worth 13*s* 4*d* yearly and now nothing because it lies waste.

And a hamlet called Grenestede formerly worth 60*s* yearly in herbage and now 3*s* 4*d*.

And a hope called Doncliwode formerly worth yearly in herbage £8 and now 10*s*.

And a hope called Waynhop formerly worth yearly in herbage £9 and now nothing because it lies waste for want of tenants.

And a park (at Wainhope) formerly worth yearly in herbage £8 and now nothing for the same cause.

And a hope called Trivetbourne with le Grene formerly worth yearly in herbage £26 13*s* 4*d* and now 20*s*.

And a hope called Poltrerneth formerly worth yearly in herbage £12 and now nothing.

And a hope called le Belles with le Bowhous formerly worth in herbage £12 now nothing.

And a hope called Stokhalgh with le Bernes formerly worth yearly in herbage £9 and now 6*s* 8*d*.

And a hope called Haucop formerly worth £10 13*s* 4*d* and now nothing for the cause aforesaid.

And a hope called Sundayhaygh formerly worth yearly 53*s* 4*d*, now 3*s* 4*d*.

And there was a water mill formerly worth yearly £30, and now nothing because it lies broken and out of order.

(Cal. Doc. Scot. III, no.979 – AD 1329)
Not extended formerly:

42 acres of demesne in Tyrsete manor, each worth 12*d*.
A hope there called Shouelburne, worth £26 13*s* 4*d*.
Another called Smal and Yerhalgh, worth £14.

In 1329, John Comyn's widow, Margaret, afterwards wife of Edmund earl of Kent, was assigned a third part of the manorial holding as a dower, as was customary, comprising a third part of Sholeburnhope, the hope of Kielderheies, the site of a capital messuage with the demesne lands in Wainhope and certain lands in Dedewaynhope, Poltrevet, land worth £14 13*s* 4*d* in time of peace in Le Green, Le Karite which was worth 106*s* 8*d* in time of peace, Dunkleywood worth £8 in time of peace, a third of the mills and park of Tarset, of the park of Wainhope and of the forest of Emelhope, and a third of some other land, name illegible, worth 12*s* in time of peace (Cal. Doc. Scot. III, no.993; Cal. IPM VI, no.252; cited in NCH XV (1940), 245).

These documents constitute one of the fullest surveys of an upland manor in Northumberland available to us. It should be emphasised that they record the manor in the devastated condition resulting from Bruce's raids during the Scottish War of

Independence. However, used in conjunction with the other principal source for medieval Tynedale, the judicial proceedings for 1279 and 1293 known as the *Iter of Wark*[6], they help to give a clear understanding of the valley's pastoralist economy and the way in which the complementary resources of the valley and the hills were organised.

Settlement in the Valley: Vills, Villages and Hamlets

The settlement pattern which emerges from the documentary sources has been mapped by Harbottle and Newman (1973, 140 fig. 2, which forms the original basis of the illustration above). A few more place names may be added, based on scrutiny of the *Iter of Wark* in particular. The permanent settlements recorded all lay in the main valley close to the river or in the major tributary side valleys, such as the Chirdon Burn and the Tarset Burn. The *Iter* mentions a total of seven vills in Upper North Tynedale, namely Bellingham, Charlton, Tarset, Tirsethoppe, Chirdon, Donkleywood (Duncliffe), and Thorneyburn (*Iter of Wark*, lii–lv, lxiv–v). These do not necessarily represent villages. Instead they were either territorial township communities or local administrative units.

In this case, since the vills are recorded in the context of judicial proceedings and principally in connection with the payment of communal fines, it is likely they represent administrative vills. Moreover, the list is not necessarily comprehensive. No vill is recorded on the south side of the river above Chirdon, although the existence of three or four inhabited places can be inferred there, and none above Donkleywood on the north side, although again a number of settlements can be identified extending far up the valley, including the chapel site at Falstone.

It is by no means clear that the majority of these vills actually contained a nucleated village in the conventional sense, as opposed to a hamlet or a scatter of dispersed farmsteads. Bellingham was probably the most substantial of the settlements, since it was the site of a chapel as well as a manorial centre (caput), complete with mill and presumably a manor house for the Bellingham lineage. There may also have been a nucleated village at Charlton which seems to have been the principal – if not the only – locus of bonded or unfree peasant tenants in the manor of Tarset.[7] The 1326 Inquisition Post Mortem for John Comyn of Badenagh, lord of Tarset, lists as part of the manorial holdings fourteen bondages 'in Charlton', each comprising one toft and twenty acres of land.

Even this was masks greater complexity, since the settlements of Little Charlton and South Charlton are also mentioned, with Little Charlton at least, if not South Charlton as well, apparently lying south of the river with rights of common in Hesleyside. (NCH XV, (1940), 251–2; Harbottle & Newman, 1973, 139). These may relate to the manor of Charlton, a sub-manor of Tarset, held by Adam of Charlton at the end of the thirteenth century,[8] whereas the fourteen bondage tenancies (in Charlton proper perhaps) were held directly by the Comyn lords. Greystead, on the other hand, is explicitly labelled a hamlet, and Snabdaugh, in the manor of Chirdon where Robert Swinburne had held five bondages each with one toft and sixteen acres of land, probably falls into the same category. Indeed, it seems likely that virtually all the sites listed in the Inquisitions, or inferred from their occurrence as part of the surnames of people mentioned by the *Iter of Wark*, were hamlets or farmsteads.

The centre (caput) of Tarset manor is a good case in point. The manor house (generally termed the capital messuage in medieval documents) was represented by a two-storey hall tower, Tarset Castle,[9] located above the Tarset Burn on a steep-sided promontory which was cut off by a deep ditch on its east and south sides. The hall tower was prob-

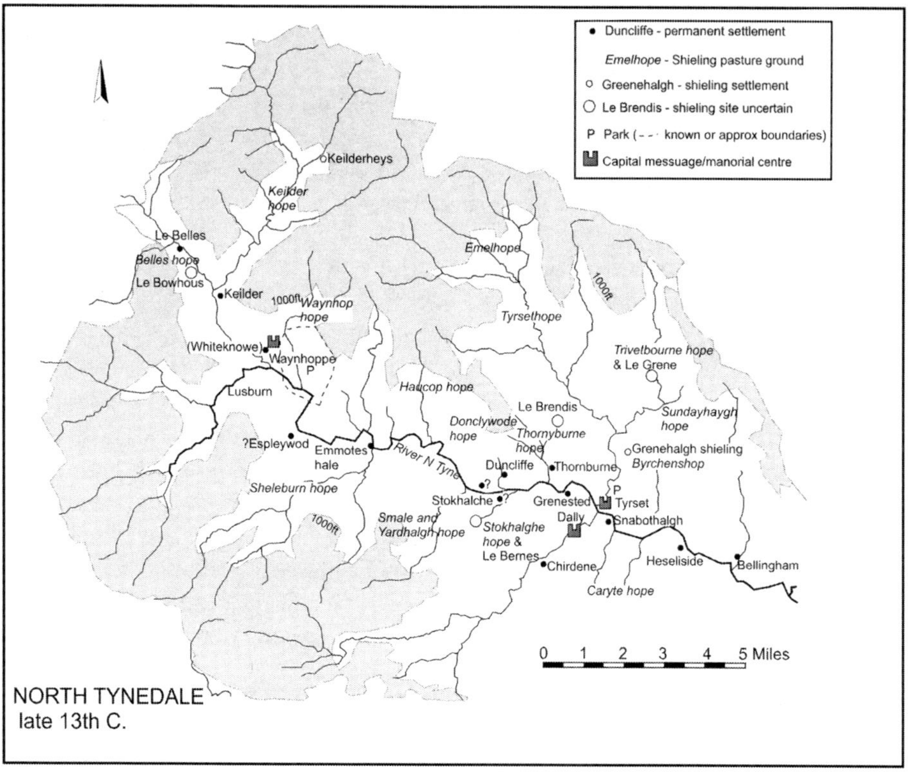

The late thirteenth-century settlement pattern in Upper North Tynedale, suggested by Harbottle and Newman.

ably erected following the issue of a detailed licence to crenelate to John Comyn in 1267 (Cal. Doc. Scot. I, no.2463; Cal. Pat. Rolls 178; discussed and reproduced by Bates, 1891, 7–8 n.30), although the castle was almost certainly in existence prior to that date, perhaps as an earth and timber-built complex.[10]

In addition there was a park, that other prerequisite of seigniorial prestige, located on the east side of the castle,[11] and a mill, which is listed repeatedly in the Inquisitions.[12] This seems to have been a fulling mill associated with the processing of cloth rather than grain, again underlining the importance of livestock and their products to the economy of the upland manor.[13] A total of eighty acres of demesne arable, perhaps distributed in two separate blocks of thirty-eight and forty-two acres, are also recorded at Tarset by the Inquisitions Post Mortem.

Harbottle and Newman suggest there was a village at Tarset (1973, 138–9), however Wrathmell is more circumspect (1975 II, 506) noting that 'no indication has been found of the size or composition of the medieval settlement there'. No bondage tenants of the kind that form the core of any lowland township and manor are recorded there in any of the early fourteenth-century Inquisitions, and no earthworks indicative of a village or even a hamlet are visible on the aerial photographs or surface examination.[14] Instead, fourteen bondage holdings at neighbouring Charlton are listed.

All this does not mean that there was no settlement at Tarset alongside the castle and its seigniorial appurtenances. The occurrence of the surname de Tyrset would imply that there was at least a hamlet there, (although it could perhaps also denote origin from an area or township territory rather than a specific settlement). However, the combined evidence, and in particular the absence of bondage holdings, does suggest that Tarset was not a regular nucleated village with rows of peasant farmers' houses and attached toft enclosures plus open fields of arable riggs and meadow beyond, such as one would expect to find in the coastal plain of Northumberland.

The Highland Pastures: Hopes and Shielings

Thus, the principal wealth of the manor clearly lay not in its control over a community of unfree tenants cultivating tracts of arable land, but in the extensive upland grazing areas it incorporated. It is not altogether clear precisely how the manor extracted value from these pastures. The Comyn Inquisitions contain no references to seigniorial cattle farms (vaccaries), sheep farms (bercaries) or stud farms in the highlands, of the kind that are clearly documented in the Umfraville manors of Harbottle and Otterburn in the neighbouring liberty of Redesdale.[15] A deed of 1360 does however refer to the 'mottes' of Kielder and Emelhope, which might represent something similar, perhaps moated farms rather than mottes in the motte and bailey sense (Laing Charters no.49; Macdonald, 1950, no.29). Shielings are mentioned at Greenhaugh and Kielderheys.

The latter can perhaps be identified with the large, regularly laid out settlement consisting of rectangular house platforms, enclosures and lazy beds at Colour Cleughs, beside White Kielder Burn (NY 675984; cf. Charlton, 1987, 59). Indeed, the size and regularity of this site is particularly striking and may give a reasonable impression of the appearance of a shieling complex of the thirteenth to fourteenth centuries, when exploitation of the uplands was under tighter seigniorial control, although the possibility that it belongs to a later date cannot be excluded. A further twenty-two shielings are also recorded in the neighbouring manor of Chirdon in the Inquisition Post Mortem for Robert Swinburne in 1326 (NCH XV (1940) 277; Cal. IPM VI no.693). These were probably all associated with long-distance transhumance (Harbottle and Newman, 1973, 140–1; Winchester, 2000, 93). However, the bulk of the pastures are simply described as 'a hope called…'. Sometimes this is associated with a further name, e.g. Belleshope with le Bowhous (i.e. Bewshaugh) and Stokhalghhope with le Bernes.

Harbottle and Newman suggest that these were additional shielings (1973, 141). However, at least one of these places figures in a surname recorded in the *Iter of Wark* (Williemus de le Bernes, cf. Hartshorne, 1858, iv) suggesting there was some form of permanent settlement there in 1279. Similarly, the references to a certain John Makam 'of Kielder', who 'dropped down dead' in the market place at Bellingham in 1293, and Emma of Waynhoppe who was taken for theft and promptly decapitated in 1279, and Gilbert, son of Peter de Belles, also mentioned in 1279, all point to the existence of permanent settlements at these remote locations at the upper end of the valley (Wilson & Leathart, 1982, 61; *Iter of Wark*, ixv and ixii).

Thus, the surname evidence, coupled with the presence of a supplementary manorial complex at Wainhope, would suggest there was a scatter of permanent settlements extending right up to Kielder and Belles at the head of the valley. The substantial stone wall of the attached park, which was later known as Kennel Park (see Armstrong's map, 1769), can still be seen in the forest on the north shore of Kielder Water. Its scale suggests a substantial investment. The capital messuage itself may have lain a little further west, again on the north shore, at White Knowe, near Gowanburn, where the remains

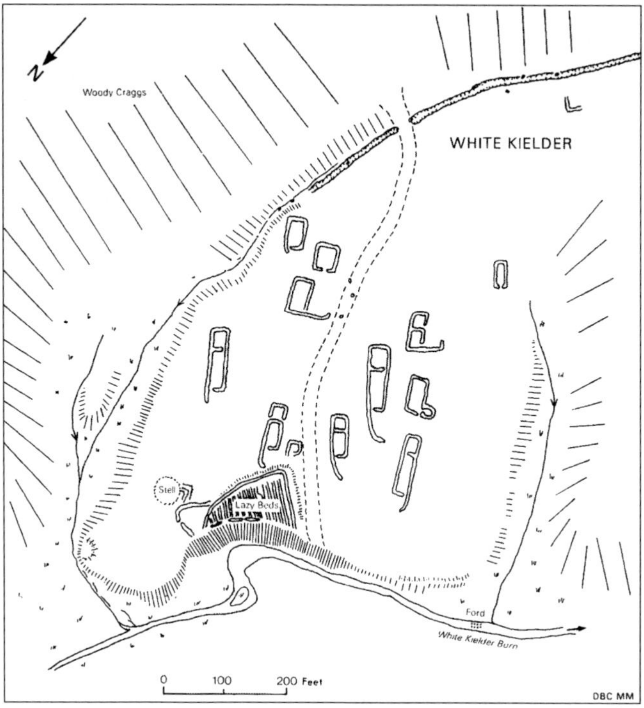

Plan of the shieling complex at White Kielder (reproduced from Charlton 1987, p. 59).

of what appears to be a medieval settlement complex can be traced beneath the trees. In addition, Tirsethoppe must have contained some permanent settlement since it is termed a vill in the *Iter of Wark* and pays communal fines accordingly. It, presumably, embraced the higher reaches of the Tarset Burn, certainly well above Tarset itself, which was also a vill (perhaps above the confluence with the Tarret Burn). Similarly, Thorneyburnehope must lie relatively close to the vill – and therefore permanent settlement – of Thorneyburne.

These areas were clearly exploited by tenants, since they were said to be worth nothing for want of such in the aftermath of the Scottish raids. However, there were clearly no nucleated settlements of bondmen in the manner characteristic of lowland manorial farming. Instead, a complex mixed pattern of exploitation of these uplands should probably be envisaged, involving both the use of extensive designated shieling grounds by tenants transhuming seasonally over considerable distances, and also the establishment of permanent farmsteads or even hamlets inhabited by tenants engaged in shorter distance stock management. The bulk of the manor's earnings probably came from charges for grazing rights paid by the tenant farmers and those using the shieling grounds. Certainly it is clear that a manor like Tarset could not have functioned without extensive movement of stock up and down the valley and from valley bottom to hillside and moor top.

South Tynedale: Transhumance Beside and Beyond the Roman Wall

South Tynedale too formed part of the great medieval liberty of Tynedale. The area around the central sector of Hadrian's Wall reveals two contrasting aspects of medieval upland pastoralist organisation. On the one hand, it provides a good example of the division of the uplands into extensive commons attached to township communities predominantly centred on settlements in the valley. However, it also shows how the vast tracts of land might be designated as forest, effectively part of the lord's private demesne, reserved, in theory, for use as a hunting range. Hadrian's Wall provided the crucial boundary between these two zones.

To the south of the ancient barrier the landscape was divided up between the territories of the various township communities of South Tynedale, like Melkridge, Thorngrafton, Henshaw and Haltwhistle, all situated lower down in the dale amidst their meadows and arable land. The townships south of the Wall thus resembled a series of transects through the Tynedale landscape, each incorporating the full range of complementary resources from valley bottom to high pasture. The waste to the north of the Wall, however, constituted a seigniorial forest demesne known as the Huntlands of Tindal and later as the Forest of Lowes, deriving the latter name from the string of small lakes or loughs found there.[16]

The extent of permanent settlement in the karst upland common south of the wall fluctuated according to a range of factors – climate, population levels and the degree of security prevailing. In the thirteenth and fourteenth centuries, permanent settlements can be identified beside or close to the Wall. Edward I appears to have stayed in Bradley Hall on 5 and 6 September 1306, en route west along the Stanegate (or the Karelgate, as it was then known) towards Carlisle and his last Scottish campaign. F.G. Simpson uncovered a tower on Peel Crags in the early twentieth century (Simpson, 1976, 109, fig. 66), and more recently a farmstead built over the ruins of Sewingshields milecastle has been completely excavated (Haigh & Savage, 1984). The favourable site of Housesteads, where lime-rich soils cover a south-facing dip slope, may likewise have been permanently occupied during the optimal climatic conditions and high population levels of the mid to late thirteenth century, as it was from the sixteenth century onwards.

For much of the period, however, the Whin Sill landscape was probably only exploited seasonally, with the population of the townships, in part at least, transhuming up on to the Whin Sill escarpment with their livestock. Two shieling settlements which must have been associated with this process have been investigated in recent years. Near to Shield-on-the-Wall Farm, a large group of shielings is laid out on the slopes of a natural north-facing arena, 'the Bogle Hole' (NGR: NY72956693), on the south side of the Wall. The site comprises a row or terrace of nine huts on the north-facing slope and mostly attached to an east–west aligned enclosing wall, with five further north–south aligned examples situated a little to the north on the west-facing slope, all hut platforms being tucked under the crest of the hillside.

Excavation by the Newcastle University Archaeological Practice in 1998 showed this site had two distinct phases, with the demarcating enclosure wall being built earlier than the shielings themselves. It has been suggested that the Bogle Hole shielings represented a principal summer habitation of Melkridge township, and were associated with the communal exploitation of the township's seasonal pasture resources (Woodside & Crow, 1999, 66). This may be reflected in the earlier name Melkridge Shiel (Melcridge Shiel/ Melcrish Sheels), apparently applied to the adjacent farmstead at Shield-on-the-Wall on the earliest map evidence, the Military Road Survey of the 1749 and Horsley's map of the Roman Wall in Britannia Romana (1732).

This suggestion is supported by the existence of a similar shieling complex located on Mons Fabricius, which may have performed an equivalent role with respect to Henshaw

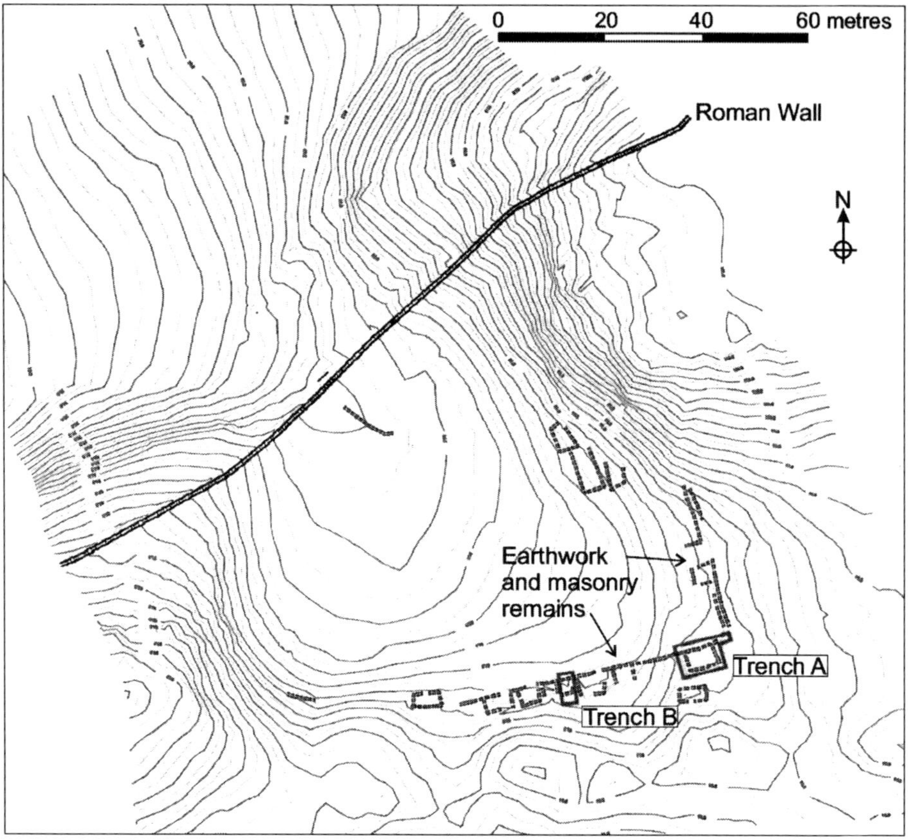

Above: Plan of the Bogle Hole shieling site on the south side of Hadrian's Wall, excavated in 1998.

Below: View of an excavated shieling at the Bogle Hole.

township as the Bogle Hole did for Melkridge. Excavations by James Crow on behalf of the National Trust in 1986 revealed structural and ceramic evidence of multiple phasing (op. cit., 63–64). The primary structures may be associated with the earliest pottery recovered from the site, which dated from the fourteenth century, but the huts were repaired many times, incorporating later flagged floors and hearths which could be dated to the early sixteenth century. Seven other shielings clustered around the lower slopes of the hill and over milecastle 39, and it is unclear whether all these groups were occupied simultaneously.

The creation of the shieling settlements on the Whin Sill escarpment suggests that the land both to the south and north of the wall was being exploited seasonally by the inhabitants of the shielings, and may reflect the opening up of the Huntland to grazing by the livestock of South Tynedale tenantry in the later medieval and early modern periods. However, even at an earlier date the Huntlands were not closed to pastoralist exploitation. Thus, in 1177 the Scottish king, William the Lion, confirmed his squire, Reginald Prat of Tynedale, in possession of 'four shielings (scalinga) wherever he pleased within the Huntland to occupy as meadow, pasture or arable', which he had earlier in free marriage along with one third of the vill of Haughton (Hodgson, 1840, 326; Moore, 1915, 25, 41–2).

Similarly, in 1282 William de Swinburne was granted a shieling at Greenlee, whilst Adam de Swinburne is recorded to have held eight shielings in the Huntlands as well as one at Bradley in the manor of Henneshalgh (Henshaw) in 1326 (Cal. IPM VI, 164, 751). The Swinburnes were prominent members of the local gentry and presumably leased these shieling grounds out to their manorial tenantry. Adam had inherited the manors of Haughton and Humshaugh from his father, John, and had acquired Simonburn in free marriage, and it was probably from associated township communities, all situated beside the lower reaches of the North Tyne, that we may envisage tenants transhuming westwards into the Huntland, to what is now designated Haughton Common and Simonburn Common.

Likewise, the pairing of Reginald Prat's four shielings in the Huntland with his portion of Haughton vill is surely not coincidental. The shielings would have been worthless without a reservoir of manorial tenants willing to pay in order to exploit the associated grazing rights. Perhaps by the later medieval or early modern periods, when any continued use of the area as a hunting forest had ceased, the Huntland seems to have been incorporated within the territories of the neighbouring township communities. The resultant configuration of township territories probably reflects the earlier longstanding patterns of transhumance routes and shieling grounds.

Pastoralism in Upper Redesdale

Medieval Settlement and Lordship

The liberty of Redesdale was held by the Umfraville lineage 'by service of defending the said lands from wolves and robbers' (Cal. IPM V, 14, no.47, cf. Hodgson 1827, 109). The liberty contained not only the valley of the Rede, as might logically be expected, but also much of Upper Coquetdale, including the entire south side of that part of the dale and the whole catchment area around the headwaters of the Coquet and the Alwin, notably the Kidland pastures. Indeed, the capital of the liberty was Harbottle Castle in Coquetdale, rather than Elsdon or Otterburn in Redesdale. The centre of Umfraville manorial administration in Redesdale itself lay at Otterburn, although Elsdon, with its large earthwork castle, must have initially played a more prominent strategic and administrative role in the Umfraville liberty than was later the case. As the site of the parish church, however, Elsdon remained the ecclesiastical centre of the dale and also the economic capital, with two market days and two annual fairs by the end of the thirteenth century. This section concentrates on Redesdale itself. The particular circumstances pertaining in Coquetdale are considered in the next section.[17]

Settlement steadily advanced up the valley during the climatic optimum lasting up until *c.*1300. Assart-men (cresmanni), associated with the clearance of new land for cultivation, are mentioned in the Inquisition of Gilbert de Umfraville in 1245 (Cal. IPM I, 12, no.49, cf. Hodgson 1827, 108). Davyshiel and Garretshiels, which probably began life as seasonal shieling sites, had clearly developed into permanent settlements by the end of the thirteenth century. They are mentioned in such terms in court cases in 1291 and 1293 (cf. Hodgson 1827, 24, 27, 129, & 134). The permanent settlements furthest up the valley, which are certainly named in the documentary sources during the mid-thirteenth to the early fourteenth century, were situated at Elishaw, where there was a hospital located beside Dere Street, and Shittleheugh on the north bank of the river, and at Blakehope and 'Smallburne' (Mod. Dargues) on the south side (Hodgson 1827, 20, 24–28, 146; Hodgson, 1916, 8; Liber Feodorum, 1122–1244).

The wide tracts beyond the zone of permanent settlement formed the Forest of Redesdale, embracing the entire northern half of Redesdale. The forest comprised a series of waste grounds, mostly based on the side valleys, or hopes (OE: hoppa), created by tributary burns. Redeshead, Earlside (the west side of the dale opposite Byrness), Ramshope, Spithope and Cottonshope are all mentioned in the detailed Inquisitions Post Mortem of the fourteenth century, where they are variously described as moor, woods, waste and occasionally pasture (cf. Hodgson, 1827, 31 – AD 1325; 1827, 109 – 1331; 1827, 110, 135 – 1363).

This upper dale area was thus under direct Umfraville control. In 1199, Richard de Umfraville was issued with a charter by King John granting or confirming the privilege that none might graze their cattle or hunt or fell wood in Richard's forests of Redesdale and Coquetdale, unless they had common rights there (Hodgson, 1827, 14; cf. NCRO 3635/13 p.7). This was presumably an attempt to prevent, or at least control, assart enclosures and need not imply that the forests were solely hunting reserves. The valuations applied to the areas of pasture, wood, and moor etc. listed in the various Inquisitions Post Mortem alone refute that notion, although hunting was certainly one of the purposes for which the forests were used. Instead these tracts were evidently utilised as extensive upland demesne, exploited through pastoralism rather than agricultural cultivation. Pastoralism was clearly a prominent element in the manorial economy of Redesdale by the mid-thirteenth century, and doubtless much earlier. In 1245, the Umfraville manors were testified to have pasture for 1,140 sheep, pasture for mares worth £12, and 1,400 acres of cattle pasture – or perhaps pasture for 1400 cattle (Cal. Doc. Scot. I: 305, no.1667).

Vaccaries and bercaries

Pastoralist exploitation of this upland demesne was effected by two distinct means. The first was through the establishment of directly managed stock farms. As noted above, this practice was commonly associated with great ecclesiastical landowners such as the Cistercian abbeys of Fountains, Rievaulx and, more locally, Newminster, and was particularly prevalent further south in the baronial forests of the West Riding's Calder valley and the Lancashire Pennines (Faull & Woodhouse, 1981, 758–761; McDonnell, 1988, 8–9). The existence of twenty-four vaccaries, or demesne cattle farms, in the manor of Otterburn was noted in the Inquisition of Gilbert de Umfraville in 1308, whilst ten were totalled there in 1330 on the death of his wife, Elizabeth (Cal. IPM V, 14, no.47; VII, 156, no.208; cf. Hodgson 1827, 109). Unfortunately, in the absence of any further detail none of these cattle farms can be located more precisely within the manor, but it is likely that at least some lay in the hopes of Upper Redesdale.

One Umfraville stock-farming enterprise can be identified in the Forest of Redesdale, however, in the form of the herd of mares which was reared on the west side of Cottonshope during the later twelfth and thirteenth centuries. The tithe foals from this herd were granted to the Abbot and Convent of Kelso, probably in the later twelfth century, and confirmed by Gilbert de Umfraville in 1227/28 (Liber de Calchou; cf. Hodgson ,1827, 15–18), when the Abbey successfully defended its claim to the foals in a dispute with the rector of Elsdon Parish. There may have been a permanent settlement of some kind associated with the maintenance of the herd, akin to a vaccary or bercary (cf. Charlton & Day 1979, 209). Such an installation would clearly be of especial interest if its precise location could be identified, and a start might be made by examining the neighbourhood of the present Cottonshope Farm. It is noteworthy that the Cottonshope ranch itself can only be identified because its stock figured in a grant to an ecclesiastical institution, which thereby ensured the preservation of the associated documentation in the Chartulary of the Abbey of Kelso and also gave rise to a legal dispute over the rights to the tithe foals.

Otherwise, exploitation of these areas was doubtless mainly on a seasonal basis by means of regular transhumance from the lower valley to the sheiling or agistment grounds in the upper valley and hopes, where stock would be grazed from April to August (Charlton & Day, 1979, 209–210; McDonnell 1988, 8, 14–15). The upland tributary hopes recorded in the inquisitions do not, therefore, comprise the full extent of Umfraville land in Upper Redesdale, the acreages recorded being far too small. Rather, they represent merely the parcels which were being leased out at any one time to tenants at will, for the grazing of livestock. The valuations recorded were the sums paid by those tenants as indicated by the Inquisition Post Mortem of Robert de Umfraville held in 1331 (Cal. IPM VII, 290 no.390). Similarly, another Umfraville inquisition (Cal. IPM V 14, no.47 – 1308, cf. Hodgson 1827, 109) specifically labels the value of four unnamed wastes in the liberty as their 'worth in agistment'.

No messuages are listed along with the 'diverse parcels' of wood, moor, pasture or whatever in the upland hopes, implying that there were no permanent farm tenancies situated there, (though there may have been demesne stock farms in these areas). The exploitation of the valley above Elishaw/Shittleheugh and Blakehope/Smallburne was, therefore, almost certainly effected by means of seasonal transhumance from lowland farmsteads to upland summering or agistment grounds. There is only limited evidence for transhumance in Redesdale at this date. The place names Davyshiel and Garretshiel suggest that transhumance was practised in the area at some date before the late thirteenth century, by which time these had become permanent settlements.

The tract of Upper Coquetdale incorporated in the Umfraville liberty has preserved more explicit evidence for this period. For example, in 1244 Batailshiel, in the Usway valley next to the lordship of Kidland, was described as the logia (lodge or perhaps shieling) 'formerly belonging to William Batalle but now to John of Letelwell'. It featured in the boundary delimitation of a land grant to Newminster Abbey by Gilbert de Umfraville (NCH XV (1940), 436–437; NC: 78). Later on, in 1398, sheilings are specifically mentioned in Redesdale in the Inquisition Post Mortem of Matilda, wife of Henry de Percy, earl of Northumberland, and formerly wife of Gilbert Umfraville (Cal. IPM XVII, 468 no.1246). The shielings were presumably located on Earlside and Over Redeshead, which figure amongst the places listed therein. However, no shielings are explicitly referred to in Redesdale prior to this date, and it is possible that agistment was the form of transhumance more commonly used by the Umfravilles and their tenants in the dale during the earlier period, before the mid-fourteenth century.

Late Medieval Recolonisation

Much reduced rental valuations are recorded for the Redesdale manors in the fourteenth-century inquisitions, reflecting population fall and settlement contraction caused by the warfare, climatic decline and devastating plague epidemics of that period. By the end of the century, however, there are hints that settlement was beginning to creep further up the valley. The 1398 inquisition (see Appendix 2) includes amongst its list of 'divers places, scalings and wastes', a series of place names not hitherto encountered, including 'Kirkestilland' (Birkhill?) and 'Mekilhyresfeld' (Horsley?). Their position in the list and tentative identification imply that these places – which probably represent farmsteads or parcels of valley-bottom arable or meadow land carved out of the waste as 'assarts' – lay above the earlier limit of cultivation and settlement, Elishaw–Shittleheugh–Blakehope.

Indeed, it is possible that the turbulent conditions of the later medieval era may, paradoxically, have ultimately favoured an expansion of peasant colonisation and seasonal transhumance, and an improvement in the status of the border tenants. Formerly, the exploitation of the uplands, whether by means of permanent stock farms or seasonal shieling pastures and lodges, appears to have been tightly controlled by the Umfraville feudal overlords or their principal vassals, such as the Battaille lineage in the Usway valley noted above. A weakening of feudal lordship over the Northumbrian dales during the fourteenth to fifteenth centuries, and the attendant growth of the kinship 'surnames', may conceivably have afforded the tenant peasantry more opportunity for assarting coupled with less strictly regulated shielding on upland pastures.

Thus, far greater acreages of pasture are listed in 1495 (Cal. IPM Hen VII, 414 no.971) in the upland hopes, by comparison with those recorded in the fourteenth century. Whereas in 1325 there were 100 acres of wood and 200 of waste in Cottenshope, 1,000 acres were rented there at the end of the fifteenth century. Likewise, twenty acres of wood and 200 of moor in Spithope in 1325, as opposed to 1,000 in 1495 (see Appendix 1). Moreover, new grazing areas figure in the 1495 document, including 'Thillez' (clearly the Sills Burn valley from its position in the list) and 'Byrdhop' (by the mid-sixteenth century the site of a settlement on the west bank of the Rede, a little way above Rochester). All this is presumably indicative of some measure of agricultural recovery, but may also signify that any earlier restriction on the extent of grazing in the upper valley, to safeguard the lord's hunting rights, had effectively been abandoned.

Patterns of Exploitation in Upper Coquetdale

Upper Coquetdale provides yet another example of medieval pastoralist exploitation, again involving the long distance driving of livestock, namely the substantial monastic development of the upland pastures in Upper Coquetdale. This monastic investment followed the granting, by the Umfravilles, of vast acreages in Kidland to the Cistercian Abbey of Newminster, near Morpeth, in the twelfth to thirteenth centuries.

The stages by which Newminster acquired its lands, pasturage and other rights and properties in Kidland, is meticulously documented in the Abbey's chartulary (NC 73–81; cf. NCH XV (1940), 449–50). The relevant documents are set out in Appendix 1.

Something of the scale of investment the monasteries were putting into the Coquetdale uplands in the twelfth and thirteenth centuries can be gauged from these, and other, documents. The monks' rights were tightly circumscribed in the initial grant of 1181. They had no right to lease grazing rights themselves. They could take what they wanted from the forest by order of the lord's foresters, but their dogs were to have one foot cut off to prevent them chasing the lord's game, and it is clear that the preservation of their hunting rights was still an important consideration for the Umfravilles at this stage.

It is likely that use of the Kidland pastures was largely on a seasonal basis, reflected in the numerous way leaves the abbey negotiated with neighbouring landowners to enable its lay brothers (conversi), servants, flocks and herds to make the journey from Newminster and the monastery's lowland granges and estates[18] in late spring, returning as autumn approached (cf. McDonnell, 1988, 10). In undertaking this transhumance, the herdsmen and livestock would inevitably have followed the drove road of Clennell Street, then known as 'the great road of Hernespeth' or Yarnspeth, and probably already an ancient routeway, before dispersing into the different tributary hopes of Upper Coquetdale.

The abbey maintained a grange at Caistron, west of Rothbury, which would have served as a useful intermediate station on the journey. From the Inquisition Post Mortem for Gilbert de Umfraville I in 1245, we learn that the monks of Newminster had another grange in Rowhope, adjacent to the Kidland pastures (Cal. Doc. Scot. i, no. 1667). Given

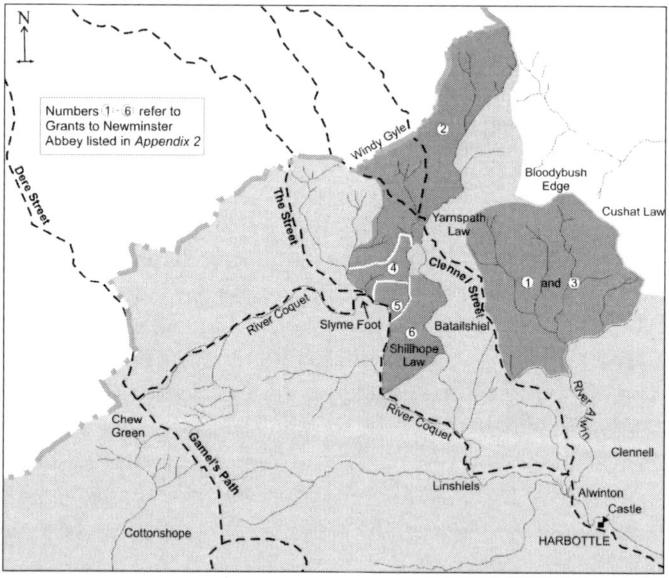

Twelfth- to thirteenth-century grants of grazing land in Kidland to Newminster Abbey. (See Appendix 2 for full boundary description of land grants 1–6.)

the proximity of the fulling mill, which the Cistercians were permitted by Gilbert to build a little further down stream at Hepden (Barrowburn), it is tempting to see these installations as part of an integrated operation, with the fleeces from flocks shorn at the grange being processed at the fulling mill.

The manner in which the abbey and the Umfravilles marked their boundaries where there were no natural or pre-existing man-made features such as burns and roads, is clearly evinced in the charters, with references to a ditch or earthen bank (fossatum) dug by the monks of Newminster (bounder 3) and several mentions of crosses (bounders 2 and 4), including the manner in which these were erected in front of representatives from both parties (‘*ad crucem quam praedicti monachi posuerunt per visum militum meorum ibi*’ – bounder 2). The earthwork can still be identified on the ground at Wholehope, running alongside Clennell Street (Charlton & Day, 1979, 227; Charlton 1996, 126–7, no.5500; NT 903094). Also hinted at is the continuing uncertainty, in the later twelfth century, regarding the actual line of the border with Scotland along the high Cheviot ridges, expressed in William de Umfraville's cautious phrase 'as much as belongs to me there' (bounder 2 – cf. Barrow, 1966, 38).

Smaller areas had already been granted to individuals, the chief tenants or followers of the Umfravilles, men like William Bataille, whose lodge (logia) has given its name to present-day Batailshiel, John of Letelwell and Henry the Crossbowman, whose holding was purchased by the monks through Richard de Umfraville *c.*1226. These individuals doubtless exploited the uplands as the Umfravilles themselves did, either by grazing their own stock on the pasture or by leasing it out to the ordinary tenants of the liberty and the ten townships who made use of the uplands through regular seasonal transhumance.

The motivations of the Umfravilles in making such extensive awards to Newminster were doubtless mixed. In part, they were probably concerned to benefit their souls and reduce their term in purgatory, which the grateful prayers of the monks could help to secure, as reflected in the conventional expressions of piety in the documents. Odinel de Umfraville may well have been partially motivated by a realisation of impending mortality when he made the first of grants, but it is clear that that transaction was essentially a straightforward lease, for which the abbey had to pay a considerable sum – 228 marks in 1181, with a further 40 marks to Odinel's heir in 1184 to confirm the lease.

Later grants by Richard, William and then Gilbert de Umfraville I appear more generous. Gilbert de Umfraville in particular expressed direct concern for the soul of his father, Richard, and his other ancestors, when he gave the monks exclusive hunting rights on the Cheviot and Coquetdale moors, which the Umfravilles had reserved to themselves in previous grants. However, in his confirmation of his predecessors grants, in 1270 Gilbert de Umfraville II revealed that up until that date the Umfravilles were still receiving a significant sum – 18 marks – every year from the monastery for the use of the Kidland pastures (NC 79–80).

For the Umfravilles, the transfer of pasturage rights to the monastery was perhaps an ideal, albeit indirect, means of exploiting the upland tracts of their liberty, enabling them to benefit from the energetic, well-managed agricultural endeavour and investment which the ecclesiastical corporation could provide. The rental brought in a steady income, with occasional opportunities for lump-sum payments in the form of further grants or fees for reconfirmation of previous agreements, without involving the lord in the trouble and expense of having to manage the sheep and cattle farming himself. Over time, the petitions of the abbey would have helped to bring about a gradual increase in the extent of the grants and the privileges attached to them, and a relaxation in their financial terms, but until the later thirteenth century, at least, the Umfravilles must have found their dealings with Newminster financially profitable, as well as spiritually beneficial.

There is a notable contrast between the extent of monastic holdings in upper Coquetdale and Redesdale. Though each valley had its own, small, religious establishment – the Benedictine nunnery at Holystone and the hospital at Elishaw – Redesdale attracted little interest on the part of external monastic houses to compare with Newminster's extensive pastures in Kidland and the Cheviot moors. The sum total, in fact, is restricted to the carucate (100 acres of ploughland) held by Jedburgh Abbey in Troughend (Liber Feodorum ii, AD 1122 – 1242), and the grant, to Kelso Abbey, of a tithe of the foals from the Cottonshope stud range, made by Odinel de Umfraville in the later twelfth century and confirmed by his successors (Liber de Calchou; reproduced by Hodgson, 1827, 15–18). The comparatively rich herbage provided by the porphyritic subsoil of Kidland may have been the crucial factor in this regard. Indeed, Newminster was not the only monastic house to be granted a parcel of land around the Coquet's headwaters. Alnwick Abbey also received a tract of land at Carlcroft, to the west of Newminster's Kidland pastures.

Hethpool and the Cheviot Pastures

The final medieval case study, which relates to Hethpool in the College Valley in the northern Cheviots, is much less explicit in its reference to transhumance and droving. Instead, these practices may be tentatively inferred, following an ingenious suggestion by Colm O'Brien, from the complex tenurial arrangements which prevailed in the vill, and the inherent likelihood of such practices in the light of its topographic situation. What is particularly interesting about this case is the evidence it provides that these practices might pre-date the Norman Conquest.

Hethpool formed one of the constituent vills of the barony of Wooler, which was held by the Muschamp lineage until the male line was extinguished with the death of Robert de Muschamp III in 1250. The lordship was established by Henry I (1100–35), like the great majority of Anglo–Norman baronies in Northumberland (Kapelle, 1979, 199, 207; Lomas, 1996, 22–25). There was already a complex fragmented pattern of landholding in Hethpool by the time of the feudal survey conducted for Henry III in 1242. One quarter of the vill was held in feudal tenure, along with the vills of Ford, Crookham and Kimmerston, by Odinell de Ford, for a single knight's fee (i.e. the military service of one knight). Similarly, Stephen de Coupland held half a carucate (approximately fifty to sixty acres) of ploughland for a thirtieth of a knight's fee. Odinell's holding was probably one of the Wooler barony's original fiefs, established before 1135. Indeed, Lomas has commented that this looks suspiciously like a pre-Conquest thanage (1996, 23), one of the larger and more important type of pre-Conquest estates held by members of the local Anglo-Saxon lesser nobility known as thegns. Typically these seem to have consisted of about three townships. Hence, there could be direct institutional continuity from pre-Conquest times here.

The remaining holdings recorded in 1242 were held in socage, a form of freehold tenure, which typically involved the performance of certain limited services, principally attendance at the baron's court and support for its operations (an obligation known as 'suit of court'), and sometimes, as in this case, the payment of a fixed cash rent or a pound of spices (Lomas, 1996, 19; Bailey, 2002, 27–8). Thus, Thomas de Hethpool held two bovates (twenty-four to thirty acres) in socage for the annual sum of 4*s*, whilst a moiety of the vill was held jointly by Ralph and Patrick for a sum of 8*s* per annum (Liber Feodorum II, 1119–20). These socage holdings figure again eight years later in the Inquisition Post Mortem of Robert de Muschamp in 1254, but here they are labelled drengage holdings (Cal. Doc. Scot., I, 371; cf. NCH XI (1922), 252, 267). Thus, two oxgangs, or bovates, were held by the widow (doubtless of Thomas of Hethpool) for a rent of 4*s*, whilst the other two drengage holdings (Ralph and Patrick's) paid two marks at Martinmas.[19] Drengages were also a pre-Conquest form of tenure, like thanages, but were significantly inferior in status to the latter and normally had only a single township or even part of a township, as here, by way of endowment. They were service tenements, and were integral elements in the large pre-Conquest administrative districts cum federated estates known as shires, to which historians now apply a variety of labels such as multiple estate, great estate or land unit.

It is in this context that O'Brien (2002, 66) has put forward the intriguing suggestion that the complexity of tenurial arrangements in this vill may reflect the arrangements of a much earlier multiple estate or shire. Within such a shire, Hethpool might have served as the point of entry to summer grazing and hunting lands on the high Cheviot hills, with Ford–Crookham and perhaps other lowland-centred thanage estates establishing manorial outposts in the vill in order to gain secure access to the upland resources. Certainly a seasonal route, following the College Valley, would represent the most logical access into the heart of the Cheviot massif from a substantial swathe of north Northumberland's lowland communities. Therefore, despite the tentative nature of this inference, it merits further investigation in the future.

'They sheylde together by surnames': Transhumance in the Age of the Reivers

As has been noted above, the later medieval period witnessed important changes in the upland economy. The insecurity caused by the prolonged warfare between England and Scotland from the end of the thirteenth century and the drastic reduction in population levels and consequent economic recession caused by the Black Death, probably resulted in an initial contraction in settlement. However, it also rendered the tightly controlled demesne farming of the earlier period uneconomic. The vaccaries and bercaries disappear from the records, and landlords reacted to the changed conditions by opening up their upland demesnes – the forests and free chases – to settlement and shielding by their manorial tenantry.

Thus, despite the devastating demographic impact of successive outbreaks of plague, by the fifteenth century, and perhaps even by the end of the fourteenth century, settlement was beginning to expand further up the valleys. Thus, by the mid-sixteenth century the tide of permanent settlement in Redesdale had reached sites like Rochester, Birdhope and Woollaw. In North Tynedale, although there is no record of this process of recolonisation reaching as far up the main valley as Kielder or Kennel Park, which it is suggested were inhabited in the thirteenth century, a much denser settlement pattern does seem to have built up in some of the side tributaries, notably Tarsetdale and Tarretdale.

A good example of this process is provided by Greenhaugh in Tarsetdale. Greenhaugh is first mentioned in the Comyn Inquisition Post Mortem of 1326 as a shieling (presumably implying a shieling ground with a summer settlement site). By the fifteenth century it may well have been a permanent settlement. It is included in a list of place names in an Inquisition Post Mortem of Henry Percy, third Earl of Northumberland, in 1464,

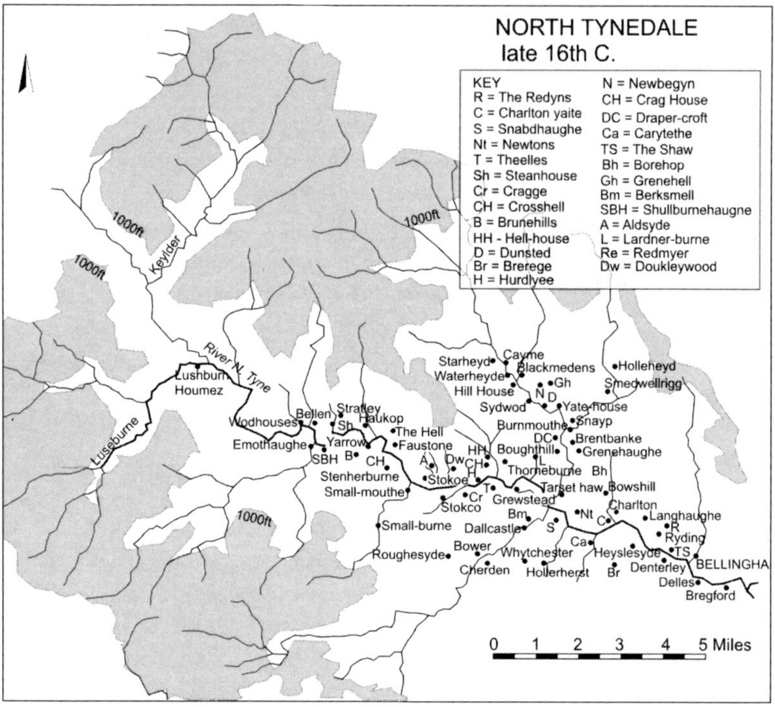

The mid-sixteenth-century settlement pattern in Upper North Tynedale, suggested by Harbottle and Newman (1973, p. 144, fig 3).

along with Sidwood, Gatehouse and Dunstead, though it is not clear which of these were settlements and which were shieling grounds (cf. Harbottle & Newman, 1973, 142; Hartshorne 1858, 260).[20] It was certainly a permanent settlement – perhaps a small hamlet – by the sixteenth century (Harbottle & Newman, 1973, 143).

The character of this settlement was significantly different. Instead of vaccaries, the settlement pattern in the valleys was composed of small tenanted hamlets and farmsteads, whilst exploitation of the hill pastures was by summering transhumance. Contemporary with these developments we see, in North Tynedale and Redesdale in particular, the emergence of kinship-based social groups known as surnames. The use of surnames became much more common from the fourteenth century onwards, but they were to have a special significance in North Tynedale and Redesdale, where they became associated with the border reiving clans. Indeed, surname, rather than the Scottish Highland label clan, was the term used to refer to these groupings in contemporary sources.

Effectively these were kinship-based self-protection groups, which emerged in the late medieval period as a result of the chronic insecurity due to prolonged Anglo–Scottish conflict and weakened lordship. Such groups provided some measure of security for the two valleys' inhabitants during these turbulent conditions through the threat of collective clan retaliation and feud. The four principal surnames in North Tynedale were the Charltons, Robsons, Dodds and Milburns. In Redesdale the Halls, Reeds, Potts and Hedleys predominated. Although relatively little is known regarding the origins of this distinctive society, since most of the available documentation derives from the sixteenth and early seventeenth centuries, such evidence as there is suggests that most of the surnames were already present in North Tynedale and Redesdale before the end of the thirteenth century and were beginning to act as armed kinship groups by the late fourteenth century (cf. Robson, 1989, 31–51).

Extract from Speed's Map of Northumberland, 1610, showing the overall settlement pattern in the uplands, with permanent wintersteeds distributed along the valleys and summering grounds in the surrounding hills.

Each surname tended to cluster together, occupying particular settlements and even certain parts of the valley, especially in North Tynedale. There, the Dodds and Milburns predominated in Tarsetdale and Tarretdale, whilst the Robsons were more prevalent towards the upper end of the valley and the Charltons lower down the dale, between Tarset Burn and Bellingham, but also in Tarsetdale. Moreover, in Redesdale, and to a large extent in North Tynedale too, the transhumant farmers summered alongside their kinsmen on the high pastures. The survey of Debateable and Border Lands, carried out on behalf of the Crown in 1604, lists the 'high lands called Summer grounds' in the manor of Harbottle,[21] which included Elsdon, Corsenside and Holystone parishes (1604 Survey, 104; see Appendix 1 no.9), commenting:

> The aforesaid groundes are used as Summer and Sheildinge grounds by the whole of the inhabitants of the Mannor, wherin each man knoweth his sheildinge steed; and they sheylde together by Surnames; not keepinge Catle accordinge to the proporcion of the rent but eatinge all in Common without stinte or number: in which grownde the Tenants claime Custome, as they doe in their other Tenements.

The 1618 Redesdale Rental provides still more detail regarding these summering grounds, recording not only the sums paid in rent but also the names of the individual tenants who occupied each of the grounds (summarised in Appendix 1 no.9). No comparable rental exists for North Tynedale, but equivalent information can be derived from the Minutes of the Court Baron for the Manor of Charlton Yate, held 7–10 October 1605, (Aln Cas C XII; reproduced in NCH XV (1940), 248–49) which set out in detail how the upland pastures of Tarsetdale were divided up by the surnames:

> Division of the open grazing lands among the families or graynes of the manor.
>
> Sandie Mylburne of Yatehouse (Gatehouse) and a number of other Milburns for themselves and the rest of their Grayne took by grant of the Earl's commissioners the waste land called Hemloppe Burne Graynes (Emblehope).
>
> Michael Hunter of Water Head and the rest of the Hunter grayne took the waste ground at Hawkuppested [*sic* Hawkhopehead?].
>
> Edward Charleton of Hesleyside for his house and the Charletons of Shitlington, Cuthbert Charleton of Bellingham and Gilbert Charleton of Boughthyll for them and their houses, Jasper Charleton of Hawcuppe for his house and the Charletons of Snabdauge, William Charleton of Charlton Yate for the Charletons of Caryteth and the Bower, have taken the waste grounds of Lystenstone hyll. The parting of the high lands among those that are of the name of Charleton in two halves by Matthew Charlton of Ellingham, Gilbert Charleton of Boughthyll, Christopher Charleton of Hetherington and John Charleton of the Bower by the consents of all the rest of the Charletons. (The bounds are set out in full).

Winchester's study of the probate inventories for Elsdon Parish, covering the period 1555–1638, gives a clear impression of the numbers and composition of livestock held by farmers in this area (2000, 18–20). Cattle were their principal possession, with only one of the twenty-three testators in the sample lacking any such beasts, however few in number. Fewer than half had any horses (none having more than three), and only one third had flocks of sheep, although five flocks of goats were also recorded. The herd sizes were generally small, averaging just over sixteen cattle of all kinds, with the great majority (eighty-two per cent) numbering less than twenty cattle. All the recorded testators had cows ('kine') and most (seventy-eight per cent) had some oxen, a reflection of the dual economy practised by the borderers – predominantly pastoralist but with some arable cultivation undertaken in the valley beside the wintersteed, for which draught oxen were essential. Similarly, none of the flocks of sheep recorded contained more than 150 animals, and some were much smaller (under fifty).

In contrast to this general picture of numerous poor farmers with small herds, a relatively wealthy surname 'headsman', Edward Hall of Monkridge who died in 1613, was in possession of forty-four cattle (including seventeen cows and twelve oxen) and 140 sheep. On the basis of references to cattle being in the hands of others, Winchester suggests that livestock belonging to the wealthy minority may often have been lent out to kinsmen, or were herded on behalf of the owner by men with few animals of their own. It is evident that in terms of the total number of stock, sheep were no less significant than cattle, but their ownership was much more concentrated, and cattle were therefore more important to the community as a whole. Thus, although the Northumbrian uplands prior to 1650 cannot be described solely as a black cattle economy, such beasts certainly constituted the single most important element.

Table showing livestock recorded in the probate inventories for Elsdon Parish and the manor of Alston Moor (reproduced from Winchester, 2000, 19, table 1.1).

Period	Elsdon 1555–1638	Alston Moor 1569–1640
No. of inventories in sample	23	27
Cattle		
% of inventories with cattle	96	93
Total cattle herd: no. (%) of inventories with herds totalling:		
Under 20	18 (82)	15 (60)
20–39	2 (9)	6 (24)
40 and over	2 (9)	4 (16)
Average cattle herd	16.4	21.7
Cows ('Kine')		
No. (%) of inventories with cows	24 (96)	25 (93)
Range of herd sizes	2–39	1–35
Average no. of cows	6.7	10.6
Oxen		
No. (%) of inventories with oxen	18 (78)	1 (4)
Horses		
% of inventories with horses	43	95
No. of inventories with:		
1–3 horses	10	19
4–10 horses	0	4
Over 10 horses	0	0
Sheep		
% of inventories with sheep	30	100
No. (%) of inventories with flocks totalling:		
1–49	2	11 (44)
50–99	0	9 (36)
100–149	2	1 (4)
150–199	0	0
200 or more	0	4 (16)
Goats		
No. (%) of inventories with goats	5 (22)	0

The predominance of cattle was not quite so marked in some of the other upland dales, as Winchester's parallel study of the probate inventories from 1569 to 1640 relating to the manor of Alston Moor, at the head of South Tynedale, makes clear. This district lay just over the county border in what is now Cumbria (formerly Cumberland), but the pattern recorded there probably holds true for the adjacent Northumbrian townships of South Tynedale. Whilst virtually every inventory examined included cattle (twenty-five out of twenty-seven, or ninety-three per cent, with an average herd size of a little over twenty), as in Redesdale, here there was a significant difference in that every single inventory listed

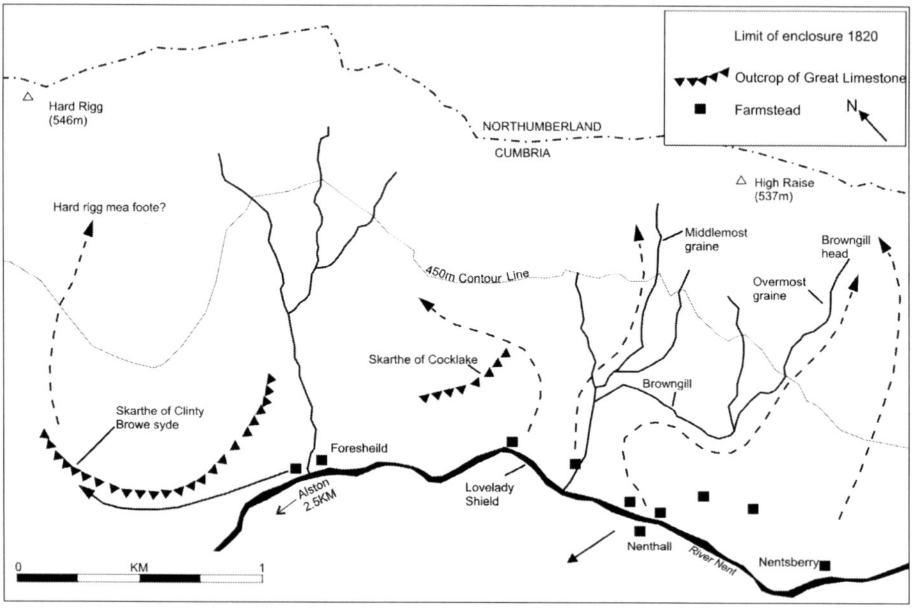

Winchester's tentative reconstruction of the drove routes from the settlements of the Nent Valley on to the high fell based on the 1597 Alston Moor 'drift roll' (after Winchester 2000, fig 5.5).

a herd of sheep. Nearly half of these numbered fewer than fifty sheep and eighty per cent mustered less than 100, but a few counted more than 200. George Lee of Garrigill, for example, who died in 1605, had 235 sheep, in addition to two horses and forty-two cattle (of which twenty-five were cows), and was clearly a substantial yeoman farmer. A further difference is represented by the fact that only one inventory recorded any oxen. Here, the pastoral economy had completely supplanted the arable, and it was lead mining which would eventually provide the second element of a dual economy.

The drift roll for the manor (NRO EP 46/85), drawn up in 1597 but based largely on an earlier version compiled in the reign of Henry VII, enables a tentative reconstruction of the pattern of routes by which the stock from each farmstead was driven up on to the fell grazings (Winchester 2000, 112–13). Two entries give a flavour of its contents (the names of the settlements and some of the upland features are still identifiable today):

> Item...The tenements called Nenthall shall drive over the Browns gill up the over moss graine and so to the fell, and over the Browns gill head and so over to the fell, and when they drive over the water (i.e. the South Tyne) they shall drive into the Hut gill graines and so to the gromall gate and then to the fell.
>
> Item...The tenements at Low byers, Spinister Croft (now Spencey Croft) and the Loneing Foot shall drive over the cowstand land and through the Dubbard moa and so to the fell.

A similar pattern of droveways is documented in West Allendale in a series of jury verdicts from the 1620s and 1630s (Winchester, 2000, 113, citing NRO 672/1/PR/A1-A3 and PR 20–105). Here, each settlement drove its stock daily up onto the moors on the east side of the valley by means of an allotted day drift or beast rake (the west side of the valley was reserved for calves and lambs outside the winter months or days when the weather was too bad or misty to venture onto the high moors).

Transhumance to shieling grounds was practised in this part of South Tynedale. Tenants settled in the upper reaches of the manor, at Garrigill beside the South Tyne and in the Nent valley, were listed as holding shielings (scalingas) in an Inquisition Post Mortem of 1315 (cf. Winchester, 2000, 160 citing PRO, C134/35 (16)). A paine roll for Alston Moor,[22] setting out the byelaws and attendant fines imposed by the manor court to regulate the use of upland grazing and other manorial resources, still contained a clause regarding the timing of tenants' date of departure for – and return from – the shieling grounds (3 May and 1 August respectively). Like the related drift roll, this paine roll was compiled in 1597, but was also reliant on an earlier version produced in the reign of Henry VII.

In addition to the shieling practised by the local inhabitants, there was some scope for the movement of stock from still further afield, just as in the earlier period. The 1605 Court Baron for Charlton Yate again records the names of those who had invited outsiders to graze their herds and flocks within the manor. This appears similar to some of the agistment arrangements followed earlier, whereby farmers might drive their beasts into a different township or manor, paying for grazing there per head of stock and hiring local herdsmen to tend them. However, this practice carried the risk of overgrazing the pasture, particularly when it was undertaken without the consent of others who had a stake in the pasture, as was the case in at least one instance in 1605:

> Presentment of the names of those who permitted persons not of the manor to graze sheep on their lands:
>
> Edward Charleton of Hesleyside hath brought in Margaret, countess of Bothwell, with a flock of sheep and a sort of neet (calves) with the consent of all the rest of the Charletons.
>
> John Charleton of Reedsmouth hath brought in one Archie Roger, Scotishman, without the consent of any with a flock of sheep and one hundreth nowte (bullocks/young oxen).
>
> William Charleton of Bogleholl hath brought in one George Niyou of Callaly with a flock of sheep and one hundreth nowte.

As conditions improved following the Union of the Crowns, permanent settlement rapidly advanced up the border dales, reaching the head of Redesdale and North Tynedale. By the late seventeenth and early eighteenth centuries, permanently occupied farmsteads had appeared in the upper reaches of Redesdale at Ramshope, Catcleugh and Byrness, for instance, with a functioning burial ground to serve these settlers at Byrness and a water mill a little further down the valley at Byrness Mill, all in an area which had been simply a summering ground in 1618[23] (1618 Rental, 334).

New farmsteads were also established in the Forest of Lowes to the north of the Roman Wall (Woodside & Crow, 1999, 66, 73–80). This entailed a concomitant reduction in the scale of transhumance. A later amendment in the 1597 Alston Moor paine roll notes the regulation regarding the timing of shielding had been withdrawn, presumably because it was no longer relevant as shielings were replaced by permanent cottages (Winchester, 2000, 162). Thus, by the end of the seventeenth century this custom, which had for so long been an indelible part of the seasonal rhythm of life in the border uplands, had largely vanished. No longer would the hills resound with the spectacle and clamour of virtually entire communities moving with all their livestock up to the high pastures in spring and returning in early autumn. Yet, just as one form of droving was dying out, another, carried out over greater distances still, was becoming increasingly prominent.

The Origins of Anglo–Scottish Droving

Haldane (1971, 6–19) has summarised the evidence for the origins of the droving trade across the Border from Scotland to England. It is clear from the number of regulations enacted by medieval Scottish kings, designed to prevent the export of livestock in times of food shortage, for example, that some trade was carried on between the two countries during the medieval period despite the prolonged periods of warfare. The great fair at Stagshaw Bank, situated just north of Corbridge at the very hub of the old Roman road network in Northumberland, was already in existence as early as 1204 (Charlton & Day, 1979, 225; Bonser, 1970, 134; cf. Cowper 1970–1971, 31).[24] It was to become, reputedly, the largest provincial cattle fair in Britain, second only to Smithfield. In 1359, a letter of conduct was issued to two Scottish drovers, Andrew Moray and Alan Erskyn, for travelling through England or the King's foreign domains with horses, oxen, cows and other goods and merchandise. Ten years later the Scottish Parliament allowed cattle to be sold to Englishmen, fixing customs dues on beasts leaving the country (Haldane, 1971, 11). Conversely, in 1451 the Scottish Parliament prohibited any trade to England except in cash, and, during the famine of 1480, banned south-bound traffic across the Border entirely. Certainly a droving trade seems to have been firmly established by the fifteenth and sixteenth centuries, although it was probably nothing like the scale that it reached in later times.[25]

In the sixteenth century of course, much of the traffic across the Border was rather more illicit, involving reiving cattle – what might be termed droving without the owner's consent. The Scottish Border surnames were at least as active in this as their counterparts on the English side, and traffic must have moved in both directions on every conceivable trackway and crossing point. The Border-watch schedules of 1541 and 1552, particularly those for the night watches which had to focus on known choke points that could be scrutinised in the dark, such as fords, give a clear impression of the multiplicity of routes which might have been used by such raiders (reproduced in Nicolson, 1747, 147–218; Hodgson, 1827, 71–2; 1828, 239–40; 1840, 118–19; NCH IV (1897), 245–6).

Following the Union of the Crowns in 1603, this reiving activity was ruthlessly suppressed and the legal droving trade gradually assumed greater and greater prominence as the seventeenth century progressed. Thus, by 1669, in the month of September alone 867 cattle and 400 sheep from the Borders were driven through the manor of Alston Moor, at the head of South Tynedale (Winchester, 2000, 160, citing CRO, Ca/2/140). It was increasingly recognised that few Scottish products were in as great a demand in the country's wealthier southern neighbour as cattle were, and that, as a consequence, this could constitute a lucrative export trade (Haldane, 1971, 17–19).

Initially the revived droving trade began in the south-west of Scotland, as Galloway had an established reputation for livestock production well before the end of the seventeenth century. Records show that it was this area that chiefly supplied the cattle for trade with England before the Act of Union, and that the animals were usually driven over the Border on the western side of the country into Cumberland and Lancashire

(Dodgshon, 1981, 252,256). Actual numbers are hard to locate, but it has been reliably asserted that in one year, 1662, 20,000 cattle passed through Carlisle (Donaldson, 1978, 387). There was trade over the eastern side of the Border, but, during the seventeenth century, this was much more localised and included a far greater proportion of sheep, as well as being generally of lesser volume than in the west.

However, as a result of the Act of Union and a rising awareness of the valuable opportunities for selling livestock in England, farmers in south-east Scotland began to produce larger quantities of cattle. A consequence of this was that the droving trade through Northumberland increased greatly so that some drovers were forced to look for new routes into the county, sometimes to the annoyance of farmers previously untroubled by the presence of droving in the neighbourhood of their holdings. It was reported that in one instance, in 1736, these activities led to a complaint from the tenant of Hindhope in Roxburghshire that drovers were crossing over his land into the Coquet Valley rather than using the traditional route through Redesdale (Dodgshon, 1981, 258–65).

NOTES

1 This does not imply that no agriculture was carried out in the uplands. It most certainly was in the valleys and in the immediate environs of the settlements, just as it was in the medieval and early modern periods. Areas of cord-rig – possibly the result of spade-dug cultivation – have been identified by fieldwork and aerial photography, notably through the work of Tim Gates in the Hadrian's Wall corridor, for example. (cf. Gates, 1999, 21; 2004)

2 The herds were generally moved up into the hills in mid-late spring and returned in late summer/early autumn; cf. Winchester, 2000, pp88–90 for a summary of the various recorded seasonal dates for this movement.

3 Camden, 720, quoted from Philemon Holland's translation (1610), cited by Ramm et al. (1970, 1).

4 Technically the term forest was reserved for royal hunting districts whilst the baronial equivalent was designated a free chase. However, much of the Northumbrian uplands was contained within a series of viceregal or palatine lordships, known as liberties, regalities or franchises, notably the Umfraville liberty of Redesdale and the liberty of Tynedale, which was held by the Scottish Crown. Hence the hunting reserves within these areas were labelled forests.

5 Evidence for settlement, population levels and tenurial development at Tarset has been collated by Wrathmell. (1975, II, 506)

6 The *Iter of Wark* comprises a summary of judicial proceedings conducted by the royal justices dispatched annually from Scotland to hold the eyre at Wark-on-Tyne, the capital of the liberty of Tynedale. The proceedings for two years, 1279 and 1293, have survived. The Latin text of the proceedings for 1279 was published by Hartshorne in an appendix in the *Feudal and Military Antiquities in Northumberland and the Scottish Borders.* (1858, ix-lxviii; cited here as *Iter of Wark*)

7 The place name Charlton may denote 'the settlement of the ceorls' or 'peasants'. (cf. Winchester, 1987, 19)

8 For the Inquisition Post Mortem for Adam de Charlton, dated 1303, see Charlton 1859b.

9 See Cathcart King 1983, pp341–2; 371–2 n.261a; NCH XV (1940) pp246–247; Pevsner et al. 2002, pp61–2, 582.

10 In 1244, more than twenty years before the issue of the licence to crenalate, Hugh de Bolbec, Sheriff of Northumberland, was instructed to take into his keeping the 'castle of Tyreset', which the King of Scots would have delivered to him; its lord, Walter Comyn, was to be allowed to remove his stores, weapons etc. (Cal. Close R. 1242–1247, 221; cf. Cathcart King 1983, 341; Harbottle & Newman 1973, 139 n.9)

11 The element 'park' figures in several place names – Park Cottage, Park Hill and Park Bank (the last being the name of the field between Park Cottage and the castle shown on a Bell estate map of 1837: NCRO ZHE 43-23).

12 The 1326 IPM records the mill had formerly been worth £30 per annum, 'but now nothing because it lies broken and out of order.'

13 The *Iter of Wark* contains a reference to 'the fulling mill of Tarset' (molendinum fullonicum de Tyrset), where Richard the Fuller (Ricardus le Fulur) suffered a burglary in 1279. (Hartshorne, 1858, liii)

14 Sixteeenth- to seventeenth-century documents indicate there had been nineteen tenants of Tarset at some stage before 1584 and there were thirteen houses registered for the Hearth Tax there in 1666 (cf. Wrathmell, 1975, II, 506), but it is not clear whether these records refer to the population of a nucleated village site or settlement dispersed throughout the township in scattered farmsteads.

15 These manorial stock farms are not named or located, with one exception, the stud farm in Cottonshope. (cf. Rushworth 1994, pp11–12)

16 Useful recent summaries of medieval settlement and landuse in this area are provided by Crow 1995, pp98–102 and Woodside & Crow 1999, pp56–66.

17 A summary of the archaeological evidence for medieval settlement in – and exploitation of – Redesdale and Upper Coquetdale has been provided by Charlton and Day (1979)

18 These may have included Filton and Tolland beside Dere Street in the barony of Prudhoe, which were also the result of Umfraville grants to Newminster. (cf. NC 63ff; Cal. Doc. Scot. i, no.1, 667–1,245)

19 In 1256, a legal action for dower was brought against three individuals by Eva, described as widow of Patrick Dreng (cf. NCH XI (1922), 267). The three defendants may all have been Patrick's heirs and two of them his sons.

20 The inquisition lists the Earl's 'lands and tenements' within the Liberty of Tynedale, called Talbot's lands, as follows (those in the upper valley are highlighted): the manor of Walwykgrange; the towns and lordships of Hawden, Charleton, Overthornburn and Netherthornburn (Thorneyburn) 28 messuages, 1,000 acres of land, 300 acres of meadow, 3,000 acres of pasture, 200 acres of wood, 200 acres of turbary (peat diggings) and 2,000 acres of moor in Walwykgrange, Hawden, Charleton, Overthornburn, Netherthornburn (i.e. High and Low Thorneyburn), the Syde, Grayside, Langhalgh, Close Hill, Bullishil, Newton, Sundaysight, Highmore. Emlopp, Smallhall, Stokhall (Stokoe), Bromehouse, Carne, Hedestede, Dunstede, Yatehouse (Gatehouse), Grenehalgh, Grenestede, Cariteth, Tresset (Tarset), Tresset Park (Tarset Park), Barnes, Yarowe and Sydewode with appurtenances.

21 The royal manor of Harbottle was equivalent to the territory of the former Liberty of Redesdale.

22 (PRO, ADM 74/1/3, reproduced in Winchester 2000, at pp162–4. A copy of 1692 is reproduced in Welford, 1912). Full discussion of the paine roll is contained in Winchester, 2000, pp160–5.

23 In 1618 the summer pasture of Ramshope was exploited by members of the local gentry, Sir Henry Witherington and various individuals belonging to the Foster lineage, including Sir John Foster. The tenants in Spithope and 'Burnies' were predominantly members of the Hall surname, the senior of the Redesdale clans.

24 Cf. NRO ZMD 115, a list of purchases at Stagshaw Bank Fair in 1298. For general discussion of the fair see NCH IV (1897), pp209–11.

25 Cf. Haldane 1971, 13: 'confused as the records are, they do show beyond any doubt the existence at least as early as the 16th century of a cattle trade to England spasmodic and interrupted but clearly recognisable as the forerunner of the great droving traffic of days to come'.

FOUR

Droving in Northumberland from the Eighteenth to the Twentieth Century

The Eighteenth Century

During the eighteenth century, two major social trends occurred that had a very significant effect on the demand for meat and, consequently, on the droving trade. These were the considerable growth in the population of England, particularly in the second half of the century, and the rise of an industrial society in England which created a number of urban centres with a concentrated demand for food. London, by far the largest urban centre in the British Isles and traditionally the largest market for food, experienced a marked growth so that, by 1801, there were over one million people – in excess of ten per cent of the population of England and Wales – living in the capital.[1]

The importance of London as a market serviced by Scottish livestock producers has been widely documented. Haldane, the most well-known historian of the Scottish droving trade, has noted that from the late fourteenth or early fifteenth centuries, Scotland

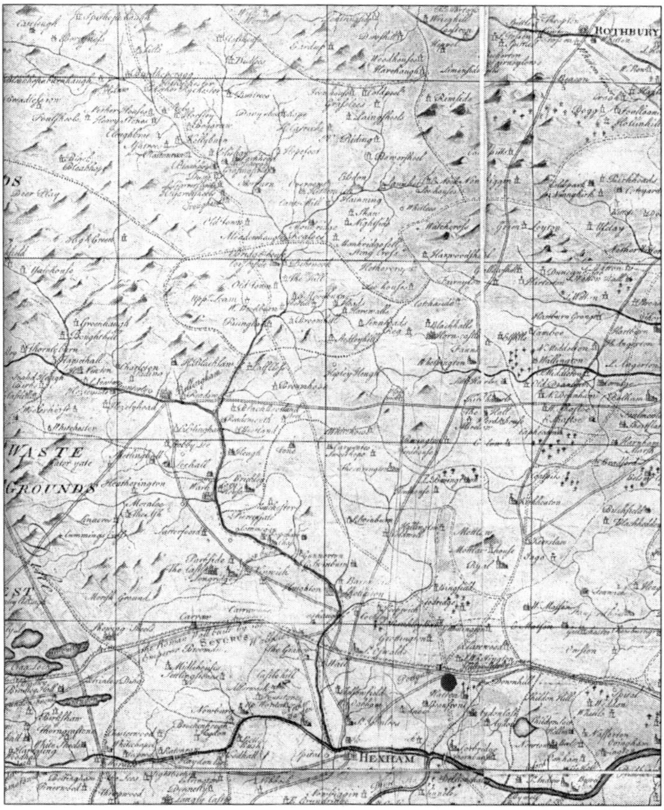

Multiple routes from the north are shown converging on Stagshaw Bank (unnamed but located just south of Portgate, marked as a black circle) on Horsley & Cay's Map of Northumberland, 1753.

Left: Photograph of a cowherd and beast at Kilham, *c.*1920, showing the typical size of animal commonly sold on for fattening by drovers.

Below: The seventeen types of standard cattle in the British Isles. Advertisement published by Bovril.

had already been involved in sending cattle south to the English markets (Haldane, 1971, 168), including London. Haldane further comments that up until the Union of the Crowns in 1603, Anglo–Scottish trade was 'always conditioned by the political and economic relations between the two countries and by the state of the Border lands', and even then economic relations did not fully stabilise until after the Union of the Parliaments in 1707. Indeed, the importing of live cattle into England from both Scotland and Ireland had been prohibited in the 1660s, but as part of the new political arrangement these barriers against the Scottish cattle trade were dismantled and renewed trading with England permitted. As a consequence, it is estimated that around 30,000 cattle were sent south across the Border in the first year following the Union of Parliaments.[2]

Thus, 1707 marked the start of an industry that was to expand steadily over the following decades so that, by the end of the eighteenth century, approximately 100,000 cattle were being driven south from Scotland each year (Bonser, 1970, 75). At this point

Engraving of shorthorned cattle from Knight's Pictorial Museum of Animated Nature, *c.*1880.

it is important to note that the demand for sheep meat was small, and there was a widespread belief among drovers that sheep could not be moved long distances in the same way as cattle (Haldane, 1971, 200). The demand for sheep from Scotland was localised to Northumberland and Durham, so that for the first half of the eighteenth century the droving trade from Scotland was principally confined to cattle. As explained below, this situation altered in the latter part of the century, and large numbers of sheep as well as cattle became regular features of droving in Northumberland.

What type of cattle were these, and from where did they originate? As Haldane and others have explained,[3] the agricultural economy of the Highlands and Islands of Scotland produced large numbers of cattle. These were usually described by contemporaries as 'black cattle', a generic term for all bovines. The animals to which the term referred were hardy, small, slow-maturing beasts with long horns. They were generally black in colour, but the term was sufficiently elastic to also cover broken-coloured, dun and even white cows (Trow-Smith, 1959, 24). Animals which were genetically hornless may also have been included, but these were comparatively rare. The breeding for sale of these beasts was the principal method by which the population in these remote areas could earn sufficient cash with which to pay rents. Moreover, the limited amount of summer grazing and winter feed necessitated the sale of large quantities of surplus livestock. The stock purchased from the Highland farmers was driven south to the large fairs held at Crieff and Falkirk, where many were purchased by other drovers and dealers who were assembling larger groups of cattle for the journey south to the English markets (Haldane, 1971, 22–24).

The Droving Trade with England

The roads and trackways used by the drovers to drive Scottish cattle from Crieff and Falkirk into England on the first stages of their journey south were chiefly located in two areas. Cattle from the south-west of Scotland, principally Galloway and Dumfries, were driven south through Carlisle into Cumberland and Westmoreland, while on the eastern side of the country the droving routes ran south from the area around Falkirk in the general direction of Hawick. From this point, they crossed over the eastern side of the Border into the valleys of North Tynedale, Redesdale and Coquetdale (Haldane, 1971, 177–78). Information about the exact course of the routes taken by the drovers is limited. The two major works by Haldane and Bonser on the droving trade north and south of the Border give very general descriptions of the routes used. Haldane is perhaps the more precise, in that he gives considerable detail about the route to the North Tyne, even including it on the map accompanying his book, as well as suggesting other routes. He is sceptical about the passage of large numbers of cattle over Carter Bar, and makes the general comment that much must remain conjectural about these routes because the evidence is so limited (Haldane, 1971, 160).

Other authors, writing more generally about the droving trade in their books, follow the leads given by Haldane and Bonser. W.G. Hoskins, in a book associated with a television series, considered the droving trade and the types of roads used by the drovers. His map shows only the valleys of the North Tyne, the Rede and the Coquet, and details the places in which the driven livestock crossed the Border. His routes follow traditional Roman and medieval pathways through the hills, although his explanation of them does not identify these origins:

> The drove-roads of the Anglo-Scottish border: there are no true passes through the Cheviots but here and there a convergence of tracks shows where it was possible to drive the Scottish cattle over the top down into the fattening pastures of England. Many of these 'roads' have their own names, such as Clennell Street, Gamel's Path, and so on. These tracks can only be traversed on foot, though an intrepid driver in a Land Ranger could just about manage the climb. Having crossed the Cheviots the cattle-drovers tended to aim for nodal villages such as Alwinton and Elsdon, where large greens accommodated them and their herds at night. (Hoskins, 1978, 120)

The accompanying map to this text does provide a good indication of the network of roads used by the drovers to cross the Anglo–Scottish border in west Northumberland, but the scale shown is hopelessly wrong – each mile on the scale is, in reality, about four miles. What is perhaps more worrying in a book produced by a noted authority on the English landscape is the notion that the cattle were being driven into England for fattening before going south for sale, and also that the roads were not linked to networks of markets such as Stagshaw, near Corbridge, or Morpeth. The names of villages and towns on the map serve only to show direction, not the purpose or destination of these routes.

One example of the uncritical adoption of the work of others is demonstrated by Addison in a chapter in his book on the lost roads of England, *Packhorse Trails, Drove Roads and Lost Roads*. The map included in the chapter is an unacknowledged copy of Bonser's map, robbed of its scale and some important details. The text simply states that, '...the journey from Scotland was more arduous and fraught with greater dangers than the journey from Wales can ever have been' (Addison, 1980, 74–5). The author then moves seamlessly into a discussion of the droving and cattle trades in Yorkshire in the eighteenth and nineteenth

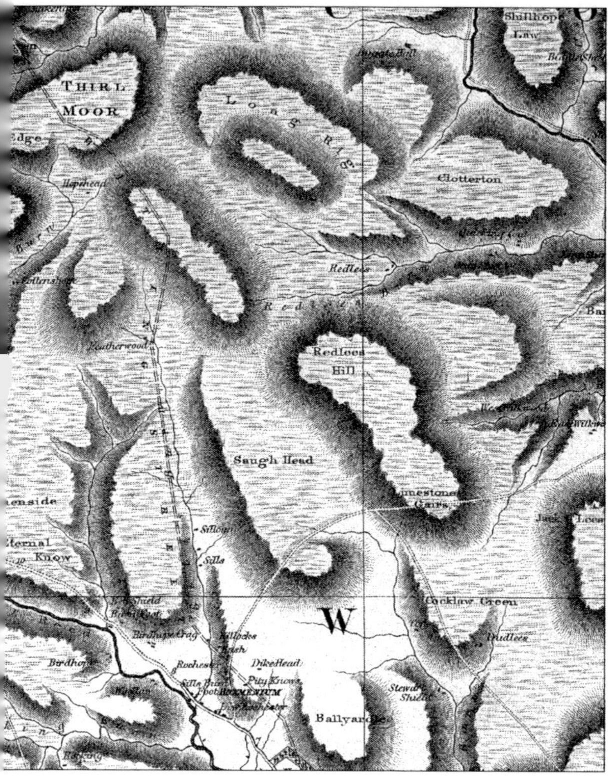

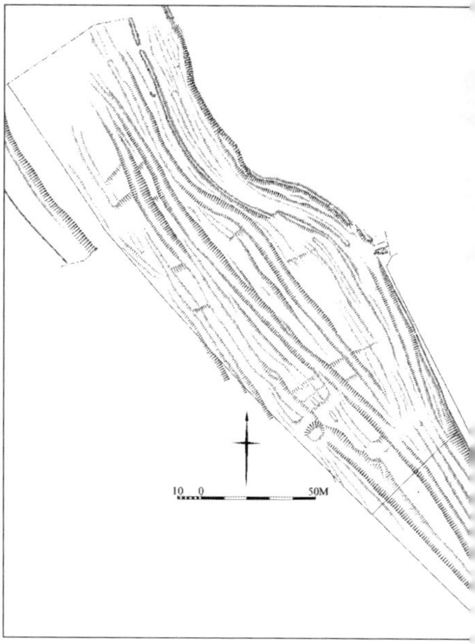

Plan of holloways at Heeston Bank (surveyed by The Archaeological Practice Ltd in 2003).

.ct from Fryer's Map of Northumberland, 1820, showing ourse of Dere Street from the Border to Rochester. of the Great Drift Road is evident to the south-east, ugh its full course between Featherwood and Cocklaw n is not marked.

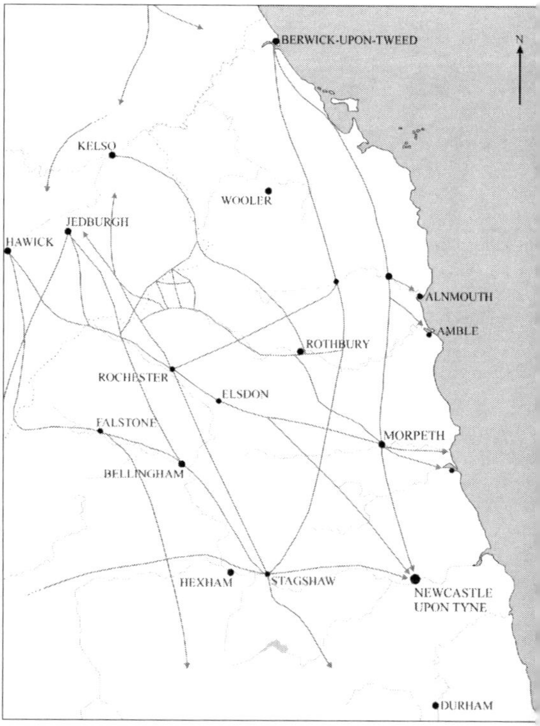

ıal photograph showing the holloways scarring andscape at Heeston Bank on a drove route Kirkwhelpington, viewed from the west.

Map showing suggested drove routes in Northumberland (reproduced from Cowper, 1970–71 p.32).

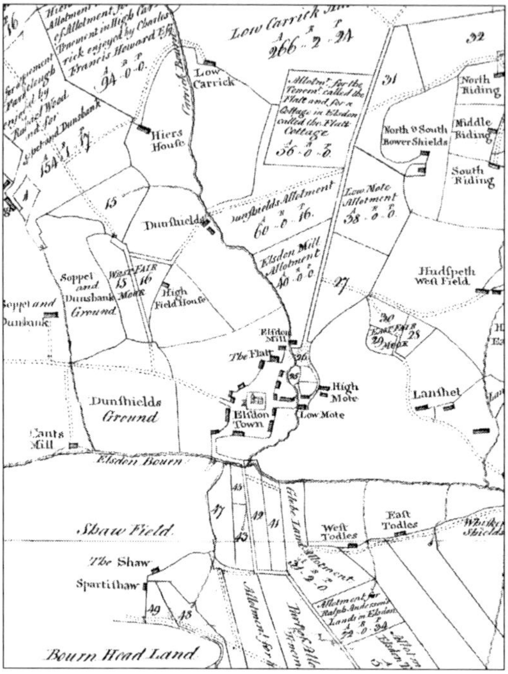

Elsdon Village and environs as depicted on the Elsdon Common Inclosure Plan, 1731. Note the two former fairgrounds, West Fair Moor and East Fair Moor. West Fair Moor is bisected by the Great Drift Road approaching the village from the north-west.

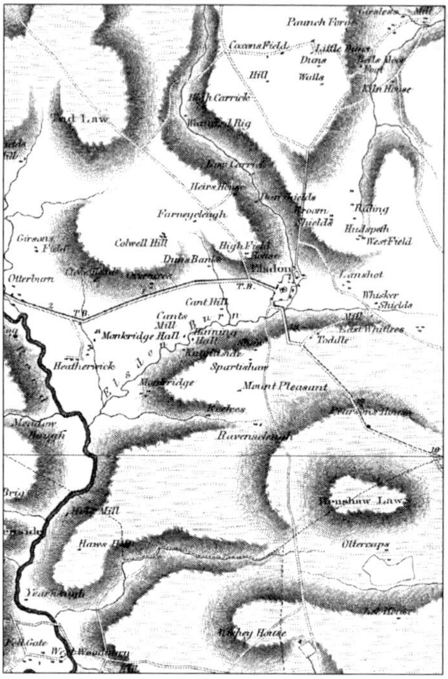

Fryer's Map of Northumberland, 1820, showing routes converging on the communications hub of Elsdon. Note in particular the Great Drift Road approaching the village from the north-west and exiting the green, heading due south towards Stagshaw Bank.

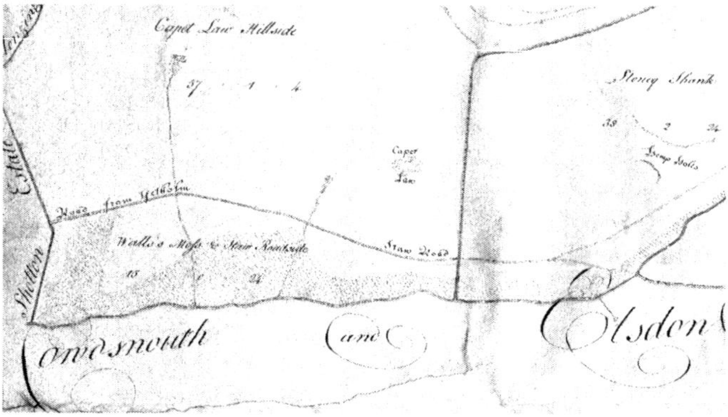

Map of Thompson's Walls Farm near Kilham *c.*1800 with the Staw Road shown (NRO KILHAM RCO13).

centuries, before considering what happened as the herds moved further south into England. Northumberland clearly does not exist, and the routes through it are unworthy of mention.

Authors local to the area have provided more detailed information. R.A.C. Cowper (Cowper, 1970–71, 30–33) suggests fifteen routes crossing the Border, giving both details of the places through which they passed as well as a sketch map of 'Some of the major drove roads'. Sadly, he lists no sources for his paper other than 'old maps' or 'official papers'. Robin Plackett, in two articles based on his research as a pathways officer for the Rambler's Association, offers greater detail of eight routes and also a list of references (Plackett, 1997, 45–61; and Plackett 1998, 2–19).

Plackett indicates that the drovers crossed the Border using many of the ancient tracks identified earlier in this book and which were also shown by Hoskins, such as Gamel's Path, the Street and the tracks used by the monks to reach the parts of Kidland that belonged to Newminster Abbey. In this he is supported by Mackenzie, a contemporary of the drovers, who wrote about a whisky house at Slyme-foot in Upper Coquetdale, where, in the first part of the eighteenth century, local farmers met to discuss business (Mackenzie, 1825, Vol. II, 83). The house was located at the point where the Street, an important droving route, came down from the hills and joined the main track down the valley. It was an ideal place

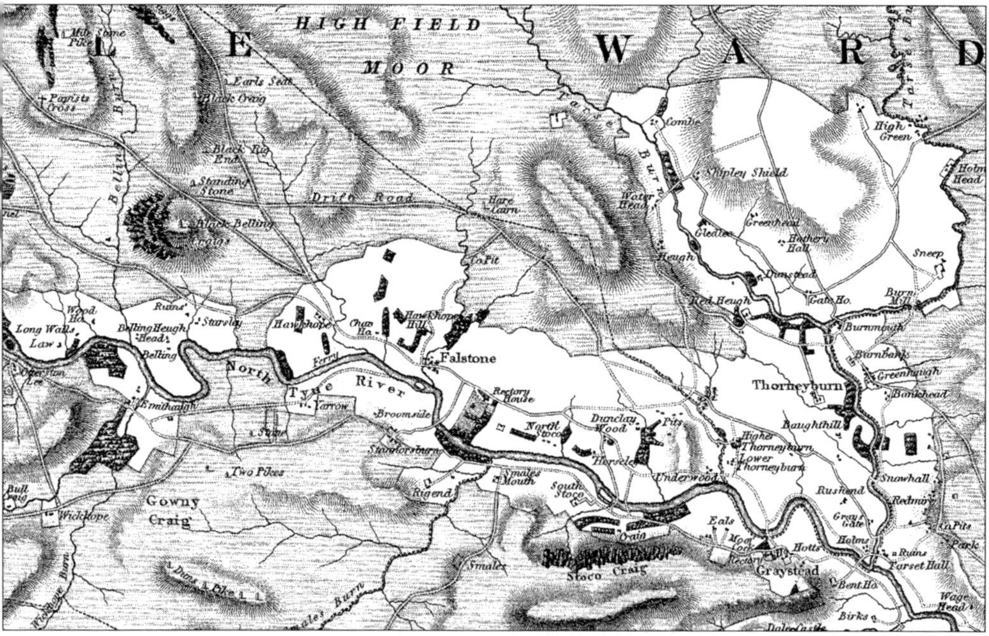

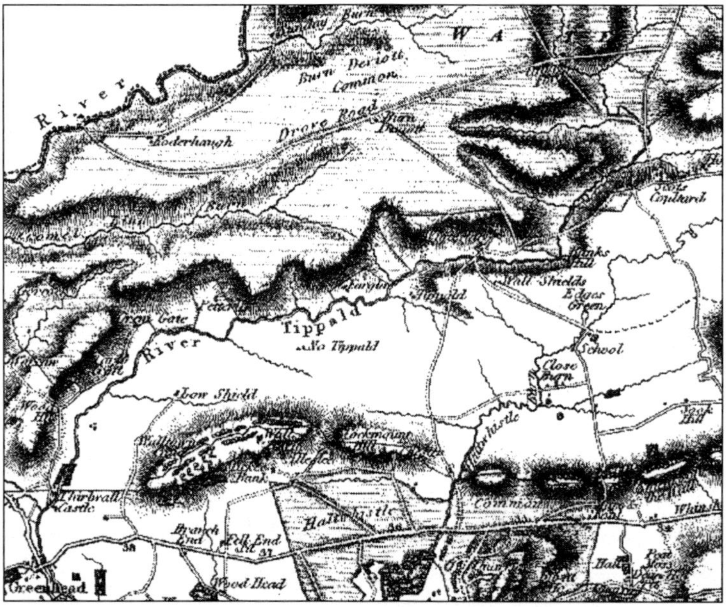

Above: The course of a drift road in Upper North Tynedale depicted on Greenwood's Map of Northumberland, 1828. Note the way it skirts the enclosed ground around Falstone.

Left: Another extract from Greenwood's 1828 map, showing the isolated drovers' inn at Burn Divot in the wastes to the north of the South Tyne Valley.

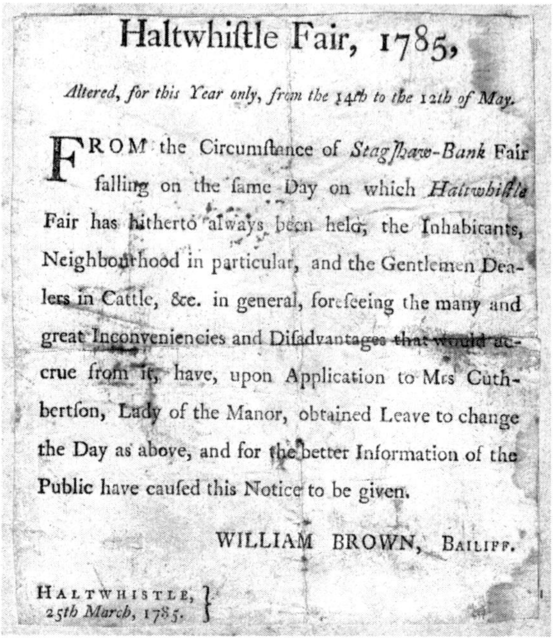

Haltwhiſtle Fair, 1785,

Altered, for this Year only, from the 14th to the 12th of May.

FROM the Circumſtance of *Stagſhaw-Bank* Fair falling on the ſame Day on which *Haltwhiſtle* Fair has hitherto always been held, the Inhabitants, Neighbourhood in particular, and the Gentlemen Dealers in Cattle, &c. in general, foreſeeing the many and great Inconveniencies and Diſadvantages that would accrue from it, have, upon Application to Mrs Cuthbertſon, Lady of the Manor, obtained Leave to change the Day as above, and for the better Information of the Public have cauſed this Notice to be given.

WILLIAM BROWN, BAILIFF.

HALTWHISTLE,
25th March, 1785.

Left: The hierarchy of fairs made manifest. Note that the date of Haltwhistle Fair was to be shifted to avoid clashing with the more important Stagshaw Bank Fair (NRO 2815).

Below: Holloways cutting into the steep hillside at the north-west end of Alnham.

where the Scotsmen could replenish their stocks of food and whisky and also conduct business with the local farmers. In addition, Plackett also shows some of the drover routes in the lower parts of the North Tyne, Rede and Coquet valleys and indicates the complex network that grew up as the trade expanded and new ways of moving livestock had to be found when some of the older tracks were converted into turnpike roads.

Further details of drover routes, and more precise evidence for a particular area, are given in Beryl Charlton's survey (Charlton, 1996, 125–26) of the archaeology of the Otterburn Ranges. In particular, she gives some sensible suggestions for the occasional use of cross-dykes, as well as suggesting that there were many minor droving or drift ways which had their origin in the reiving period or in the transhumance agriculture of the area.

What do these sources tell us about the nature of droving in the Borders and, more particularly, in Northumberland? Paradoxically, the most helpful of these three authors,

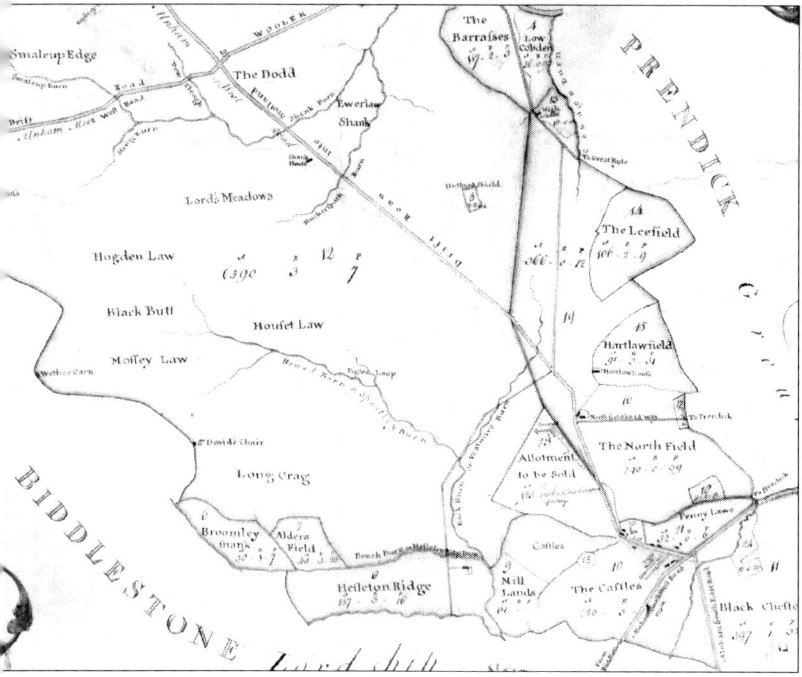

The Drift Road into Scotland and Drift Road to Wooler shown to the north-west of Alnham on an estate map of 1775 (Aln Cas O.II.12.I NE).

despite the limited scholarship of his paper, is Cowper. The map he provides suggests four general directions taken by the drovers, all of which are consistent with other information that is known about droving in the county in the eighteenth century. One route runs from Berwick and early in its course divides into two, with one branch leading inland to Whittingham while the other branch leads to Alnwick, Morpeth and Newcastle, with side branches to the coastal ports. A second road leads from Kelso over the Border and through Rothbury to Morpeth. A third set of roads is shown originating from the headwaters of the Tyne, Rede and Coquet via Elsdon and Bellingham to either Morpeth and Newcastle, or to Stagshaw Bank just north of Corbridge. Finally, another route leads down the valley of the North Tyne to Haydon Bridge and southwards. Together, these routes describe the probable markets for which the cattle being driven from Scotland were destined.

The rising prosperity of the towns on the northern coast and within the immediate hinterland was linked to the development of the coal trade and has been well documented[4]. These areas had a growing demand for cattle, both for immediate sale into the meat trade and also for fattening for future consumption. Some of this market was supplied by cattle from farms in the county, but more came from Scottish sources.

One of the few detailed descriptions of an eighteenth-century droving route is available in Morpeth for the trade from Kelso and Berwick. It is an article entitled 'The Old Cattle Market at Morpeth', which was printed in one of the Northumberland papers and is to be found as a newspaper cutting in a collection of materials associated with the town now lodged in the County Record Office (NCRO/SANT/BEQ/28/1/12). The article is not dated, but from internal evidence was probably written around the middle of the nineteenth century, after Morpeth had been replaced by Newcastle as the main urban meat market in the late 1830s and 1840s. It consists of the reported recollections of a former drover, George Robson, who, at the time the article was written, was about eighty years of age and who had taken an active part in the droving trade in the later eighteenth century.

Early twentieth-century view of market day at Morpeth.

The article begins by stating that the sales of cattle at Morpeth began to take place all the year round from the late eighteenth century onwards. Initially they began as sales 'off the grass' and were smaller in winter, as fewer numbers of cattle were brought forward than in the summer and autumn months. However, as the cultivation and feeding of turnips to cattle in winter increased so the trade in that season became stronger, with more cattle being brought forward. The author then describes the way in which the cattle from Scotland came to the market:

> The cattle and sheep supplied to Morpeth market came principally from the counties of Roxburgh, Berwick and North Northumberland, with a few at certain seasons from Cumberland and East Lothian. Of course, the stock were all driven by road, being lifted from Roxburgh and Berwick on the Fridays, crossing the Tweed at Kelso or Coldstream, and generally stopping at some place near there on the first night. The next night's stopping place was at Bender, a small inn north of Wooler and 33 miles from Morpeth, with fields attached for the accommodation of stock. As regards the stock coming through Berwick, some came on by Barmoor and Doddington, joining the Kelso and Coldstream lots at Wooler, and some went on the Great North Road by Belford and Alnwick.
>
> The next stopping places for the Wooler and Bender route were Glanton, Powburn or Whittingham. By that time it was Sunday night, but we were not so far advanced in civilisation at that time as to pay much regard to the Fourth Commandment, and if at all remonstrated with in this respect, we very readily pleaded the works of necessity and mercy. On the Monday morning large quantities of sheep and cattle might be seen laid off for an hour's rest among the heather at the old inn and farmhouse on Rimside Moor, well kept by Mr and Mrs Wardle, while the drovers were supplied with a good breakfast. Then the road was taken again from Longframlington and that night's resting stations were Weldon Bridge and Longhorsley. Next morning [Tuesday], the seven

> miles to Morpeth were easily performed, where the stock generally arrived between 10 and 12. They were then put into fields and fed and rested until next morning [Wednesday] – Market Day.

The above extract indicates that relatively short distances were travelled each day, and that the adequate resting of stock was a major consideration. It was important to the drovers that the stock in their charge were not hurried or unduly stressed by the process of droving, as this would impact upon their condition, with resultant financial consequences that could be drastic. Therefore, the daily distances travelled by driven stock, as well as the nature of overnight resting places, were determined by experience and tradition with the comfort and condition of the stock in mind. Pawson (1960, 199), reports the results of an experiment in droving carried out by the University of Durham's Cockle Park Research Farm in 1920, when two small groups of cattle were driven over a distance of four-and-a-half miles from Cockle Park to Morpeth. The first group of six fat cattle, driven at a constant steady pace, lost two stones per head over the course of the drove; the other group, driven faster and made excited by the process, lost seven stones per head, equivalent to a £15 10*s* financial loss at the time. The results of this limited experiment attest to the financial desirability of droving at a steady slow pace without upsetting or overexciting the cattle.

On market day, the cattle and sheep were driven into the town before daybreak and up to the market square. This is the area in the centre of the town in front of the town hall and the town clock. This area has now been partly paved over, but it is still possible to see the extent of the square and obtain a sense of the space used for the market. It was said to be capable of holding 200 cattle, and that there were pens elsewhere if the market was particularly busy. The cattle were sold in the square and along the stretch of road leading up to it from the east. The sheep were housed in pens which lined the remainder of the street from the market house down to the old bridge at the end of the street. Six pence a pen was charged to the sellers of sheep. The market began at daybreak and was reckoned to finish by noon. At this point the work of some of the drovers was over and they returned home on foot. For others, there was further employment as they would be hired by the purchasers of the livestock to drive them to their new homes. The article states that most of these buyers came from South Northumberland and County Durham, but that in the three spring months when there were quantities of winter-fed cattle offered for sale, there were buyers from Yorkshire, particularly from the larger towns such as Leeds and Wakefield.

In addition to the article cited above, the same record office volume contains a shorter newspaper cutting entitled 'Morpeth: its Cattle Market and its Inns.' Although reproducing some of the same information as the first article, it testifies to the growth of the market in the late eighteenth century. In 1761, the average of weekly sales throughout the year was forty cattle and 600 sheep. By 1811, these figures had increased to 100 head of cattle and 2,000 sheep, leading the writer to state that it was widely acknowledged that this made Morpeth the second largest market in the country, only being outdone by Smithfield in London. This changed within the next twenty to thirty years, as Newcastle replaced Morpeth as the principal trading point for livestock in south-east Northumberland as a result of the growth of the town as a market in its own right, and also the coming of the railway with its added advantages to buyers and sellers. A market continued to take place in Morpeth, but its size decreased as the quantities of Scottish stock driven to it declined, although there was a slight revival in the period after 1870 when Irish cattle sellers brought numbers of their animals to the market. The old market site continued to be used until the twentieth century, when it was replaced by marts closer to the railway station. Photographs were taken of the old market in operation and have been included in books about the history of Morpeth (see Rowland, 1989, photographs 41–50).

It is important to realise that the route taken by the Scottish stock to the Morpeth market was also used by local farmers supplying stock to the town. The routes which appear on Cowper's map, as well as those shown elsewhere, were often ones which had been used before the major period of droving in the eighteenth and nineteenth centuries, and went on being used after the trade had passed to rail and road transport. In addition, there were many smaller tracks and pathways that fed into the larger drove roads that were used by local drovers for many hundreds of years and which have only ceased to be used since the widespread adoption of motorised transport in the late twentieth century.

Two such minor routes associated with the Kelso to Morpeth drove road lead from Wingates Village in Coquetdale to Morpeth. The village of Wingates (OS ref. NZ 098951) lies on an upland plateau about three-and-a-half miles south of Pauperhaugh in the main Coquet Valley. The village and its surrounding area have a number of long-established farms which have supplied stock to Morpeth market. One track leads south from East Farm in the village to Wholme Farm, and thence to Southward Edge and Harelaw where it joins a metalled road that leads to the present A697 just north of Morpeth. A second track leaves East Farm in an easterly direction to intersect with a metalled road just north of Croftside. The road then leads into Longhorsley, a village on the Kelso to Morpeth drove road. Local oral tradition[5] testifies to the use of these tracks for the movement of livestock, and there are distinct signs of such activity still visible. In the late twentieth century such tracks, when not parts of the road network, have tended to become recreational footpaths or bridleways, but there is considerable evidence of their use by farmers up until that time. (Directions to view parts of these routes are given in Chapter 6 of this book.)

Scottish cattle could also be purchased at local fairs, such as Elsdon, or the major fair located at Stagshaw Bank, just to the north of Corbridge.[6] Stagshaw Bank was one of the most important fair sites in the county, with two important sales held at Whitsun and in July. The only other fair of comparable size was that held at Newcastle in October. Cattle purchased at Stagshaw Bank were not intended solely for use in the county, but were also bought for sale further south at fairs and markets along the way to London (Bonser, 1970, 134). Thus, Cowper shows a route leading from Stagshaw Bank to the south which runs parallel with the route he shows from Haydon Bridge. Both would probably lead to Skipton in Yorkshire, which was one of the largest markets for Scottish and other cattle in that county.

Thousands of animals were exhibited at Stagshaw Fair, and large numbers of buyers and sellers of all forms of livestock attended it. It became a byword for riotous behaviour as a result of some of the rowdier altercations that took place over disputed sales and other inflammatory incidents, but its significance for livestock sales and the droving system in Northumberland is difficult to exaggerate. Contemporary illustrations show the prominence that it achieved and the way in which it was regarded by contemporaries as the most important of the county fairs. Although the fair declined in importance after the end of droving, sales of stock continued to be held on the site until after the First World War.

Hubert Robinson, a local resident who lived all of his life around Stagshaw, recalled being taken by his parents to the last three fairs held in the late 1920s.[7] Although he remembered geese being driven along the road to the fair, by this time the majority of hooved animals sold at Stagshaw were horses, and these in modest numbers. In its later years, most of the fair consisted of stalls selling a variety of wares, the most prominent of which were Hexham tans – the gloves produced in the nearby town of Hexham – as well as various entertainments. The products of blacksmiths, particularly those relating to horses and farming, probably also continued to appear until the end.

Hubert Robinson also recalled that the long association of the Stagshaw Bank Fair with gypsies, or Roma (amongst whom horse-trading and blacksmithing were traditional activities), continued for some years after its final demise. Drawn by a long-term association with the place, caravans and carts would appear on the common at fair time, as if compelled by echos of the past, or unable to escape from a deeply entrenched and cherished cyclical pattern of seasonal activity, until the echos faded and the Roma families no longer felt obliged to visit. After its abandonment, the fairground reverted to moorland under the gaze of Hubert Robinson, who lived all his life in a cottage below the Errington Arms and whose passing in 2009 extinguished perhaps the last living link with the fair.

In addition to the great regional fair at Stagshaw Bank, local fairs were also important in supplying customers in rural Northumberland. Two of the most notable after the drovers had crossed the Border from Scotland were in the villages of Elsdon and Harbottle, in Redesdale and Coquetdale respectively. The village of Elsdon was on the line of one of the most important droving routes in Northumberland, the Great Drift Road which crossed the Border on Brownhart Law, following the course of the ancient Roman road, Dere Street, known locally as the Kemelspethe or Gamels (Gemmels) Path (see Chapter 6 for information on surviving remains of droving on the course of Dere Street and the Great Drift Road).

The Great Drift Road diverged from Dere Street proper near Featherwood, at the head of Sills Burn, and continued south-eastwards along the moorland watershed of the Rede and the Coquet systems, providing a direct link between the Gamelspath border crossing and Elsdon. This moorland route possibly has a very long history. It has been suggested that it was derived from a prehistoric ridgeway (Charlton & Day, 1976, 229; and see case studies in Chapter 6). The Great Drift Road approached Elsdon from the north west actually passing through West Fair Moor, one of two fairgrounds outside the village, before entering the settlement on the west side. It then passed through Elsdon Village and out on to the Ottercops, which it traversed by way of Cuddy's Cleugh to Sweethope Lough, and thence to Stagshaw Bank.[8]

Drovers who did not wish to go to Elsdon but wanted to proceed down the Great Drift Road were able to leave the moorland road before entering the village. About three miles short of Elsdon, on Leighton Hill, a track led southwards past the ancient fort of Camp Hill to cross the Jedburgh to Elsdon turnpike road next to Overacres Farm. From here the track led down to a point where the Elsdon Burn could be crossed, just by the present Monkridge Bridge. From this point, another track led up to the Drift Road. A short distance before reaching the bridge, there was an overnight stance for the cattle, the site of which is marked by the presence of an ancient well with a strong supply of water which is reputed never to have run dry (see case studies in Chapter 6 for directions to view a section of this track).

The importance of this particular route was considerable, since drovers always sought to avoid major river crossings and toll roads (Bonser, 1970, 74–92). The former were difficult to cross, because where the river had to be forded the water might be high or in flood, and in those places where stock had to be driven over bridges there were tolls to be paid, which could add considerably to the costs of the journey. Turnpikes were often expensive, and there were frequently difficulties with other travellers who did not wish to be held up by herds of slow-moving cattle. The Great Drift Road was an ideal route for cattle, as it avoided these difficulties. Moreover it did not cross the River Rede, and where it encountered the Wansbeck that river was narrow and easily forded, as were the other streams along the route. Although the main road into Redesdale from Carter Bar was not turnpiked at the beginning of the eighteenth century, an Act of Parliament passed in 1774 created the Elsdon and Redewater Turnpike Trust.[9] This permitted the road to be repaired, widened and altered, and tolls for its use to be charged. The Great Drift Road lay to the east of the turnpike and entered Elsdon Village to the east of the last toll house in the same place as shown on the Inclosure map on page 58.

Another major droving corridor identified by Cowper was that down the North Tyne, also described by Haldane (1971, 160) and Plackett (1997, 50). There were no turnpike roads down the North Tyne Valley, and contemporary maps show several drove roads running down it, both to the north and south of the river.[10] In the case of the northerly routes, although passage to Bellingham involved crossing the Tarset Burn, the North Tyne itself did not have to be forded. Despite the fact that the Rede had to be crossed south of Bellingham, there was a ford, and later a bridge, which permitted easy access to a road leading to Stagshaw Bank or to the longer road south into Durham and Yorkshire.

Finally, Bonser's map shows an additional drove road in the far west of Northumberland. This road is one of two shown leaving the town of Hawick in southern Scotland. The eastern road runs south to Falstone in the North Tyne Valley, and is similar to the other drove roads in that valley described in the preceding paragraph. The western road from Hawick leads south-west through Riccarton and crosses the Border into Northumberland as it traverses the Larriston Fells. At Christianbury Crag the road divides into three, and the most easterly branch crosses Spadeadam Waste to the village of Gilsland. From Gilsland, the route ascends the South Tyne Valley to the town of Alston in Cumbria. Alston was a notable market town and was on a drove road that eventually led to the important market town of Skipton in Yorkshire (Shepherd 2003, 180–2). Although little evidence has been found during research for this book concerning the activities of farmers in west Northumberland and their participation in the droving trade, Shepherd suggests that Alston market was used by farmers from the South Tyne Valley for buying and selling stock.

One interesting feature arising from a consideration of maps of the drove roads is that the drovers and livestock using them moved relentlessly south from Scotland, or only diverted from the main route when the stock was taken to a market town such as Morpeth. Bonser, for example, attaches arrows to his routes to show the direction of the drove (Bonser, 1970, e.g. 150–51 and 162–63). As a broad generalisation this may be largely correct, but there is evidence that suggests that the assertion that all stock moved in the manner shown by Bonser needs some qualification. Using the example of the tracks leading from the village of Wingates referred to above, attention has already been drawn to the subsidiary droving routes that were used to drive stock to and from local farms and which were often linked to the main drove roads. In southern and south-west Northumberland, the tendency to drive stock against the general direction of droving was particularly marked.

As explained above, Stagshaw Fair was, for many years, the most important market place for farmers in Northumberland and possibly for many others in northern England. As a result, farmers, butchers, cattle dealers and anyone else wishing to trade in livestock in the southern part of Northumberland had to travel north if they wished to attend the fair. Should they have wished to bring livestock to the fair, then there was a possibility that they had to drive their animals in the opposite direction to the bulk that were using the drove road. Such activity was liable to lead to congestion and disturbance if groups of livestock attempted to pass one another on the roads, so in some places alternative routes were opened up to assist in the northerly movement of some stock. In Allendale, livestock often used the packhorse trails that were the principal method of conveying lead from the dale to the company offices in Hexham. As some of the farmers in the dale were often also responsible for organising the transport of lead, arranging the movement of livestock was simply an extension of their usual activities (Hunt, 1970, 1984 edition, 108, 145–56).

Further west, oral testimony of local tradition has identified a drove road linking the town of Alston to Stagshaw Bank (William Bolton of Fourstones, personal communication to I.D. Roberts in an oral history interview, 7 April 2006). This road may have been used by some of the main droves, but tradition links its use to the local farmers. Earlier information about the common at Alston indicates that farmers in this area were familiar with moving stock in this manner, as they had instructions for accessing their stints via droving routes laid down for the individual properties that they occupied (NCRO/EP 46/85, Alston Moor Drift Roll, 1597; see Chapter 3).

The road from Alston to Stagshaw is as follows and may be traced on OS Landranger 87, *Hexham, Haltwhistle and Surrounding Area*. The description tendered by Mr Bolton in his interview began in Alston, from whence the road ran to Whitfield via Blagill, Blagill Head, Mohope Moor, Mohope Head and Hawkuplee and then, following the left bank of the River West Allen, to Whitfield. Leaving Whitfield, the road ran via Staward and past Ridley Hall, before crossing the South Tyne to the village of Bardon Mill. The road then ascended via Crindledykes to the line of the Roman Wall. It then passed through Busy Gap to the east of Housesteads Fort, where it crossed the line of one of the north/south drove roads before following to the north of the Roman Wall and the Military Road to Chollerford, and thence to Stagshaw. Thus, apart from crossing drove roads frequented by the Scottish drovers, those driving livestock to and from west Northumberland and north-east Cumberland were able to attend Stagshaw Fair without hindrance to other traders.

The Agricultural Context in which Droving Took Place

The preceding section on the droving trade with England described the main drove roads that developed in Northumberland in the eighteenth century. At the same time, it has also been possible to indicate something of the nature of the subsidiary network of local routes and tracks that grew up around the principal drove roads, livestock markets and fairs to serve the needs of local farmers, dealers and butchers. This section seeks to explore the agricultural context in which these developments in the droving trade took place. As the drove roads were principally located in the western part of the county, their greatest impact and subsequent influence was on agriculture in the valleys of the North Tyne, Rede and Coquet rivers and the uplands surrounding them. For this reason, an examination of what happened in this particular part of Northumberland forms most of the contents of the following section, but the significant effects on the agriculture of the remainder of the county will also be considered.

Farming in the valleys of the North Tyne, Rede and Coquet in the seventeenth century was based on a pattern of small farmsteads located close to the valley floor, where there were fields of flat land on which hay and corn crops could be grown. In general, a farmer's livestock was a mixture of cattle and small flocks of sheep. The livestock was wintered on the cultivable land close to the farm, but in spring the stock was taken out to common grazing on the surrounding moorland. During the summer period, the ground on which the stock had been wintered was used to grow crops such as oats and hay. The animals returned to the farmstead in the late summer to graze on the aftermath of the harvest, before spending the winter close to the farm once more. This type of farming was essentially an extension of the transhumance subsistence agriculture that had once formed the basis of life in the valley in the late middle ages.[11]

During the latter part of the seventeenth and the early part of the eighteenth centuries, local landowners encouraged the development of farms that were leased out to rent-paying tenants. Although S.J. Watts described the beginning of this process very clearly in the paper cited above, less work has been done on the development of the farming system it produced. The most valuable contribution has been made by Paul Brassley, and much of what follows is taken from his work, but there is a need for further research on this topic. The tenant farmers he described were principally livestock farmers who cultivated some corn, usually oats, and potatoes. Their main source of income was from the cattle they raised and then sold on, either for breeding or for slaughter. On many of these farms, landlords added some enclosed hill pasture in order to create more viable holdings and to enable farmers to summer their stock on hill land closer to their homes. This, in turn, resulted in the abandonment of the distant pasturing of stock on unenclosed waste land.

Brassley examined a number of inventories of deceased farmers in the uplands as part of his study, concluding that 'in all, the cattle usually accounted for about half the value of all the goods on the farm, but even so most farmers had less than twenty head of cattle in total, and many had less than ten.' About ten per cent had no sheep at all and, among those who did keep sheep, flocks of more than 100 sheep were as common as those with less than fifty (Brassley, 1985, 137). The size of the flocks on farms in the Coquet Valley may have been greater than those in the North Tyne and Rede Valleys, but on all farms, Brassley found that the value of the livestock greatly exceeded that of the crops (Brassley, 1985, 140).

In view of the value of the livestock, Brassley made some attempt to investigate the types of cattle and sheep on these holdings. His information was limited and he was forced to rely on that given by Bailey and Culley in their survey published in 1805 (Bailey & Culley, 1805, 139–154). From the limited evidence he examined, Brassley was prepared to support the information from Bailey and Culley about the breeds of sheep (Heath/Blackface and Linton) that were on the upland farms. However, he was reluctant to accept that the Shorthorn cattle they stated to be universally present would always have been hardy enough to withstand the rigours of winters in Northumberland (Brassley, 1985, 139).

The small size of the farms had important consequences for the relationship of local farmers with the drovers. Production on such small farms must have been very modest, and even had the stock from a number of farms been ready for market at the same time there would hardly have been enough cattle available to interest a drover in assembling a herd from the uplands. Brassley even suggested that, in view of the lack of hardiness in Shorthorns, some of the farmers may have actually been purchasing cattle from the drovers in order to have hardy beasts to fatten for the market. What seems more likely is that the upland farmers took their stock to local fairs, such as the ones at Elsdon and Stagshaw Bank, where they were purchased by drovers and dealers who were assembling large herds to drive south or adding to droves of cattle already bound for urban markets. This means that such droving that was taking place in the valleys of the North Tyne, the Rede and the Coquet, was of travelling herds of cattle which rested in these areas overnight on their passage south and were driven by professional drovers not drawn from the farming population of Northumberland. Any local droving was confined to small-scale movements of a few head of cattle or sheep to the nearest available market, and was usually carried out by the farmer and his family.

The Turn of the Century – A Period of Change

How long the pattern of farming in the upland valleys described by Brassley continued is uncertain. Brassley himself suggested that even by the middle of the eighteenth century, some of the farmers he studied had found the size and profitability of their farms too small to make ends meet, and as a consequence they had to find additional rural employment (Brassley, 1985, 76). He also drew attention to the rising rentals which would have exacerbated this situation. The twofold dilemma of wishing to capitalise on the ready livestock market by charging tenants higher rents and the non-profitability of the small farms prompted landlords to amalgamate farms into larger, more economic holdings. Certainly in the 1760s one landlord, the Duke of Northumberland, began this process at his farm at Catcleugh, which lay just north of Byrness in the Rede Valley,[12] and then extended it into the North Tyne Valley in the early years of the nineteenth century.[13] There may have been other motives for amalgamation,[14] but the first decades of the nineteenth century saw an emerging pattern of extensive holdings stocked with large flocks of sheep and small herds of cattle.

Agriculture in eastern Northumberland differed considerably from that in the west of the county. Although the economy had been disrupted at various times by the wars with Scotland, patterns of settlement and farming had not been dislocated as seriously as they were in the uplands in the north and west of the county. The land was also more fertile and there was considerably more arable cultivation. At one time, it was considered that improvements in agriculture common elsewhere in England in the eighteenth century did not affect eastern Northumberland until well into the second half of that century, but Brassley has shown that there is evidence that changes such as the enclosure of open fields and more productive patterns of crop rotation were taking place much earlier in the century (Brassley, 1985, 172–180). In his view, some farmers were already beginning to make profits from improved cultivation and stock management by the 1730s.

The extent of these improvements is qualified by the observations of one important contemporary commentator, Arthur Young. Young visited the county as part of his tour of the north of England and reported his findings in a published account of his journey in 1770. His description of the farms in the south-east of the county, i.e. south of Warkworth, was particularly critical as he found them to be small in size, lacking recent improvements and giving poor yields of livestock and crops to their occupiers. The situation in the north-western part of the county was much better and Young drew attention to the work of Mr Dickson and some of his tenants in improving their farms (Young, 1770, 158–168), as well as landlords such as Sir Walter Blackett at Wallington, who gave strong leadership in modernising their estates (Young, 1770, 193).

One important stimulus for these improvers was the growing prosperity on Tyneside, arising from the increased demand for coal, and the associated developments in manufacturing taking place in that part of the county. As the article cited earlier in this section which described the drove road from the Border to Morpeth indicates, the market in Morpeth was not only supplied with beasts driven from Scotland but was augmented by cattle and sheep bought in Northumberland. Most of these animals were purchased from improving farmers in the northern part of the county and used the same droving routes as the stock brought from Scotland. At the same time, evidence from the papers of one of the most important improving farming families in the north of the county, the Culleys, indicates that they were buying cattle to feed and fatten from the drovers (Rowe, 1971).

The situation had changed again by the time the Government-inspired general report on the agriculture of the county was written in 1794 (Bailey & Culley, 1794, 1805 3rd edition). Bailey was the land agent to the Earl of Tankerville, and one of the most knowledgeable figures in Northumberland on the subject of estate and farm management, while Culley was a member of the most prominent family concerned with the practical improvement of crop and livestock husbandry. The picture that they painted of farming in the county was one of considerable improvement. In particular they drew attention to the methods used to raise the quality of sheep farming in the western uplands, and to the continuing advances being made on farms in the north-east of the county. Attention was also drawn to the improvements made in breeding shorthorn cattle and the resulting increases in killing weight and milk yield achieved by breeders. Only in south-eastern Northumberland were farms still small, leases of short duration and profits marginal.

What part did droving play in these changes? And what effect did they have on droving? The answer to the first question is that, in the west of the county the droving market stimulated sheep production. There was a ready market at Stagshaw and the local fairs for the products of the upland sheep farms and farmers did well. Prices for sheep and wool were buoyant and farmers prospered, as evidenced by returns from such farms as those belonging to the Ridley family (NCRO 414/11a/ Ridley of Park End Papers, Returns from 1792–1801). In the east of the county, the situation was more complex. As a result of changes to the rotation of cultivation on farms, there were larger quantities of root crops available, and, particularly on farms in the north of the county, it became possible to keep and fatten more stock over the winter. The strength of the market at Morpeth meant that more cattle and sheep were sent on the drove roads to take advantage of it, and this provided more employment and financial opportunity to the drovers.

Changes had also taken place elsewhere in the economy. The market for livestock continued to grow, but more rapidly than previously. This was partly due to the increasingly rapid urbanisation of England, but in the short term was also due to the demands from the Victualling Boards supplying the armed services during the wars with France (Bonser, 1970, 110–11). The market demands were so large that the barriers preventing importation of cattle from Ireland had been abolished. During the 1790s, large quantities of cattle were imported from Ireland into south-west Scotland, and frequently accounted for over half the Irish cattle exported to the British mainland during that decade. The peak year was 1796, when 21,510 cattle arrived in Scotland from Ireland. Once in Scotland, most of the Irish cattle were driven to Dumfries where there was an established market for the sale of Scottish cattle bound for the English market. From here, the Irish beasts would pass to new owners, most of whom took mixed herds of Scottish and Irish cattle into England (Cochran, 1985, 119–120).

The nature of the meat market had changed in that there was now a much more significant market for sheep meat. Haldane reported that the Scottish drovers had discovered it was possible to drive sheep the same lengthy distances as cattle, and as a result in 1757 over 150,000 sheep had been driven over the Border from Scotland (Haldane, 1971, 200–201). By the turn of the century, this figure had grown considerably higher. These consequences, together with increased opportunities to sell wool, encouraged the development of the large sheep farms in the North Tyne, Rede and Coquet valleys and in the Cheviots, north and west of Wooler. The increased droving trade from these valleys was now concerned with the delivery of sheep, rather than cattle, to southern markets.

Sheep and other livestock were delivered to local fairs; there were very few direct sales from farmers to buyers made at the farm gate (Mingay, 1989, 87). The list of fairs provided by Bailey and Culley is given in the Appendix, and shows the distribution and frequency of fairs throughout the county in 1794 which were used by the overwhelming majority of farmers. Despite their popularity, these fairs were beginning to be regulated and a hierarchy was emerging of the more important ones, often because they were located closest to a ready market.[15]

The Nineteenth Century

The first few years of the nineteenth century saw the agricultural industry faced with much the same demand for meat as in the 1790s. Until the end of the war with France in 1815, military demands added to the increasing market in the growing towns and had a distorting effect on supply and price. The end of the war brought a fall in prices for livestock products, as well as for agricultural commodities in general. Although this trend became established within a few months of the end of the war, the decline in price was particularly sharp during the 1820s and early 1830s (Mitchell and Deane, 1962, 471).

Gradually during the 1830s a recovery took place, generated mostly by demand from the industrial towns where general prosperity, after 1850 in particular, led to an increased spending on diet and a greater consumption of meat (Perren, 1978, 216; see also Burnett 1979, 28–29). Manchester provides a helpful case study of market forces within one of the new industrial cities of the north-west of England.[16]

Manchester – A Case Study

The population of Manchester was measured as 75,000 in 1801. By 1821 this number had grown to 126,000, and by 1871 it had reached 351,000 (Mitchell and Deane, 1962, 21). The demand for commodities, including meat and meat products, grew with the increasing size of the city. Imports of cattle from Ireland, shipped into the north-west on the Dublin–Liverpool route, increased from 53,158 in 1829 to 167,584 in 1852, partly in order to assuage the appetite of Manchester as well as other Lancastrian towns. Roger Scola has demonstrated that the overall consumption of cattle in Manchester alone rose from slightly over 50,000 in 1820 to approximately 400,000 in 1870. This represents an eightfold increase, as measured against a fivefold growth in the population of the city. Although the demand for sheep meat was not as great, the supply of sheep and lambs to the city increased fivefold in the same period.

Scola not only analysed the supply of different types of meat to Manchester, but also investigated the way in which livestock was delivered to the market. In the late eighteenth century, most of the meat supplied to Manchester came from local sources in Lancashire and Cheshire. Some additional supplies were bought in from the Craven district of Yorkshire. It is likely that some of these animals were obtained from the Scottish droves passing through Yorkshire. As Manchester grew, the local sources of supply proved to be inadequate. More stock was purchased from the drovers bringing cattle and sheep from Scotland and the north of England. Scola discovered that livestock was purchased at local fairs from the two main droving routes – the Cumberland and Westmorland route, and the eastern route through Northumberland and Durham. Drovers delivered livestock from all these sources into Manchester.

Even with the opening of the first railways into the city in the 1830s, it was found easier to bring cattle and sheep into town on foot, only slower moving pigs and poultry arrived by rail. This practice included the majority of the Irish cattle in the 1830s and 1840s that arrived through the port of Liverpool and were then driven to Manchester. Gradually the railway network expanded and competition for business between the companies grew fiercer. As a consequence, by the 1850s all livestock transported to Manchester arrived by rail. So convoluted had the situation become that by the end of the decade some cattle were sent directly by rail from Newcastle-upon-Tyne to Manchester (Perren, 1978, 30–31). What had transpired in Lancashire was a microcosm of what was taking place all over England. The adoption of the railway as the principal means of animal transport was being repeated all over the country – the age of long-distance droving had ended.

Droving in Northumberland in the Nineteenth and Early Twentieth Centuries

Scola's study of Manchester, because of its thoroughness and detail, provides an important model of the way in which industrial and population growth in a large city transformed the distribution and supply of food to its inhabitants. During the first half of the nineteenth century, towns elsewhere in the north of England were growing in ways similar to those described by Scola in Manchester, and these changes were having important effects on the droving trade.

The drovers who went through Northumberland at the beginning of the century had already begun to change their practices. They were now purchasing and driving large numbers of sheep as well as the cattle which had formerly been their sole trade. Many of the sheep reared on the large hill farms in the upland valleys of north-west Northumberland were sent to stock fairs and markets for purchase by the drovers, and delivered to towns in the south of England. However, an increasing proportion was also being bought for the growing market in Newcastle and Tyneside.[17]

Although the depression in trade and the parallel adverse effects on prices and wages were as apparent in Northumberland as in other parts of the country, it did not affect the growth in towns on Tyneside in much the same way that towns elsewhere in the north of England continued to develop. Thus, there was still an increasing demand for foodstuffs, of which meat was one example. It may be the case that, because of the low wages among some of the population, the increase in the volume of food required did not exactly match the growth in the number of the people in a town, but, nevertheless, the drovers continued to supply stock to the urban markets and, generally, those numbers continued to rise. The increasing size of the potential urban market is demonstrated in the following table which shows the increase in the size of the populations of three Tyneside towns – Newcastle, Gateshead and Tynemouth – in selected years between 1811 and 1881 (Mitchell & Deane, 1962, 24–27).

TABLE TO SHOW POPULATION GROWTH IN NEWCASTLE, GATESHEAD AND TYNEMOUTH IN FOUR SELECTED YEARS BETWEEN 1811–1881

Year	Newcastle	Gateshead	Tynemouth	Total
1811	33,000	9,000	18,000	60,000
1821	42,000	12,000	23,000	77,000
1851	88,000	26,000	29,000	143,000
1881	145,000	66,000	44,000	255,000

Stock destined for these towns were driven through Morpeth to Newcastle and, until the 1830s, most of the cattle sales took place in Morpeth. Figures given in the earlier section on the droving trade indicate that, by 1811, over 5,000 cattle and 200,000 sheep were being sold each year in the market at Morpeth, many of which were destined for Newcastle and Tyneside. The rapid growth in the size of the market for meat on Tyneside and the increasing difficulty of supplying it through Morpeth was one of the most significant reasons for the opening of a new larger market in Newcastle in 1836 (Perren, 1978, 30). Henceforward, although Morpeth still retained a market, Newcastle became the major meat-trading centre on the eastern side of Northumberland. By 1852, when, as shown in the table above, the population of the three towns had more than doubled their sizes since 1811, 38,109 cattle and 250,369 sheep were sold in the market in Newcastle (McCord and Thompson, 1998, 292).

In addition to the demands of the Tyneside trade, Newcastle also became a market in which butchers from Yorkshire came to purchase stock for the meat markets of Leeds and other industrialising towns in the county (Grady, 2000, 140). Besides increasing droving to Newcastle, the stock purchased in Newcastle had to be taken to Yorkshire, and this created further employment for the drovers. However, such employment was to be short lived as changes in the transport system created problems for the drovers.

Richard Perren explains the various pressures on the drovers, which principally came from two sources. One was the development of alternative quicker means of transport, initially by coastal steamer and then by the railways. Stock arrived at the urban markets more quickly and less stressed, and therefore in better condition. At the same time, the extension of the turnpike road network made it increasingly difficult to avoid travelling on such

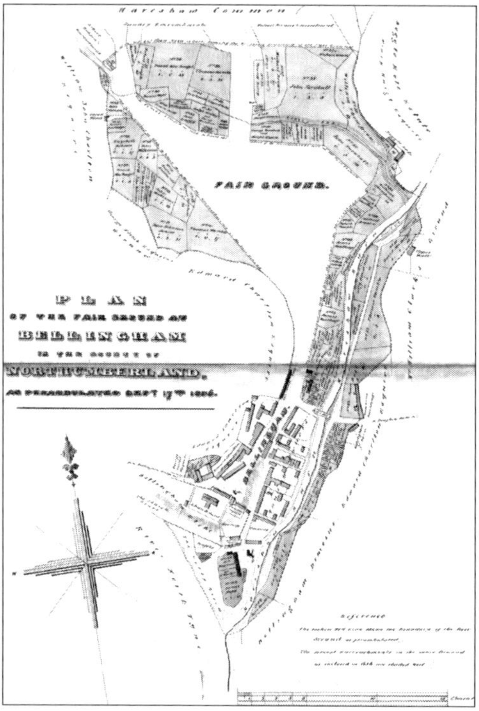

Plan of Bellingham Fairground, 1836, showing encroachments (NRO ZHE 43/15).

The last lamb sale of the season at Bellingham mart in October 2004, prior to closure.

roads and paying the tolls levied. Moreover, the enclosure of much common land meant that there were fewer places to rest up the cattle at night. Under these circumstances, it was inevitable that livestock began to be transported by rail and boat rather than on the hoof.

These changes were welcomed by the farmers. Stock arrived in better condition at market and thus could command better prices. The money realised returned to the farmer more quickly than in the past. Some farming operations were improved by the railway transport of stock. For example, John Robson and James Hedley, farmers of West Kielder and Bewshaugh respectively in the North Tyne Valley, hired a special group of wagons each year following the construction of the Border Counties railway line.[18] These wagons were used to transport the draft ewes from each farm – a total of over 700 sheep. The speedy and complete removal of these animals permitted tupping to begin at once, without the danger of older stock getting in the way. Family and farm staff acted as the drovers when driving stock from the farm to the station. Hedley's diary includes many other examples of the way he and neighbouring farmers adopted rail transport for the carriage of livestock.

Although long-distance droving disappeared from the mid-century onwards, the job of the drover did not. The term drover as a description of an agricultural occupation continued to be used by the census enumerators into the twentieth century. At a national level, the number of men listed as drovers reached a peak of 9,300 in 1861, but by 1911, 7,800 continued to use this as term as a description of their employment

(Collins, 2000, 1179–80). The reason for this is that drovers were still employed in the railway yards and town markets to supervise the movement of livestock. This is what happened in Northumberland. According to the census returns of 1851 and 1861 there were 117 and 104 drovers, respectively, employed throughout Northumberland during those years. In 1901, the figure had reduced to 83, and by 1921 it had dropped to 66.[19] Gradually, over the series of four returns consulted, the residence of the drover was increasingly reported as being around the markets. Drovers were now essentially urban employees, not rural workers.

That their presence was required is easily explained by the following figures. The size of the population of the three Tyneside towns, as shown in the table above, continued to grow after 1851, so that by 1881 they contained over a quarter of a million people. Numbers of livestock sold also continued to rise so that in 1882 it was reported that 111,705 cattle and 302,504 sheep were sold in the market in Newcastle (McCord & Thompson 1998, 292). The return of livestock for the entire county of Northumberland lists that the quantity of cattle of all ages was 93,550 and that of sheep 880,230, of which 336,702 (Agricultural Returns 1884, 36). Thus, the quantity of cattle sold exceeded the total herd in the county by approximately 25,000, and the number of sheep sold would have required nearly every lamb in the county to be sold into the meat market to satisfy demand. As such an event is pure fantasy, the demands of the Newcastle market had to be satisfied by large quantities of stock being brought from places well outside the county, many of which were in Scotland, mostly by train but also by coastal steamer. Drovers who lived close to the market were needed to handle such quantities of animals, and this explains their presence as residents of Tyneside rather than rural Northumberland.

A detailed examination of the census notebooks for the two North Tyne parishes of Greystead and Thorneyburn for the six returns between 1841 and 1891 supports this

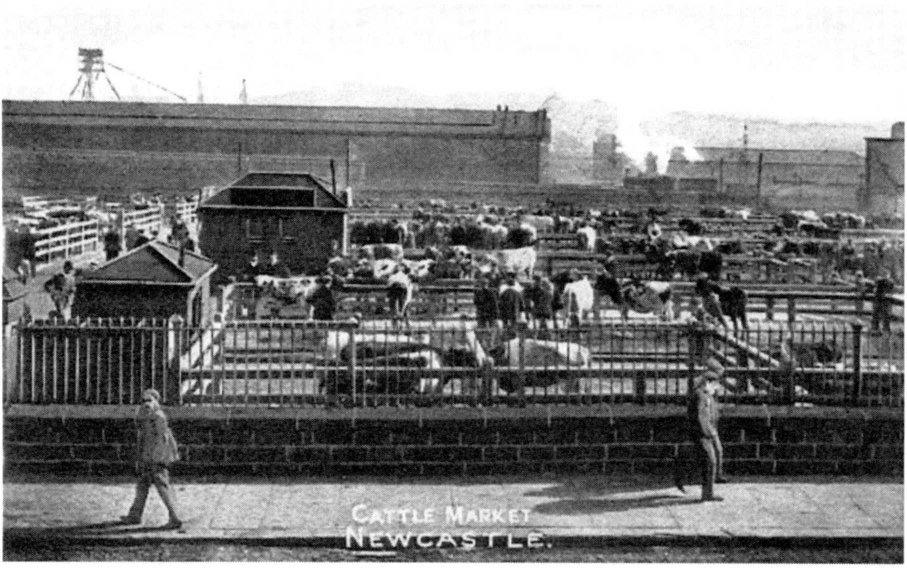

Newcastle cattle market in 1905.

idea; no resident of either parish claimed the occupation of drover in any return, and yet this was an important stock-farming area. As the *Agrarian History of England and Wales* claimed, '[drovers]...became the intermediaries between railhead, auction mart and fair, little diminished in numbers but employed in very different patterns of work' (Collins, 2000, 1183).

Undoubtedly, some of these trends were accelerated by changes in the marketing of livestock. Appendix 3, Table 2, shows the pattern of fairs throughout Northumberland in 1841. As indicated above, some of these were more important than others and continued to grow, while others declined. Some, such as the fair at Newcastle, were replaced by urban markets. In other places, auction marts replaced fairs. The first auction mart in the Borders was Oliver's Mart at Hawick, which commenced selling stock in 1859 when it did £25 3*s* 5*d* worth of business.[20] By 1869 this had grown to over £100,000, and to over £200,000 by 1872. Although it was 1915 before the £300,000 mark was passed, the mart had become a permanent fixture and a highly profitable venture. Clearly popular with buyers and sellers, other marts were gradually opened elsewhere in the region and had replaced the fairs by the early twentieth century. Details of those operating in Northumberland are given in Appendix 3, Table 3. Static in their operation and more regular in their trade than the fairs, the marts employed drovers to oversee stock movement – yet another variation on the newly emerging pattern of work.

Agriculture in the Upland Valleys of Northumberland in the Nineteenth Century

The pattern of livestock farming established in the uplands in the latter part of the eighteenth and early nineteenth centuries, i.e. one dominated by large-scale sheep farms, continued through the remainder of the nineteenth century and for nearly three decades into the twentieth century. The first piece of evidence of the dominance of sheep in this agricultural economy occurs in the Tithe Commission File for Elsdon parish in 1838.[21]

In the wake of the Tithe Commutation Act, all parishes had been surveyed for the purposes of creating a uniform tithe payment structure throughout the country. The extent of investigations carried out by the commissioners depended on the size of the parish and the problems encountered therein. In the case of Elsdon, the type of agriculture was so overwhelmingly pastoral that some remarks on this were included. The parish was confirmed as being over 77,000 acres in size and was described as 'for the most part wild and mountainous and consists of very extensive moors'. Noted as being ideal for the breeding of Cheviot sheep, it was stated that the livestock consisted of 30,000 Cheviot sheep, 10,000 lambs and 500 cattle of 'the improved shorthorn breed' with 500 calves; a ratio of forty sheep to each head of cattle.

Much the same distribution of livestock was to be found throughout the North Tyne, Rede and Coquet valleys from then into the twentieth century. The table opposite shows stocking rates on five farms in the North Tyne and Rede Valleys rented from the Duke of Northumberland. These figures demonstrate clearly the preponderance of sheep on these holdings. Indeed, in the case of Cranecleugh correspondence in 1830 between the tenant, Percy Hedley, and the Duke's agents shows that the farm was only stocked with sheep and that it was not paying its way. The Duke's officers wondered if the introduction of some cattle might remedy this, but show some uncertainty about their proposal.[22]

Early twentieth-century view of sheep being driven to market from Bow Rigg near Bellingham (Collier P4.33.15).

TABLE SHOWING STOCKING RATES ON FIVE FARMS IN NORTH TYNEDALE AND REDESDALE[23]

Bewshaugh	**3,100 acres**	
Stock 1850	12 cattle	1,500 sheep
Stock 1872	40 cattle	1,800 sheep
Catcleugh	**5,800 acres**	
Stock 1850	16 cattle	3,200 sheep
Stock 1865	25 cattle	3,200 sheep
Cranecleugh	**6,700 acres**	
Stock 1850	20 cattle	2,000 sheep
Stock 1865	40 cattle	2,000 sheep
East Kielder	**6,100 acres**	
Stock 1850	13 cattle	2,600 sheep
Stock 1869	20 cattle	2,600 sheep
West Kielder	**8,000 acres**	
Stock 1850	20 cattle	2,840 sheep
Stock 1867	0 cattle	3,000 sheep

The table makes it clear that these five farms had all become very large holdings with vast numbers of sheep. Cattle only formed a tiny part of the enterprise, and despite some effort on four of the farms to increase the number of cattle, the effect was only marginal.

On a larger scale, Appendix 4 shows the stocking rates of five upland parishes at four selected dates between 1870 and 1931. The area covered by these five parishes exceeds 240,000 acres. The figures are abstracted from the annual returns made by farmers to the Government since 1866 (TNA, MAF 68). The way in which the data has been collected has varied over the sixty-one years covered by the table, but the way in which it has been abstracted and presented is based on the categories used in 1870 and permits clear comparison between the returns.

Although over the period as a whole stocking rates of cattle and sheep had increased slightly, it is apparent that the ratio of cattle to sheep had changed very slightly in favour of cattle. This led to an increase in the acreage of grass cut for hay over all, although the total acreage of hay in 1911 was greater than in 1931. It is also noticeable that the ratio of lambs to older sheep had moved in favour of the lambs, probably in response to a demand for lamb rather than the older sheep meat preferred in the early nineteenth century. Feeding before lambing had improved, as had the techniques used at lambing by shepherds, and these factors led to better survival rates in the latter part of the period studied. This maintained the preponderance of sheep in the upland economy up until the start of the Second World War.

The Twentieth Century

Although some aspects of the droving trade after the coming of the railway system have been considered in the previous pages, there are other facets of droving in the late nineteenth and twentieth centuries which have not. Professional droving may have mostly been confined to the urban railway station, market and abattoir, but the driving of livestock on foot continued to be an important part of farm life into the second half of the twentieth century. Those involved were usually members of farming families or farm workers employed on the holding, but some of the routes they continued to use were ones over which stock had been driven for many years, and some of the trades associated with droving (albeit non-exclusively), such as blacksmithing and innkeeping, persisted in this environment. Evidence of this type of droving has been explored specifically using oral history techniques and is the subject of a chapter in its own right.

The smithy at Stannersburn, near Falstone, *c.*1910.

NOTES

1 The population of England and Wales in 1801 is recorded as 9,061,000 while London (county) had a population of 1,088,000. See Mitchell & Deane, 1962, 8 and 20.

2 Bonser, 1970, 71. At this stage, apart from some localised trading along the Border, sheep were not yet part of the droving trade.

3 For the economy of the Highlands, see Gray, 1957, Devine 1993 and 1999.

4 For a typical account see, for example, McCord & Thompson, 1998, pp221–234.

5 Interview with Thomas (Tommy) Wood of Wingates, farmer, by Ian Roberts, 27 August 2006.

6 Bailey & Culley 1805, pp171–4. The list of fairs given in this volume is shown in Table 1 in the Appendix.

7 Interview with Mr Hubert Robinson by Ian Roberts and Richard Carlton, 15 June 2006.

8 The route is shown as the Great Drift Road on the enclosure maps for Elsdon 1729 and for Corsenside and East Woodburn 1794 (NCRO QRA 12). The Highland drover, Alexander Munro, was obviously following the moorland drift road when he died at Dudlees on 15 June 1801, as recorded in the Elsdon parish records (EPR, 226).

9 Papers deposited in NCRO by Mrs D. Murray of East Woodburn and yet to be catalogued contain a document relating to the turnpike and give details of its history.

10 In addition to Greenwood's county map of 1828, several maps of North Tynedale in the Duke of Northumberland's archives depict drove roads. The map of the Belling, Starsley, Woodhouse, Law and Kennel Estates in 1826 (Aln Cas. O 21.19) shows two drift roads on the north side of the valley, running parallel to one another on a WNW–ESE orientation. The more northerly of the two passed through Bellingburn Head, its course marked by a series of standing stones. The southerly example passed through Swinsey Gate along the south side of Lonon Syke. Both are marked on Greenwood's map, though only the northern one is labelled 'Drift Road'. An earlier map by John Robertson (Aln Cas O 21.3), depicting the Duke's Cranecleugh and Whickhope farms on the south side of the valley in 1735-7, shows a 'Road from Scotland to Stagshaw Bank' which enters the estates from Leaplish ground and runs past Kateshaw Hill along the north side of Cranecleugh Burn. Plackett (1997, 50) also cites John Leadbitter's map of moors and waste lands on the south side of the valley belonging to Sir Edward Swinburne in 1772, which shows several tracks in North Tynedale marked 'Drift Road from Scotland to Stagshaw Bank'.

11 Details of agriculture and the tenurial arrangements found in the 17th century can be found in R.P. Sanderson (ed.) Survey of the Debatable and Border Lands adjoining the Realm of Scotland and belonging to the Crown of England in 1604 (cited here as 1604 Survey); S.J. Watt 1971 and in Butlin 1973.

12 Hodgson 1827, 153-4, reported that in 1658, Sir Charles Howard and his trustees sold the summer pastures at Catcleugh and the neighbouring Spithope to Henry Widdrington of Black Heddon. Widdrington, in turn, sold the property, which, together with other neighbouring land, ultimately came into the possession of Gabriel Hall. By his death in 1733, Hall had accumulated a substantial estate that mainly passed to his son Martin, but he also made some bequests to other children. The whole had been divided into farms and when subsequently some of the property was sold in the 1760s, the Duke of Northumberland bought Catcleugh, Spithope, Babswood and Chattlehope. Previously all of these four properties had been created by Widdrington or Hall from the commonly used summer grazing in Upper Redesdale, which in total in 1604 had exceeded 21 000 acres, but now this portion had been amalgamated to form a single farm of approximately 6,000 acres.

13 By the early nineteenth century, at over 40,000 acres in extent, the Duke owned the largest estate in the North Tyne valley which was divided into ten large farms ranging in size from Gowanburn (1,208 acres) to West Kielder (8,005 acres). Evidence from the Bell Collection of papers (NCRO ZAN Bell 65/1) shows that one of the farms, Cranecleugh, with over 6,000 acres, was an amalgam of two farms, Cranecleugh and Bull Crag, while another, The Belling (over 4,300 acres) was made up of at least four earlier, smaller farms and at the north end of the valley. Bewshaugh (over 3,000 acres) at the north end of the valley was also created from four farms.

14 In considering the formation of the Belling farm, Harbottle & Newman 1973, 137-176, give consideration to a number of reasons for farm amalgamation. The reasons that they suggest could well apply to properties owned by a wide range of landed proprietors, not just the Duke.

15 Mingay 1989, 89-90. In Northumberland in 1785, the date of the Haltwhistle fair was moved from the 14 May to 12 May as it clashed with the bigger, more important fair at Stagshaw Bank. The notice announcing this change made it clear that if this was not done, the more important gentlemen cattle dealers would not attend at Haltwhistle, see NCRO 2815, and fig. 29 opposite.

16 Information about Manchester is taken from Scola 1992, in particular 38-70. This is one of the few thorough studies of the food supply of a nineteenth-century industrial city.

17 Perren 1978, 30. Perren explained that at the beginning of the century the Tyneside trade was supplied from Morpeth, but, in 1836, a market was opened in Newcastle which shortly became the dominant one for the meat trade in the north-east of England.

18 NCRO 4341, Hedley of Bewshaugh Diary, Vol. II, entry for 25 September 1863.

19 NCRO Census Returns for the County of Northumberland 1851, 1861, 1901 and 1921.

20 Hawick Auction Mart Papers (Private collection). Stock sold at Hawick Auction Mart 1859 – 1951. I am grateful to the late Kenneth Oliver for sight of this material.

21 The National Archives (TNA) file IR 18/6955, Elsdon Tithe Commission Agreement.

22 NCRO ZAN Bell 65/2, Letter of 27 February 1830 to Mr Colbeck.

23 NCRO ZAN Bell 65/18 for 1850 and ZAN Bell 65/1 for the remainder.

FIVE

Droving in the Twentieth Century: Local Events and Personal Recollections

Although there are a number of written records of droving in the twentieth century, some of which are cited below, much of the driving of livestock went unrecorded. One reason for this is that it was no longer a trade. As explained previously, professional drovers were mostly employed to deal with livestock in urban situations – there were few long-distance drovers, and they were employed only infrequently. Another reason is that driving stock in the twentieth century was an informal task, carried out by family members or employees as part of general farm duties. The distances over which they drove livestock were also much shorter than the heroic distances undertaken by their eighteenth- and nineteenth-century professional predecessors.

Nevertheless, the work that was done was important, though practically disappeared as motorised transport became widely and readily available. In the absence of written evidence, oral recollections of individuals who have driven stock or know about droving in the twentieth century have been collected through oral history interviews. The information supplied in these interviews has subsequently been used to help reconstruct a picture of this essential agricultural activity. Although the sample of those interviewed is not large, there is considerable consistency in the statements made, both between the respondents and also with the published evidence about droving in the twentieth century. A list of the informants interviewed has been given in an appendix to this section.

The Marketing of Cattle in the Twentieth Century

As explained earlier, long-distance droving ended with the development of a railway network around the middle of the nineteenth century. As this change took place, so did the way in which livestock was bought and sold. The traditional fairs at which these transactions had occurred began to be replaced by auction marts, almost all of which were close to railway stations.[1] In order to sell their cattle, as well as sheep and other farm stock, farmers had only to deliver them to the mart where they would be sold by auction to a purchaser who then assumed responsibility for any further transport. In cases where the animals were destined for the meat market, this usually entailed a short journey to an abattoir. Store animals were either conveyed most of the way to their new homes by rail, or were driven away by the purchaser or his employees.[2]

As a result of these changes in marketing, droving became a short-distance occupation, mostly carried out by farmers and their families and employees.[3] Mr Tommy Simpson provided an example of such droving which occurred in the 1880s and 1890s in the area to the north-west of Newcastle (Mr T. Simpson in an oral history interview with I.D. Roberts, 20 March 2006). Mr Simpson's father, also called Thomas Simpson, left school and went to work for a Mr Dickenson, a farmer and cattle dealer based at Bolam West

Tarset station in North Tynedale, 1914 – one of the many small stations from which beasts could be transported following the demise of droving.

House. It was part of Thomas's duties on a Sunday afternoon to take a pony and dog and to ride around a number of Mr Dickenson's clients in the area around Middleton, Cambo and Belsay. He collected up a mixed drove of cattle and sheep that had been purchased from these farmers by his employer and drove them via Ponteland to part of the Newcastle town moor near Cowgate. Cowgate was the location of an important fair (McCord & Thompson, 1998, 292) where there were enclosures in which the stock could be confined. Thomas left the stock that he had brought to Cowgate in these enclosures and they were collected on the following day by staff from the Newcastle market for sale on the next market day.

Professional drovers were usually only employed in organising stock in the area of the mart. Some of them were employees of the mart, while others might work for municipal authorities[4] and were responsible for delivering the stock to stations and abattoirs in the town. In some places, they were given special badges and employee numbers which invested them with some authority for controlling the movement of the animals within the town area. This mixed type of droving continued until the coming of motor lorries in the 1920s, when some changes began to be introduced as the stock was usually driven directly to and from the mart in the wagon so that the drovers additionally became responsible for directing motor traffic. Eventually, when many of the rural railway lines were closed as a result of the Beeching reforms in the 1960s (Simmonds & Biddle, 1997, 29), motorised transport became practically the sole form of conveying livestock from place to place. Marts and markets adapted their practices to meet these changes, and loading and wash docks for cattle wagons were introduced to all marts.

Before the advent of cattle wagons, lorries and other petrol- or diesel-driven vehicles, the only form of mechanised transport available to farmers was the railway. Thus, for many years members of the farmer's family or farm employees had to drive stock to and from the nearest railway station, sometimes at all hours of the day or night. Mrs Davy, now living in retirement in Thropton, (in an oral history interview with I.D. Roberts, 21 July 2006) recollected her father, Mr J. Walton, purchasing Irish cattle at the mart at

Scots Gap. The cattle were loaded on to a train when the mart closed and then sent to Rothbury, the nearest station to the Walton Farm at Flotterton. Mr Walton insisted that the cattle were collected when they arrived, and Mrs Davy vividly remembered driving the beasts from Rothbury through Thropton to Flotterton, a distance of approximately four miles, on dark autumn nights.

There were also places which had access to the railway, but from which it was not convenient to send livestock by train. One example of this was the village of West Woodburn in the Rede Valley, which was only four-and-a-half miles from the nearest mart at Bellingham where the mart was close to the railway station. However the two villages were not on the same line, and to travel from West Woodburn to Bellingham would entail taking a train to Redesmouth Junction and then changing to a train to Bellingham. Although this was possible and was done by passengers, moving stock in this way was unnecessarily time consuming and expensive. Mr Simpson remembered that, as a boy, he had participated in driving stock between the two villages. As part of the road lacked a fence or wall on one side for some of the route, children from West Woodburn assisted those driving the animals by running alongside the stock in order to prevent them straying away on to the unenclosed ground.

There continued to be a number of farms which were not conveniently located close to the railway, and some instances in which farmers wished to use a mart which held special sales which had to be reached by driving the stock rather than using a railway. One example of this was the use by Scottish and English farmers living on the Borders of Northumberland and Scotland who wished to send their sheep to the sales at the Rothbury Mart. Andrew Purves states that shepherds from the Kale, Bowmont, Oxnam and College valleys took a three-day journey stopping at places such as Barrowburn, Quickening Cote and Harbottle for the two overnight stops on their journey to Rothbury (Purves, 2001, 192), while David McCracken recollects being told that farmers from Akeld stopped at Threestoneburn and Scrainwood when driving their sheep to the same mart (interview with A.D. McCracken of Burdonside, Tarset, March 2005).

Walter Brown has explained that there were a number of droving routes from farms such as Langleeford and Broadstruther in the Cheviots which connected to this route. These particular drove roads had been used by travellers and packhorses for many years, and continued to be used for moving livestock until well into the twentieth century (personal communication to I.D. Roberts, November 2009). In order that the animals taking such long trips to the mart could rest before the sale, the auctioneer, Robert Donkin, provided fields for this purpose at Gallowfield and Pondicherry, two farms between Thropton and Rothbury (interview with L.I. Hedley of Overacres, Otterburn, March 2005).

In the inter-war period, all such journeys were usually conducted by farm employees and only occasionally by specialist drovers. Most of these men were locally employed and drove stock over short distances compared to their eighteenth- and nineteenth-century predecessors. Bill 'Kayfer' Wilson was a well-known character in the Rothbury area who lived in a blacksmith's hut at Cove Quarry and drove stock between the farms of Tosson, Scrainwood and Old Bewick and the local marts (information supplied by R.M. Tindall of Fourstones, June 2005). Geoff Logan recollected a drover called Gold or Gould who worked around Berwick (interview with Geoff Logan of Fenton Hill, near Wooler, 14 May 2009). This man was employed by Geoff Logan's father to drive stock from

Reston Mart to the Logan family farm at East Fenton. As the mart took place on the Saturday, he drove the stock out on the Sunday morning and was rewarded by being given his Sunday lunch, a 10*s* note and a car ride back to Berwick for himself and his dog!

The recollections of most of the interviewees date from the early 1930s, and all are therefore within the period when motorised transport was beginning to be used by farmers. One feature of the transport of livestock revealed through oral interviews is the highly individual way in which farmers adopted the new form of transport. W.A. Robson, who spent his early years at Willowbog, a 3,000-acre farm in the Upper North Tyne Valley rented from the Swinburne family, recalled that his father had all sheep driven to the station at Kielder and sent to the mart at Bellingham by rail. He refused to use any of the new lorries as they were twin decked, and he considered it detrimental to the health of the animals on the lower deck that they should travel underneath the ones on the upper (interview with W.A. Robson of Charlton, near Bellingham, March 2005).

A few miles further down the valley, Laurence Dagg recalled that at the Hott Farm in the 1930s his father adopted motorised transport as soon as he was able, and that the minimum of droving was employed (interview with Laurence Dagg of the Hott Farm, Tarset, March 2005). In 1931 in the Rede Valley, the family of James Johnson moved from Heatherwick near Otterburn to Tuthill at Hartington near Cambo. The family and their chattels were moved by lorry, but all the livestock was driven the ten miles between the farms along the public road (interview with James Johnson, Tuthill Farm, Hartington, Cambo, April 2005).

Motorised transport was sometimes not as speedily adopted as the railways had been in the previous century. During the depression of the 1930s, cost provided a hindrance to its use. Ian Hedley recollected driving sheep from his farm at Overacres to both Rothbury and Bellingham for sale at the marts in these places (Mr L.I. Hedley in an oral history interview with I.D. Roberts, March 2005). One particular instance remained in his mind above many others. He took a flock of lambs to Rothbury for sale in the autumn of 1933, a distance of about twelve miles. He was only offered 11*s* a head and brought them home. The abortive sale had taken up to two days for driving the stock. Three weeks later he took the same sheep to Bellingham where he was able to obtain 11*s* 3*d* per head for the flock. He sold them. Having taken a full day to drive the lambs the ten miles to Bellingham, he vowed never to pass out a parcel of sheep again. However, Mr Hedley remained pleased that he had not had to pay for the transport of the sheep, as he would have lost any profit on the sale if he had done so as margins were so small in the depression.

Wartime created other circumstances in which stock had to be driven rather than moved by lorry. During a study of traditional cattle farming and droving undertaken by the Northumberland National Park in 2004, the staff undertaking the study reported the experiences of Bob Telford (Northumberland National Park 2004, 2). Mr Telford's family had to move cattle from a farm in the North Tyne Valley to a new holding near Glanton, some forty-five miles away, in May 1943. Because of fuel shortages and the great difficulties in obtaining motorised transport, it was decided to move the herd of seventy-five – which included cows with calves, replacement heifers and young bullocks – by driving them. Mr Telford managed to accomplish the journey in only two days with the help of two men, one of whom drove a horse and cart to carry any tired calves. At the end of the drive, both men and stock were exhausted, but it was the only way in which cattle could be moved over such distances in wartime.

Where rail transport was convenient, it usually continued to be used up until the line was closed. Farmers like the grandfather and father of Bill Robson of Chesterhope, who had farms located close to the Wansbeck Railway and who also used the mart at Scots Gap which was on the same line, continued to use the railway for cattle transport throughout its life. They were able to contact the station master at the station closest to the farm, order a wagon, load it on the day of travel and it would then be attached to the first convenient train travelling to the station nearest the ultimate destination to which the beasts were being sent (interview with W. Robson of Chesterhope, April 2005). Yet, during the same interview, Mr Robson was able to recollect the names of road-haulage firms, such as Reeds of Otterburn, who were able to provide motorised transport if the railway was not convenient. It is thus difficult to be specific about the time when road haulage completely supplanted droving other than when the railway closed. The absence of information about the numbers of livestock conveyed by the railway adds to this difficulty.[5]

Farming Policy

A further complication in assessing the nature of the droving trade in the twentieth century arises from changes in farming policy in that century. In the nineteenth century and the early part of the twentieth century, farming policy was usually dictated by the farmer in response to market forces (Roberts, 1992, Chapter Two). For example, the number of lambs produced on each farm and their sale into the meat market (as lambs) increased significantly from the 1870s onwards, as lamb became the favoured form of eating sheep meat as opposed to the mutton and wether meat of former times (Perren, 1978, 191–197). Occasionally landlords influenced farm policy, as demonstrated on the Redesdale Estate in the 1880s when the estate constructed hay sheds on many of the farms (Roberts, 1992, Chapter Four) in order to help the farmers improve their sheep stock and keep a few additional cattle as an antidote to the depressed market conditions in this period. The increased stocks of cattle created additional droving tasks for the farmers, as the stock had to be moved at different times of the year from the sheep stock and sometimes also to different markets.

In the twentieth century, farming policy has been dictated by different factors. The most important of these has been Government agricultural policy. Although the Government collected statistical information about agriculture from 1866 onwards and there were occasional Parliamentary investigations into certain agricultural events, such as the cattle plague in the 1860s, it was not until 1889 that a Board of Agriculture was created with ministerial responsibility for matters dealing with the agricultural industry.[6] The Board as an agent of Government became increasingly influential in forming the policy of the farmers for their holdings. Initially more advisory than directive, the Board became much more authoritative during the First World War, and this paved the way for more interventionist policies in the post-war period.

One of these was the subsidy paid for the production of beef, which began to be paid in the 1920s and which continued up until 1939 and was resumed and extended after the war ended in 1945 (Pawson, 1961, 113–115 and 191–192). This policy had a direct influence on farm policy in the Northumbrian uplands. Farmers were encouraged to keep more cattle, and thus stock on farms of both breeding cattle and stores increased.

This is shown clearly in the Table of Parochial Returns by comparing columns five, six and seven of the 1911 and 1931 returns. It was also a point referred to by two of the interviewees in their statements about the numbers and types of cattle kept on their farms.[7] Government policy was also responsible for changes in farming policy during and after the Second World War. The War Agricultural Committees were responsible for the direction of farming policy during the conflict and a separate study is required to demonstrate the effect that this had on the production and marketing of livestock during the war.[8]

After the war, the Government continued to exercise considerable influence over farming policy (Holderness, 1985, 70–74). In the North Tyne Valley, both Laurence Dagg and W.A. Robson have described how they and their families became employed in the production of liquid milk for the dairy at Stocksfield. For some years the milk was transported by train to the dairy, but after the closure of the line it was taken by lorry. The dairy closed in the 1960s and both farmers kept suckler cows thereafter instead of dairy animals.[9] In both cases, changes in farming policy and practice were made as a result of Government and other external agencies acting on the farm, and were carried out more rapidly than in the past. Dairy farming provided additional work in moving stock on a daily basis for the task of milking. Although not onerous and regarded as part of the task of milking, the fact that this had to be done twice each day restricted the amount of time available for moving other stock on the farm. Consequently, it encouraged the use of motor transport and the role of professional hauliers in farming in Northumberland. Thus, when the dairy herds were replaced by suckler beef production, the business of transporting livestock had changed completely to the one found at the present time.

With minor variations, these patterns of livestock transport were repeated throughout Northumberland. The adoption of motorised transport occurred more speedily and thoroughly on farms which were closest to urban areas where the road system was better and also where the volume of motor traffic very much prohibited the manual driving of livestock. In the more remote communities it is still possible to see herds of cattle and flocks of sheep being moved from one place to another on public roads, but the journeys are usually short and the animals closely supervised. Recent changes in the regulations governing the movement of livestock and slaughtering have meant that all movements of farm animals have to be recorded and the ways in which they are moved have to follow a comprehensive code of practice. These latter are particularly strict, especially when animals are moved over very long distances or between countries. The modern equivalent of the drover probably requires an intimate knowledge of bureaucracy and a laptop computer rather than a pair of stout boots and a good dog!

Irish Cattle

Pawson states that in 1957 a total of 86,000 Irish cattle were brought into the county of Northumberland (Pawson, 1961, 113). All the interviewees were asked about the Irish trade with the county, as this was clearly a very important factor in livestock husbandry and had a powerful influence on marketing. Unfortunately, no extensive survey has been carried out of this trade and the part that it has played not only in farming in Northumberland but also in the agriculture of northern England in general.[10]

From the late nineteenth century, Irish cattle were purchased for fattening in

Northumberland before sale into the meat trade (Turner, 1996, 58–61). The interviewees described how, in the period from the 1920s up to the 1980s, the cattle were bought in Ireland by Irish dealers who then arranged for them to be transported by rail and boat to the English markets at places like Scots Gap, Hexham, Belford and Alnwick. Different types of cattle were sent to the different markets in order to suit the differing types of weather and grazing found throughout the north of England. Those sent to north-western Northumberland came from Sligo and Donegal, as they were hardier than cattle from other places and thrived well on the farms in this part of England. Both Bill Robson of Chesterhope and James Johnson of Tuthill[11] explained that some cattle were purchased in the autumn for keeping over winter and fattening in the following spring and early summer, while others were bought in the spring for summer grazing and sale in the early autumn.

The number of cattle purchased depended on the availability of feed on the farm and therefore varied from year to year. The cattle were also not grazed on the fells but were kept on some of the better ground on the farm. In the earlier part of the century, these cattle were usually of the Shorthorn breed, but were later crossed with Aberdeen Angus or Herefords in order to produce a better type of beef animal. The cattle were much sought after as they were easily handled and responded well to the type of feed they were given. The trade died out in the 1980s, probably as a result of the political unrest in Northern Ireland, but also because the entry of the British and Irish into the EEC changed the nature of agriculture in both countries.

In terms of the droving trade, Irish cattle dealers in the 1920s and 1930s brought cattle over from Ireland and then took them around the country to sell them. Many of those who came to Northumberland shipped their beasts from Dublin to Silloth in Cumberland and then sent them by train to Hexham or Scots Gap. From these stations, they might take some to the local marts to sell while others drove them from farm to farm selling to the farmers who usually traded with them (personal communication by Mrs M. Robinson, West Cocklaw Farm, Northumberland, 30 April 2005).

Gradually but increasingly after the war, this practice ceased as the number of sellers grew fewer and the quantity of cattle each dealer brought increased. Instead, the dealers used the railways and motor transport to bring their cattle to the auction marts. It was also the case that most of the dealers became associated with one or two marts in particular and did not hawk their animals from farm to farm, or mart to mart. George Strachan, in his personal memoir of his career as an auctioneer, listed a group of ten dealers that he associated particularly with the mart in Morpeth in the 1950s (Strachan, 2005, 40). Some droving did take place, particularly to farms close to the marts, as the Irish cattle were used to being driven. However, more work is being undertaken on this aspect of farming by one of the authors of this book in order to provide a definitive picture of the Irish aspect of the cattle farming industry in Northumberland in the twentieth century.

NOTES

1 The first mart opened in the Borders at Hawick in 1859 by the Oliver family was close to the railway. Others at Wooler, Ponteland, Belford, Alnwick, Acklington, Wark, Bellingham, Rothbury and Scots Gap were also close to stations. At Hexham, the station was slightly further away, but livestock was driven through the town to the railway loading dock. The important urban markets at Newcastle and Morpeth were established prior to the arrival of the railway, but their proximity to the railway stations in both towns

may be as a result of the use of this form of transport by farmers delivering cattle to the market.

2 The droving system in the early part of the twentieth century is clearly described in Purves 2001, 191–3.

3 The droving of sheep to market by shepherds may have been more widely practiced than cattle driving. In terms of visual imagery of sheep and cattle driving, the Heritage Centre in Bellingham has a collection of over 2500 photographs and post cards (including the pictures taken by W.P. Collier between 1912 and 1937). This collection contains six images of flocks of sheep being driven to marts but none of cattle.

4 Interview with W. Robson of Chesterhope, West Woodburn, April 2005. Mr Robson has two badges from Perth and Newcastle dating from the early part of the twentieth century. These were worn strapped to the drovers' arms.

5 G.W.M. Sewell, The North British Railway in Northumberland (1991, 1993 reprint) contains very little information about livestock traffic. Mr Sewell has explained (personal communication April 2005) that he has seen no details of this traffic but he believes that further research may reveal the location of ledgers giving details of numbers and costs of livestock movements on both the Wansbeck and Border Counties lines. Time limits preclude this research for this study.

6 This is a vast topic. Further information can be found in volumes such as S. Foreman, Loaves and Fishes (1989), Sir John Winnifrith, The Ministry of Agriculture, Fisheries and Food (1962) and E.H. Whetham, *The Agrarian History of England and Wales* Vol. VIII 1914 – 1939 (1978).

7 Interview with Laurence Dagg of the Hott Farm, Tarset, March 2005, interview with W. Robson of Chesterhope, April 2005.

8 Pawson 1961, 8–10 gives an indication of some of the changes introduced by the Committees in Northumberland.

9 Interview with Laurence Dagg of the Hott Farm, Tarset, March 2005, interview with W.A. Robson of Charlton, near Bellingham, February 2004.

10 Smailes 1960, 188-302 makes several references to the trade across the north in the section on Rural Areas in his book. More anecdotally, Harold Slight 2000, 58–60 describes the work of some of the drovers associated with this trade.

11 Interview with W. Robson of Chesterhope, April 2005, interview with James Johnson, Tuthill Farm, Hartington, Cambo, April 2005.

SIX

What to See and Do: Remains Of Droving

The movement of livestock by droving within and through the Northumbrian uplands probably occurred continuously over several millennia since prehistoric times, and its history over the last millennium is well documented. The scale of droving increased when the population of the towns grew, particularly after the onset of industrialisation in the eighteenth century when the demand for meat could not be met from local supplies alone. Thus, at the height of the droving trade it has been estimated that around 100,000 cattle were driven each year from Scotland to England. The routes used were often long-established by tradition, usually taking twisting courses from north to south, thereby making them easily distinguishable from local packhorse trails up the valleys and from new roads of straighter course established at the time of the enclosures and turnpikes in the eighteenth and nineteenth centuries.

Drovers using such routes travelled with herds of up to 2,000 sheep and 200 cattle, halting every six–twelve miles at regular resting places where overnight pastures and inns were available. Such resting locations were important also as places of business and trade, as were the fairs and markets at the end of the drove routes, since drovers were often men of status carrying messages and credit notes, as well as valuable stock. The commercial and social importance of droving, however, is not matched by the scale and permanence of monuments associated with it in the landscape, which means that it is easily overlooked. Closer attention, however, reveals that in addition to the songs and stories of droving preserved in folk memory, numerous physical traces of droving can be seen within the county.

Many droveways used regularly by professional drovers preserve upon their routes a number of features associated with their former use, most often including the road surfaces themselves and linear boundary features such as walls and ditches. The droveways crossed rivers and streams principally by means of fords, but bridges were provided on some of the major routes into market centres and over major rivers such as the lower Tyne, and more were constructed in the later period of droving, the eighteenth and nineteenth centuries. Important crossing points on the droving routes sometimes acted as foci for the establishment of trading posts and the development of permanent settlements.

Amongst a range of smaller or more ephemeral structures often associated with droveways, but also existing independently, are the remains of ponds and troughs for watering stock, smithies for shoeing cattle before they reached metalled roads in the lowlands, and field systems linked to inns and other semi-permanent settlements. Compounds such as stells, often used to house stray animals as well as to gather sheep for shearing and lambing are a common sight on the fells, and at Elsdon one survives in a village location.

Some routes, notably Clennel Street and The Street, are associated with cross-dyke earthwork features (see below) which may have been used, at various times since the prehistoric era, to control and toll the passage of people and stock. Some of the many prehistoric and later settlement sites upon the roads, as well as other remains of buildings and enclosures, may also have been related to the movement of people and stock, perhaps providing rest places for both, as at Slyme Foot on The Street in Coquetdale. Some roads, such as the A697 between Morpeth and Cornhill-on-Tweed, are associated more with structures and features – including coach- and post-houses, entrance lodges to estates, mileposts and signs – related to their contemporary and later use as highways for passengers and goods, than with droving. A large range of other sites and features, including hill forts and cultivation terraces, may well be unrelated to drove roads, but on the other hand could have been used as route markers and temporary shelters, and are nevertheless essential components of the landscapes through which the droveways pass.

Drove Roads

Pre-eminent among the remains of droving activity are the routes of the drove roads themselves, many of which can still be followed on the ground by walkers today. Indeed, these ancient byways traverse some of the highest and most spectacular scenery in Northumberland. Many of these roads are corridors of land, sometimes quite wide and characterised in places by a number of separate paths meandering within the corridor. These paths, now often visible as holloways, were formed by the

View west from Redmire Bridge over the Tarset, with earthwork remains of multiple holloways down a steep approach slope at the top left of the view.

View across lower Clennel Street to the earthwork remains of an enclosure.

Cross-dyke on the course of Clennel Street north of Alwinton, viewed from the north.

View across a trackway on the major droving route connecting Coquetdale and Redesdale, with Harehaugh hill fort in the background.

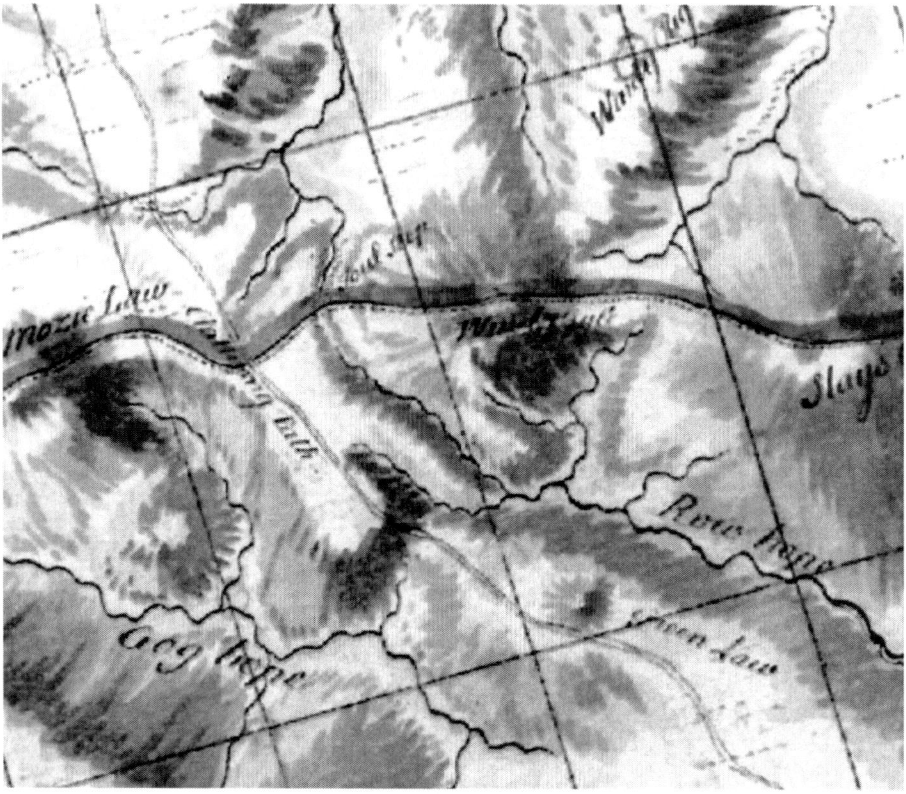

The Street, labelled Clattering Path, depicted in Roy's Atlas of Scotland 1747–55. The old road from Cambo into Coquetdale, skirting the northern edge of Simonside, was also known as the Clattering Way in the seventeenth century and may have been regarded as a continuation of the Clattering path further north.

natural tendency of stock to choose the easiest course, abandoning boggy, heavily rutted paths in favour of drier courses which themselves became rutted in time. Multiple hollo-way courses, whether caused by droving or regular farm stock movements, tend to occur on steep gradients. Examples shown here include those on the approach to the village of Kirkwhelpington from the north-west, the northern approach to Alnham, Landshot Hill above Hudspeth, adjacent to the site of Elsdon East fairground and the approach to Redmire Bridge, probably an older fording point, over the River Tarset near its confluence with the North Tyne.

Amongst the most important, still visible drove roads in Northumberland, The Street and Clennell Street both cross the high Cheviot watershed, dropping into the head-waters of the Coquet and continuing on via Alwinton and Harbottle. Although these routes are now clearly defined by modern mapping, principally the Ordnance Survey series which began to be surveyed in this region in the 1850s, earlier historic maps suggest that such routes began as wide corridors within which numerous routes were possible; multiple courses taken by cattle and stock being driven to summering grounds or to market would have been followed within a broad swathe of ground determined by herdsmen or drovers on the basis of ground conditions and wayleave.

The Street as it joins the Coquet Valley route at Slyme Foot, with a possible enclosure on the west side of Rowhope Burn.

Holloway at Fiddler's Elbow near Wingates, Coquetdale.

Course of the Great Drift Road at Ferneyrigg, looking north.

Thus, several potential courses of Clennel Street are shown on historic maps south of the Border, while The Street is even less well defined, early maps both north and south of the Border showing radically different routes from that now taken. Even apparently clearly defined routes such as Dere Street, which crosses the Border at the head of Coquetdale and leads down into Redesdale, became less well defined in places due to continued use in the medieval period and intensive re-use as droveways. Indeed, Dere Street was so heavily used as a drove road in the medieval and later periods that the Roman road surface has suffered serious erosion along many sections, and in others has been removed entirely.

At Featherwood, another important droveway branches off Dere Street and follows the moorland watershed between the Rede and the Coquet before descending to reach the major droving hub of Elsdon, with its inns and annual fairs. This route, known as the Great Drift Road, then ran due south from Elsdon towards Stagshaw Bank. For most of its length the route is marked on the modern Ordnance Survey map by a bridle path, but despite the former importance of this road its course is often difficult to trace on the ground. A branch off this route led south-east towards Newcastle via Kirkwhelpington, where its course is particularly evident north-west of the village on Heeston Bank, beside the A696, where numerous holloways have been scored into the hillside by the repeated passage of livestock and other traffic (see page 56).

Another important droving corridor was provided by the valley of the North Tyne, where the long-distance movement of livestock was not obstructed by turnpikes. Several drove or 'drift' roads ran parallel to one another along this valley, particularly on the north side of the river, merging near Thorneyburn where the route can still be followed as a country lane.

Finally, it is worth re-emphasising that, in addition to the droving routes named here, numerous other border crossings and a greater network of routes included on historic maps, or today visible on the ground as minor roads, tracks and earthworks, may well have been just as important in the past.

Cross Dykes

Other monuments on the high moors which have been linked to droving include the cross-dykes – linear earthen banks and ditches – evident on many of the Cheviot ridges, such as that located beside Clennell Street on Wholehope (NT 903094; see page 91). Some of these may have played a role in channelling stock as they negotiated the moorland ridges, whilst others have been interpreted as barriers constructed to impede the escape of reiving raiding parties. However, it has also been suggested that at least some of these cross-dykes may be much more ancient, perhaps Neolithic or Bronze Age in origin, and that they may have functioned as communal boundary markers. In practice, it is likely that such dykes were constructed and used for different purposes in different periods, extending over a very long timespan. Documentary evidence suggests the large earthwork on Wholehope, for example, represents the work of the medieval monks of Newminster Abbey, demarcating the boundary of their pastures, but aspects of its morphology – such as the presence of pits in the bottom of the ditch – might also imply a prehistoric date, so perhaps the monks adapted an already ancient landscape feature.

Fairgrounds

The location of many of the principal fairs associated with droving can still be seen, although there are scarcely any traces of their former role. For example both of the Elsdon fairgrounds, the East Fair Moor and West Fair Moor, still exist as patches of moorland on either side of the village, though there is little to indicate their former function. The latter is bisected by a lane which follows the course of the Great Drift Road, descending from the moorland watershed towards the village.

Amongst the Northumbrian fairgrounds, none was more important than that at Stagshaw Bank straddling Dere Street (now the A68) just north of Corbridge and south of Portgate. The Stagshaw Bank Fair is known to have been a seasonal gathering since at least the twelfth century, providing the means to exchange cattle and sheep from the Highlands with ironwork and other goods from the Tyne Valley for centuries. In addition to its commercial role, it provided a gathering point for gypsies and a meeting place for other dispersed communities. Sports, games and drinking played a large part in the carnival atmosphere of the fair, as remembered by one of the last living witnesses to the fairs before they ceased in the late 1920s.

Mr Robinson of Stagshaw remembers geese, as well as cattle and sheep, being driven into the fairground, and cart racing on the A68 which passes through it. For decades afterwards, gypsies continued to camp on Stagshaw Common at the time of the fair just after midsummer, as if drawn to the place by historic tradition. Today, Stagshaw Bank simply offers a broad expanse of moor and pasture with little clue to the periodic intense activity which the fair hosted. Something of the tradition of Stagshaw and the other large seasonal fairs is maintained, however, as in the late summer and autumn stock fairs and shows are held at small towns around the periphery of the National Park, such as Bellingham and Wooler, and in some of its villages, such as Alwinton, Harbottle and Rochester.

View across the site of Elsdon East Fairground towards Hudspeth, with holloways caused by the passage of stock on Landshot Hill beyond.

Left: The site of Stagshaw Bank Fair viewed from the Dere Street (the modern A69).

Below: Falstone Show in 1913.

Rochester showground, 2003.

Above right: Judging traditional breeds of sheep at Alwinton Show in October 2003.

Above left: Judging sheep at Rochester Show, 2003.

Above: Alwinton Show, October 2003.

Left: Quoits: one of the traditional games of the Borders region. Here a team from the Scottish Lowlands demonstrates at Alwinton Show, October 2003.

Inns

Droving could not have functioned without the numerous wayside inns which provided overnight board and lodging for drovers and a secure pen with fodder for the livestock in their care. Inns were also dispersed around fairgrounds such as Stagshaw – where there were at least three in the modern period, although two have since closed – and clustered within market hubs such as Bellingham, Wark and Elsdon. Inns which were especially closely involved in the droving trade are often revealed by their names. Thus, the importance of the cattle trade to the communities of North Tynedale is demonstrated by the group of inns at Wark-on-Tyne, where the former Highland Drove can still be seen on the opposite side of the main street from the Black Bull and the Grey Bull, although unlike those two it is no longer in use as a public house.

Above: The Black Bull and Grey Bull public houses and a neighbouring butcher's shop at Wark, on a droving route down the North Tyne Valley.

Left: The former Fox and Hounds public house at Stagshaw Bank.

The Black Cock Inn at Falstone.

The Rose and Thistle public house at Alwinton.

CASE STUDIES

Elsdon – A Droving Village

Nowhere in Northumberland was droving more significant in the local economy than Elsdon. Indeed, when droving began to decline in the early nineteenth century so did the relative fortunes of the village itself, losing out to neighbouring Otterburn, which was more favourably positioned beside the newly constructed turnpike in relation to continuing general Anglo–Scottish trade. No less than three inns dating to the eighteenth and early nineteenth centuries are located around the green at Elsdon, although of the three – the Bird in the Bush, the Crown and the Bacchus (formerly the Scotch Inn, a name which betrays its role) – only in the former is it still possible for the weary traveller to buy a drink today. Their involvement in the carrying and droving trade from Scotland was noted during the mid-eighteenth century by the Reverend Dodgson, and the Bacchus in particular exhibits some measure of architectural pretension, suggesting a degree of local prosperity at this time. Peter Ryder's description of the three inns is set out below:

Inns around the Green in Elsdon (by P.F. Ryder)

Further to the south, on the junction with the road to Otterburn, the Bird and Bush Inn is an early eighteenth-century building with an old mounting block outside. The oldest part is of three bays, the north end, facing the Otterburn Road, only has one window to the attic. This has a chamfered surround and, even at this height above the ground, sockets for vertical iron bars – proof of concern for security. To the right here is a rear wing, probably of the early nineteenth century, that has a Gothic-arched stair window, later altered to a square-headed form. The front has chamfered jambs to its doorway, but the present windows, four-pane sashes, are set in openings that have probably been enlarged; their sills are clearly nineteenth century. The age of the building is, however, given away by its steep roof pitch and shaped kneelers to its gables. To the south is a two-bay extension, probably of the later eighteenth century.

The best range of buildings is towards the north end of the west side of the green. At its south end is the former Bacchus Inn, which has a three-bay main block with a taller hip-roofed cross-wing at its north end. The main block, of early to mid-eighteenth century date, is of coursed squared stone and has a central segmental-arched doorway with a chamfered surround with keystone, above which a corbel in the form of a cherub supports a rustic figure of Bacchus sitting on his barrel and holding a flask. The windows of the block may have been enlarged. Linking the block to the wing is a half bay containing a round-arched doorway with fanlight; the wing has a plinth, sill and first-floor bands and tripartite sash windows, the upper of Venetian form a radial-glazed head. The half bay and wing are probably of the later eighteenth century; the north side of the wing has nineteenth-century openings.

The next block was a stable block or coach house to the Crown Inn. It is now of two storeys and three bays. The windows on either side of the central door are set in blocked elliptical-headed arches. There is a band above and the upper floor may possibly be an addition. This is followed by the former Crown Inn, a range with a more steeply pitched roof, with rendered walls and a doorway in an architrave surround, with its head inscribed 'JOHN GALLON ANNO 1729' and a moulded cornice on bold console brackets. The windows have probably been altered. Adjacent to the north-west corner is an old mounting block. The adjacent single-storeyed range, of good-quality squared stone, is probably of the early nineteent century, and consists of a three-bay cottage and then, as the ground drops away, a slightly lower cart shed with an elliptical-arched entrance and small windows.

Besides the inns, the pinfold (see page 106), one of the former smithies and the village green at Elsdon, it remains possible to visit the village and its neighbourhood in order to view sites and follow routes that illustrate various aspects of the droving trade. Elsdon was connected to the Scottish Border by the Great Drift Road which branched from Dere Street near Featherwood, north of Rochester. Various sections of this road can be traced, but particularly clear is a branch road near Overacres, which allowed drovers to bypass Elsdon on their way south to Stagshaw and beyond. The route described here departs from the village of Otterburn, located on the A696, and travels via Overacres to Elsdon.

Otterburn to Elsdon

Leave Otterburn by driving southwards on the A696 in the direction of Newcastle upon Tyne. After about a quarter of a mile (400 metres) bear left on to the B6341, signposted Rothbury and Elsdon. In approximately 350 yards (300 metres) is Overacres Farm on the left-hand side of the road. Opposite the end of the farm, on the right-hand side of the road, is a gate and wooden signpost indicating a bridle way. (Note: This is a working farm, so careful parking and closing of field gates is essential.) Through the gateway is a cinder track which follows a section of the drove road, with banks on either side of the track which confined the cattle or sheep to the drove road. Some of the banks had stone walls at their bases and the remains of these are visible, as are some of the remaining stone gate posts that gave access to the fields on either side of the drove road. The track

Above: View towards Overacres from a route which bypassed Elsdon to the west.

Left: Drystone dyke on the Overacres–Monkridge route past Elsdon.

View south from the Elsdon East bypass route towards Monkridge and Raylees Common.

View south from the Elsdon East bypass route towards Raylees Common, with a drinking trough on a natural spring in the foreground.

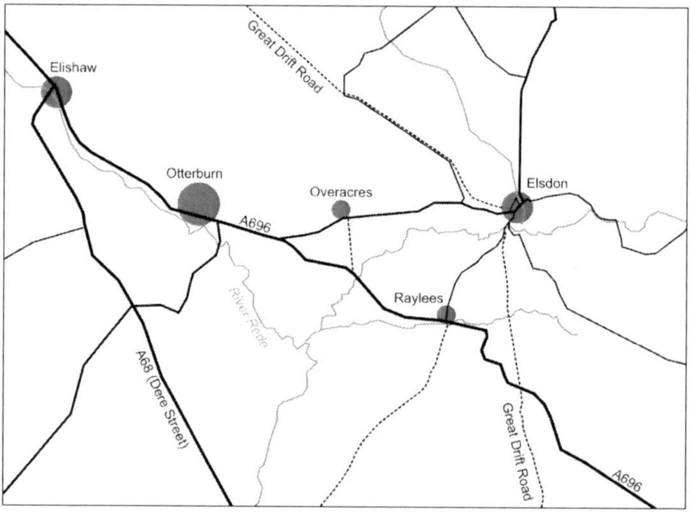

Map of Elsdon and district showing locations referred to in the text.

gradually descends down towards a burn and the Monkridge Bridge on the A696. In the distance is the range of hills called the Ottercops over which the Great Drift Road ran in the direction of Stagshaw Bank and the great fair held there. At the end of the penultimate field, through which the track runs before coming to the A68, is a large trough on the left-hand side of the track. This trough is fed by a spring and is never known to have run dry. It was situated at the side of a substantial lairage where the stock could be rested before they climbed up the hill and north-eastwards to the Great Drift Road, or south-west towards Dere Street at East Woodburn, skirting Raylees Common via Monkridge in the Rede Valley.

Elsdon Gate and Elsdon

Leaving Overacres and continuing along the B6341 in the direction of Elsdon for about a mile the road passes Soppit Farm, after which is a lane leading off the left-hand side of the B6341 just in front of a small cottage, Elsdon Gate, the turnpike toll cottage at the end of the Turnpike Trust road that operated from Carter Bar to Elsdon from 1773 to 1881. Turn into the lane and on the east side of the lane are earthworks in the field, the remains of banks and holloways connected to the drove road. These earthworks are not very regular, as they have been disturbed by mining operations and the recent construction of a covered reservoir to supply water to the village of Elsdon. Following the lane to a cattle grid, a road to the right leads to Dunshield Farm, while the main road bears away to the left in a northerly direction. This road is built on the track of the main drove road which leads from the Scottish Border down into Redesdale. Further north, close to Rochester Village, this drove road followed the line of the Roman road, Dere Street, but

View westwards towards Elsdon Gate, a former toll house, with earthworks running parallel with the modern road separating the turnpike road from the course taken by drovers.

Boundary earthworks marking the course of the Great Drift Road north of Elsdon Gate.

Course of the Great Drift Road north-west of Elsdon.

moved away from the Roman road to head down to Elsdon. It is possible to drive along the drove road and see the remains of banks and ditches, but ultimately the road leads into the army training area and it is advisable to turn back and rejoin the B6341 and turn left to Elsdon.

Turning towards Elsdon, it is clear that the drove road passed behind the toll gate cottage in order to avoid the turnpike and then turned towards the village. In the village, it is possible to park by the green which is known to have held a fair since Elsdon was given a charter for an annual fair and weekly market in the thirteenth century. The fair continued into the nineteenth century and is mentioned in Appendix 3 in the tables dealing with fairs in 1794 and 1841. The village was an important trading centre and a key point for the drovers, with roads arriving from Coquetdale and the head of Redesdale to the north and west, heading south-east to Morpeth and Newcastle and south to Stagshaw Bank.

The road into the village from the west is the only one that does not cross a stream to water stock. However, the road passes between a public house, the Bird in Bush Inn, and an area of land opposite on which two new houses have been built. The new houses

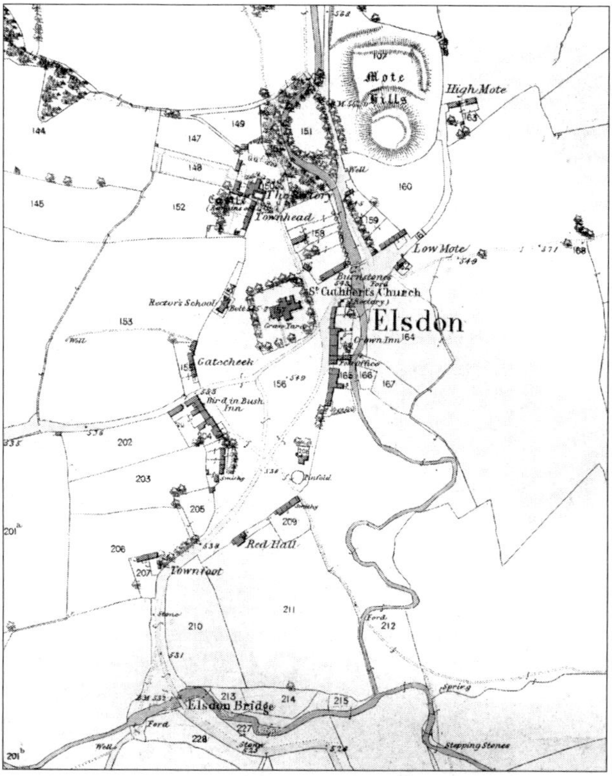

Above: Extract from the Elsdon tithe plan (NRO DT 164-4M).

Left: The village of Elsdon depicted on the first edition Ordnance Survey plan of *c.*1860, showing, in addition to roads, a number of features related to droving, including Gatecheck, a pinfold, smithy and public houses.

The Bird in Bush Inn at Elsdon, *c.*1915, on the occasion of the riding of the village bounds.

View of Elsdon showing, from right to left, the Bacchus and Crown public houses.

Left: Elsdon pinfold, formerly used to hold stray animals.

Right: Water trough near Gatecheck, Elsdon.

Raylees farmhouse, a former inn which served travellers when the turnpike was diverted away from Elsdon in the early nineteenth century, and which may have earlier origins as a drovers' inn.

View southwards from Raylees farmstead over the A696 towards the earthworks of a suspected medieval moated farmstead (occupied by modern house) which is large enough, potentially, to have been used as a lairage by drovers leaving Elsdon.

occupy a site called Checkgate that was called Gatecheck on the first edition of the Ordnance Survey map. The two new houses were built at the end of the 1990s and occupy the site of a former barn, but the site has had houses and buildings on it since at least the seventeenth century and has a trough (on its land) situated next to the road. The trough is spring fed and has a local reputation for never failing to supply water. The trough and the name of the site may well suggest a connection with the livestock trade. Returning to the village green, a short walk to the right leads down the green to the site of one of the old smithies and also the pound for the holding of stray cattle or sheep to be reclaimed by the owner on payment of a small fine.

Leading out of Elsdon to the south were two main routes, one towards Morpeth and Newcastle from the east fairground near Hudspeth, then south-westwards via Landshot and Whiskershiel, or via Winter's Gibbet, onto a moorland route towards Rothley. The other route to the south was by the Great Drift Road towards Stagshaw Bank and the Tyne Valley. The Great Drift Road left Elsdon by various routes between the former inn at Raylees and Ravenscleugh to the east (Greenwood shows the Great Drift Road running east of Ravenscleugh). It crossed the present A696 somewhere in the area of Blaxter and continued for some six kilometres across Ray Fell to the Ray Burn, where its earthwork remains can be seen crossing the present Knowesgate–Ridsdale minor road some two kilometres west of the medieval village of West Whelpington. In order to arrive at Stagshaw Bank it must have taken a turn to the south-west somewhere in this vicinity, and it is perhaps of relevance to note the place name Cowstand Hill overlooking Sweethope Lough some three kilometres to the south-west.

The Wallington Estate

Wallington, the estate formerly belonging to the Trevelyan family and now owned by the National Trust, has a number of droving routes both within the boundaries of the estate and close to it. Harry Beamish, the National Trust historian, has given the following account of droving in this area, and indicates where it is possible to see the remains associated with the places to which he refers. The estate and the places mentioned by Harry are easily reached from Elsdon following the road from Elsdon to Cambo that leads past Harwood Forest.

A brief reference in Hodgson's *History of Northumberland*, published in 1827, describing the township of Catcherside on the western edge of the Wallington Estate, gives a tantalising suggestion of an old droving route south from the Border which predated the turnpike era:

> This place, now so still and lonely, seemed in former ages to have known something of life. The Scotch Street ran through it; and it had an ale-house, where the carriers and cadgers in the bell-horse times baited...

A droving route running across this part of the county seems a reasonable assumption, given the geography and settlement pattern. Before the organised enclosure of the eighteenth century, the country would have been relatively unimpeded with stock-proof boundaries, particularly to the west of the more settled land around the settlements at Hartington and Cambo. A drover coming south over the Border streets, and heading for a rendezvous such as the great fair at Stagshaw Bank above Corbridge, would have found the going relatively straightforward, with water and grazing to hand and small settlements such as Catcherside along the way for refreshment.

The estate maps at Wallington and the early editions of the Ordnance Survey show a route across Harwood Head which is reflected by public rights of way today. There is a strong possibility that antiquities served as waymarkers along this route, in such open country a large prehistoric earthwork or a medieval boundary marker, such as Steng Cross, would have been useful reference points. Today, only the base stone of Steng Cross survives, beside the better-known Winter's Gibbet. The cross stood on the watershed ridge and would have been easy to pick up on the skyline from some distance away. Further south, a large rectangular prehistoric earthwork is passed on the way to Catcherside. There is a deeply incised holloway beside it, suggesting that it was a well-used route. Catcherside Camp may well have been another waymarker. The prehistoric enclosure would have made an excellent nightfold to keep the stock secure!

The presence of an old droving route is further suggested by a long-standing tradition recorded in the excellent book *In the Troublesome Times*, first published in the 1929.

This tradition indicates that there was a smithy at The Shop Trees, a short distance east of Steng Cross on the Harwood Gate to Elsdon road. Here, it is said, cattle had been plated to defend their feet from the metalled roads which they would meet on the next stage of the journey. Until that point most of the travelling would have been on the old green roads over the Border. The origin of the smithy is unknown, but by the mid-eighteenth century a good turnpike road ran past the site from Elsdon to Morpeth which had an important cattle market. Further routes via Cambo led to Newcastle and Hexham. The same source records that, within living memory, farmers from the Cambo district had travelled to the great cattle fairs at Falkirk to obtain Kyloes. The tradition of driving cattle south from Falkirk had been brought to an end by the development of the railway network in the second half of the nineteenth century. Scots Gap on the Wallington Estate established a thriving cattle market for the district because of its situation on a railway junction. Much of the trade in this later period was with Ireland rather than Scotland.

An Allendale Drove Road

As explained earlier in this book, drove roads in Allendale tended to be shared by pack-horses used to carry lead from the mines and smelt mills to Hexham and other places in the Tyne Valley. Several such roads are marked on the Ordnance Survey Landranger 87 map, *Hexham, Haltwhistle and Surrounding Area*, crossing over Hexhamshire and Allendale commons. One road which provides a long walk between the East Allen Valley and Whitley Chapel begins at Sinderhope on the B6295 road that runs between Allendale and Allenheads. Travelling north to Allenheads, the drove road can be reached by turning left off the B6295 on the bend at Sinderhope (NGR NY84852) then proceeding along the lane. The metalled lane, walled on both sides, gives way to a stone track which leads to a gate on to the common. Thereafter the track is no longer walled. The series of photographs on page 110 shows the transformation of the route from bounded metalled road to unbounded track.

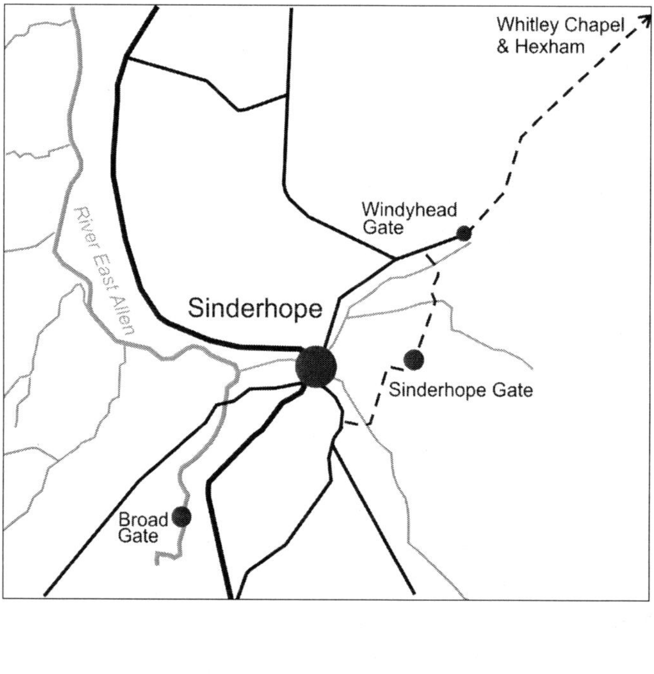

The location of Sinderhope in Allendale.

Above: Looking south-west from Windyhead Gate across the East Allen Valley and Sinderhope to Longwell Moor.

Left: Looking south-west towards Windyhead Gate at Sinderhope, Allendale.

The track here is a designated footpath and bridleway that leads seven miles across Hexhamshire Common to a lane which leads past Springwell House before entering the village of Whitley Chapel. This lane connects to the B6306 which runs north to link with the B6307 which, in turn, runs to Dilston and Corbridge, thence to Stagshaw Bank. It is still possible to find a relic of the former packhorse route, as this trail departs from the drove road just after leaving Whitley Chapel and turns north along a lane to Steel and Dye House. There is now a bridge over the Ram Burn between Steel and Dye House, but a lane to the right of the bridge leads down to a ford over the burn which was used by the packhorses and any droves of cattle making their way to Hexham rather than Corbridge.

Left: Longwell Moor to Whitley Chapel/Stagshaw route, west of Whitley Chapel.

Below: The west side of a droving and pack-horse route between the lower East Allen and Hexham, crossing the minor road near High Shaw, two kilometres north-west of Catton.

The east side of a droving and pack-horse route crossing the minor road near High Shaw, two kilometres north-west of Catton.

Also in Allendale, but closer to the confluence of the East Allen with the South Tyne, is another east–west road which, like the Sinderhipe–Whitley Chapel route probably served jointly as a packhorse trail for minerals from the North Pennines and as a drove road to or from the Tyne Valley and Newcastle. At the point where this road approaches from the west a minor road near High Shaw, two kilometres north-west of Catton, it is a very impressive wide 'green lane' enclosed on both sides by drystone walls. East of the minor road it continues as a well-made track but has lost the drystone wall on its north side. Various features, including springs and enclosures, along this route are probably associated with its former functions as an economically important routeway.

Burn Divot

In a ruinous state, but dramatic in their setting, are the isolated remains of the drovers' inn at Burn Divot, north of Cawfields (NY 694708 see page 113). Both gable walls have collapsed, but the longer sides of the building still stand as do the walls of the large surrounding paddock where the animals would have been penned overnight. However, it is Burn Divot's location which is truly striking. Standing on a hillock in desolate countryside, seemingly at the world's end, commanding extensive views to north, south, east and west but with no other building in sight, few places in Northumberland better epitomise the marginal and often lonely existence of the drover. The former drove road running past Burn Divot is depicted as a drove road on Greenwood's map of 1828, where it is shown running eastwards from the Border near Roderhaugh (modern Rotheryhaugh) on the Irthing, one branch turning south at Burn Divot towards the Tippalt Burn, thence to the valley of the South Tyne, while another continues to a point north of Scots Coultard, from where it drops to the Tyne Valley. Modern maps indicate that much of this route has been lost to moorland or forestry, but some sections remain, including a walled section of road west of Burn Divot, while the road south from Burn Divot survives as a grassed-over farm track, or 'green lane'.

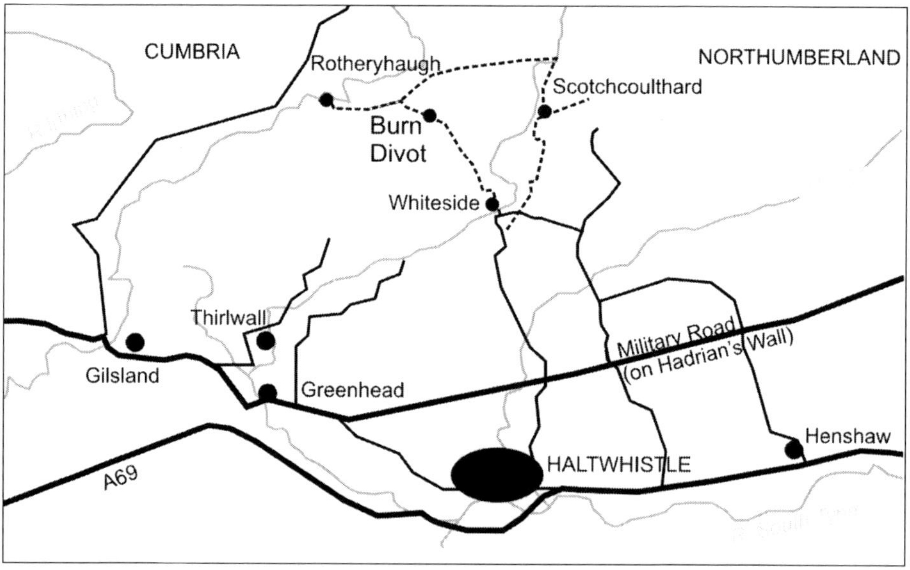

The location of Burn Divot north of Haltwhistle.

Remains of the former drovers' inn at Burn Divot near Cawfields, north of Hadrian's Wall.

View of the road leading south from the drovers' inn at Burn Divot.

A697 Coldstream to Morpeth

The A697 is a modern road based on older tracks and turnpikes which now serves as an alternative to the A1 for travel between Scotland and England via the east coast, but was formerly an important, perhaps even the pre-eminent, droving route around the east side of the Cheviots from lowland Scotland. Details of this drove road are known from accounts such as that of George Robinson in the eighteenth century, and from surviving features such as the distinctive droving inn at Bendor, now a private house.

The A697 runs into Coldstream from the west, passing Lees, a large planned farm of the early nineteenth century. Several public houses and inns beside the road through the town are of nineteenth and perhaps later eighteenth-century origin, and the extensive Newcastle Arms at the junction of Main Street and Market Street may have marked the point at which traffic formerly dropped to the market place and on to fording points on the Tweed before the current bridge replaced them in 1762. Potential fording points shown on Roy's map can be seen from Henderson Park and other locations in the town. These positions also afford views of the large haugh-land in the Tweed bend south of the town, which may have served as lairage, and of the Cheviots far to the south.

The road now exits Coldstream on the north-east side of the town, but prior to the 1760s did so from the haugh-land south-west of the town, allowing more immediate access to Cornhill via Cornhill House, which still preserves within it the remains of a medieval tower house. Cornhill retains the basic form of a planned village of two parallel rows of houses, a form which probably originated in or before the eleventh century, with the main

Right: The route of the A697 from Coldstream to Morpeth.

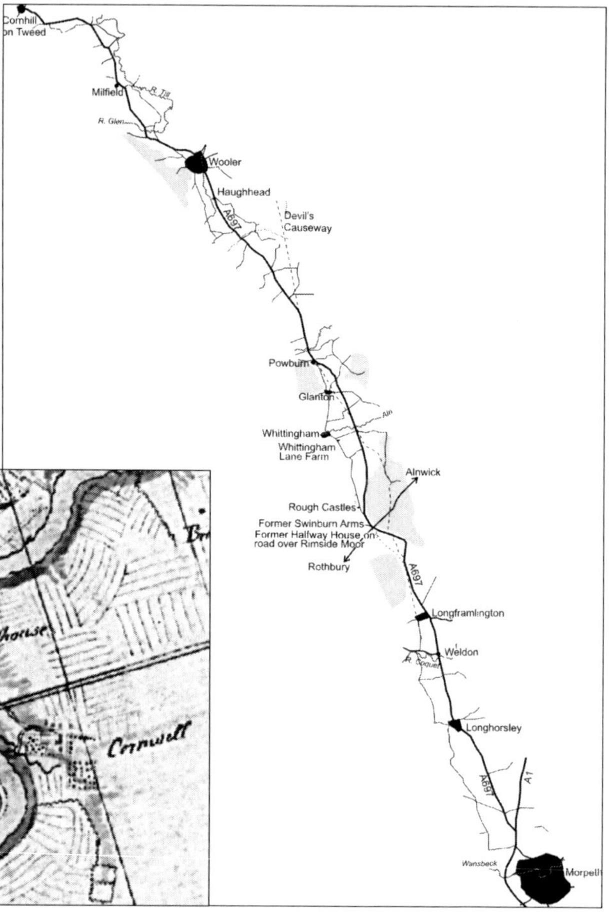

Below: Fording points over the River Tweed depicted on Roy's Atlas of Scotland 1747–55 prior to the construction of the bridge downstream in 1762.

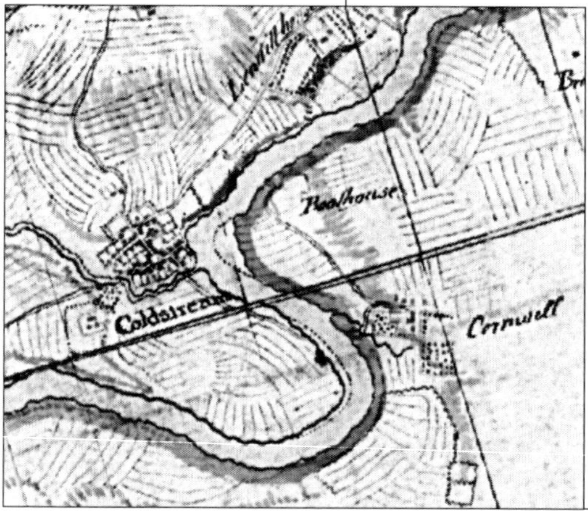

road passing through it. The present road through the village enters from the north and turns sharply north-east past the Collingwood Arms, a former post house and coaching inn, but perhaps also used by drovers, before turning again to the south-east at a junction with the A698, the angle which contained the railway station and the associated auction mart, the building of which in the mid-nineteenth century effectively made the practice of droving redundant. George Robinson in the late eighteenth century recorded that an overnight stop would be made by drovers at or near Cornhill; some large enclosures visible on early maps on the south side of the village may have provided lairage for stock on such occasions.

The road then passes prehistoric standing stones which may have acted as guide-posts through good farmland near the successful eighteenth- and nineteenth-century planned farms of Bendor and Crookham West Field. The rich arable land of this district was the site of early attempts to intensify agricultural production and went hand in hand with improvements to the road following turnpiking in the 1760s. The Blue Bell at Pallinsburn, near Crookham, is a former coaching inn associated with the turnpike, while the nearby Coach House hotel is an earlier place of rest which may have been used by drovers as well as coaches, perhaps as an intermediate rest station if not for overnight stops.

It is possible that, following turnpiking of the road in the mid-eighteenth century, drovers avoided sections of the road by taking smaller parallel tracks to the west, but

The Black Bull, former drovers' inn at Bendor.

they are likely to have rejoined it after crossing the River Glen, where the Cheviot Hills rise abruptly to form a barrier on the west side of the road. Historic maps show that the main road in the eighteenth and early nineteenth century did not run via Akeld as now, but headed south-east from just south of the Glen to the Black Bull Inn at Bendor, the roof space of which contained cubicled divisions for individual drovers on their first night out of Cornhill. The main road via Akeld was established sometime in the first half of the ninteenth century, but the earlier route now survives as a back road.

East of Bendor the road divides, with the present A697 heading due east, while an alternative and perhaps older course heads south-east to provide a more direct route into Wooler through the High Street, which contains a number of former coaching and droving inns, notably the Black Bull, standing on the edge of the market place, first recorded in 1199. The road south from Wooler is through Haugh Head, site of an early post house and possible droving inn, now known as Surrey House (following the legend that the Earl of Surrey, commander of the English Army at the Battle of Flodden, rested there prior to the Battle in 1513), the core of which is believed to be earlier than the mid-nineteenth-century exterior.

After Haugh Head, the road passes through a landscape dominated by features of nineteenth-century estate farms and country houses which grew from the profits of agricultural improvement, aided by developments in transport, particularly the turnpikes and railways which provided access to growing industrial markets. However, within this landscape of estate farms, improved workers' cottages and roadside lodges are older features perhaps related to droving, including a pond, Dunny's Well (NGR NU 014242) marked on nineteenth-century maps, and still surviving on both sides of the road near Lilburn, and houses at and south of Lilburn Glebe which are served by the old bypassed road course. A minor road running between farms parallel with the west side of the A697 may also have been used by drovers as far as Powburn, Glanton and Whittingham which, in addition to providing the next overnight stop after Bendor, also formed a hub for droveways coming out of the south-west side of the Cheviots, such as the Salter's Road.

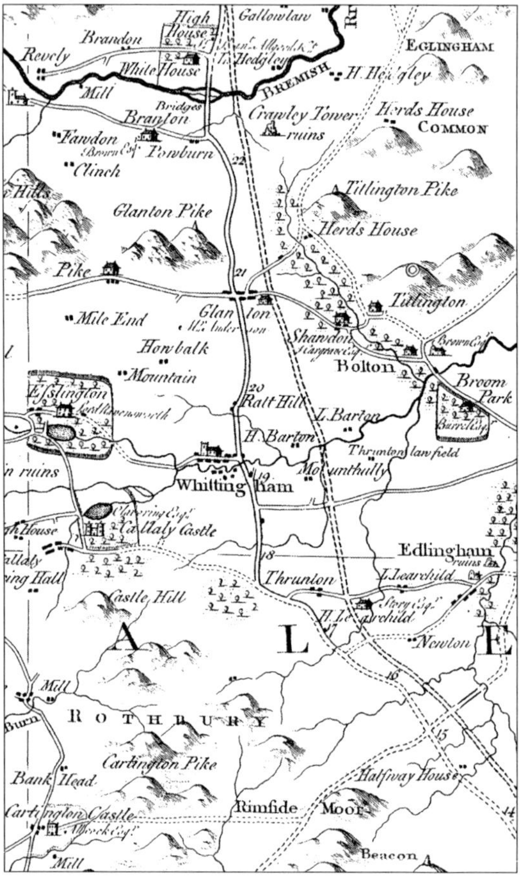

Roads between Halfway House on Rimside Moor and Powburn, as depicted on Armstrong's map of 1769.

After Powburn – where, between the bridge and turn to Glanton, a public house and old smithy (see page 117) may be an echo of the droving trade – the drovers probably did not follow the line of the current A697, established as a turnpike in the 1750s, but went via Glanton and Whittingham, leaving the latter at the south-east end of the village. A known drover's inn at Whittingham is the Hole in the Wall – named after the method of serving drovers whilst keeping them outside the premises – but inns at Glanton and Powburn probably served the same clientele. After Whittingham, the road passed through Whittingham Lane Farm, where a natural spring supplies old stone drinking troughs and a smithy appears on the mid-nineteenth-century first edition Ordnance Survey plan, then ran along current farm tracks to meet the present road, part of the 1752 Longframlington to Powburn turnpike, running alongside Thrunton Woods.

The road takes a straight course via Rough Castle, a farm associated on early maps with some large stock enclosures, past some Iron Age or Romano-British earthwork enclosures which may have been re-used as stock enclosures in the modern droving period. Upon reaching the modern A697 at the junction with the Rothbury road, former site of the Swinburne Arms public house, the drove road probably followed the 1750s turnpike over Rimside Moor, through a copse of beech trees within which are the remains of a remarkable complex of structures, including the roadway, culverts, enclosures and a multi-period house, formerly known as Halfway House, latterly Moorhouse, and mentioned by George Robson as a resting point on the way to Morpeth.

The road then passed over moorland to Longframlington and beyond to overnight stations at Weldon Bridge and Longhorsley, from where the last stretch into Morpeth could be tackled in a morning. Alternative courses to the current A697 are available west of the road, particularly between Weldon Bridge and Longhorsley, and may well have been taken by drovers, especially after the main route was turnpiked in the mid-eighteenth century.

Surrey House at Haugh Head, Wooler.

Powburn smithy and public house.

The 'Hole in the Wall' at Whittingham.

The present and earlier courses of the road north from Whittingham.

Above *Left:* Drinking trough at Whittingham Lane.

Above Right: View from the north of the road over Rimside Moor.

Rimside Moor
Halfway House
viewed from the east.

View towards the north of the road over Rimside Moor.

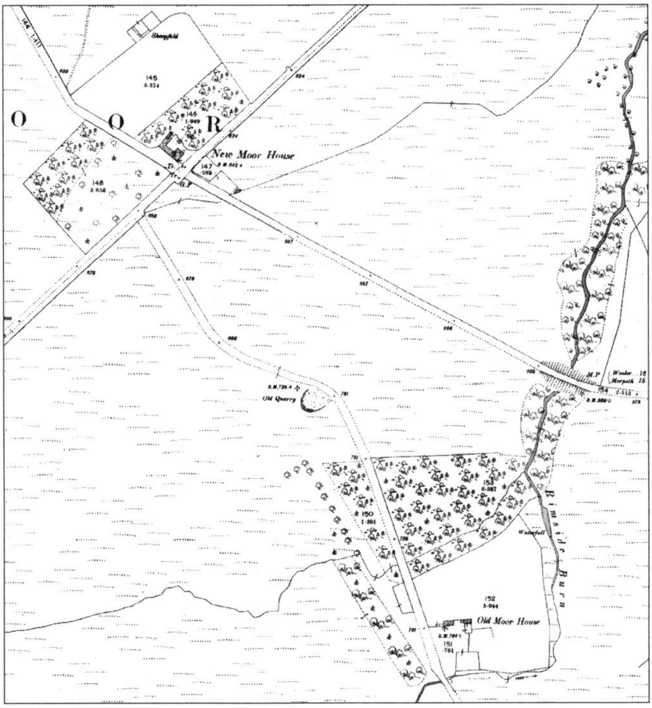

The road over Rimside Moor shown on the second edition Ordnance Survey plan, *c.*1898, showing the former Halfway House, now renamed Old Moor House and New Moor House, formerly the Swinburne Arms public house, both with attached enclosures. Note the former course of the road past Old Moor House, marked by still-extant lines of beech trees.

Rimside Moor enclosure and bridge on a later course of the road past 'Halfway House'.

Dere Street

Dere Street, for much of its route, closely follows the present A68, crossing the Tyne at Corbridge and passing northwards through Hadrian's Wall at Portgate near Halton Chesters, but finally deviating from the A68 near Bremenium Fort at High Rochester, from where it continues along modern military roads northwards, via Featherwood farmstead, to the Roman military complex of Chew Green at the head of Coquetdale and on into Scotland. Its route was mapped and surviving features discussed in publications by McLauchlan, the Duke of Northumberland's surveyor in the 1850s, since when parts of it have been further eroded.

Although perhaps based on earlier tracks, Dere Street was different to many of the other drove roads through the Borders region in that its route has been formally defined since it was laid out by Roman army engineers in the first century AD However, after the Roman period it was neither maintained nor improved, so that by the time it came to be used as a major droving route in the eighteenth century, parts of it had probably diverted away from the Roman course. Its continued use as a droving route into the nineteenth century led to extensive erosion as successive generations of cattle forged their own routes within a wider corridor around the original road.

Much of its course south of West Woodburn follows precisely the line of the A68, although there are deviations, notably within Little Swinburne and Colwell Townships in Chollerton Parish, where the A68 diverts eastwards away from Dere Street, which, until the eighteenth century, separated the above townships from those of Great Swinburne

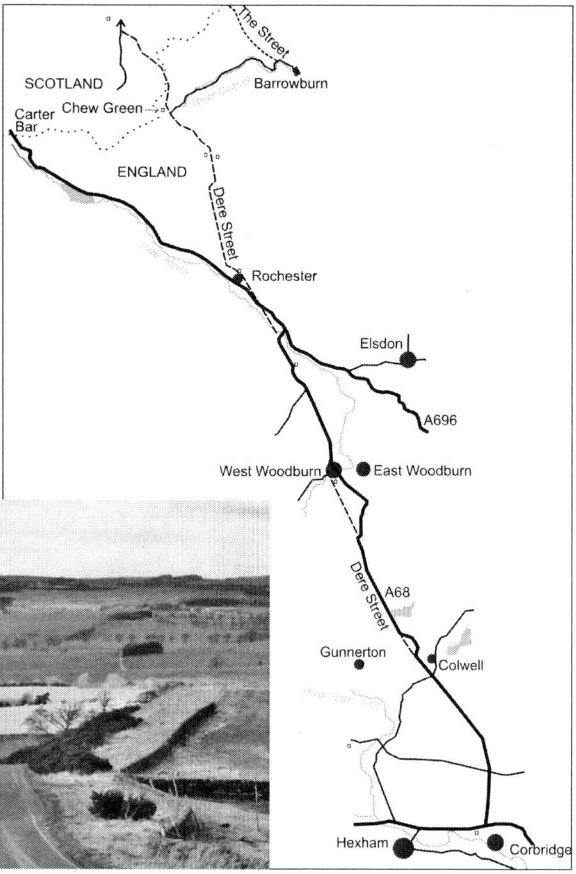

Right: Map of the course of Dere Street from the River Tyne to the Border.

Below: The course of Dere Street running north from Portgate.

and Gunnerton. The original course of Dere Street in this locality is still partially evident and may have been used by drovers, as may a parallel track to the west, alongside which are the remains of an old house, possibly an inn, and some very earthworks which may have been used to channel stock from the road to holding pens of enclosures.

Further north, from Four Laws, the modern road again takes a course east of Dere Street, its route to the east side of Risingham only partially marked by earthworks, tracks and field boundaries until it rejoins the A68 at Woodhouse north-west of West Woodburn. A branch of the Dere Street droveway (or, alternatively, a means of crossing the Rede) was provided by a road east from a point just north of Woodhouse, leading to the still-standing Old East Woodburn Bridge and continuing to East Woodburn, from where Dere Street could be regained or a route taken eastwards towards Kirkwhelpington and Morpeth. North of Woodside, the present A697 continues with only a single minor diversion around Troughend until Brownrigg, near the Roman fort site at Blakehope, where it finally leaves Dere Street, though does not head decisively away from it until after High Rochester. Little is visible of the historic course of Dere Street in this section until just south of High Rochester, where it appears as a raised green track in moorland, passing through the prominent tumuli of the Roman cemetery there. After High Rochester it crosses the Silloans Burn and is then incorporated in the modern military road system, which sits upon or directly adjacent to it all the way to the Golden Pots south of Chew Green, where its course is again obscure.

Above: An alternative course of Dere Street at Coulson's Close, Chollerton Parish.

Left: The earthwork remains of stock management earthworks on the west side of Dere Street at Coulson's Close.

Not surprisingly, the features most closely associated with this route are Roman military sites, including some of the best-preserved fort sites in England at Corbridge, Risingham, High Rochester and Chew Green, and marching camps in between, particularly in the stretches of road just north of High Rochester and Featherwood. Although some of these Roman earthworks may have been used as lairages for droving – notably at Chew Green – few features specifically associated with droving are apparent. Perhaps the most obvious traces of droving are the alternative route courses visible along certain sections of road, most notably in the section of Dere Street immediately south of Chew Green, where the road ascends a steep hill towards the first of the 'Golden Pots' – sockets for medieval waymarking crosses positioned along the ill-defined moorland course of the road. The moorland stretches in the vicinity of the Golden Pots present a confusing multiplicity of trackways, to the extent that it is difficult to determine the line of the original Roman route on the ground. Where it can be defined and has not been

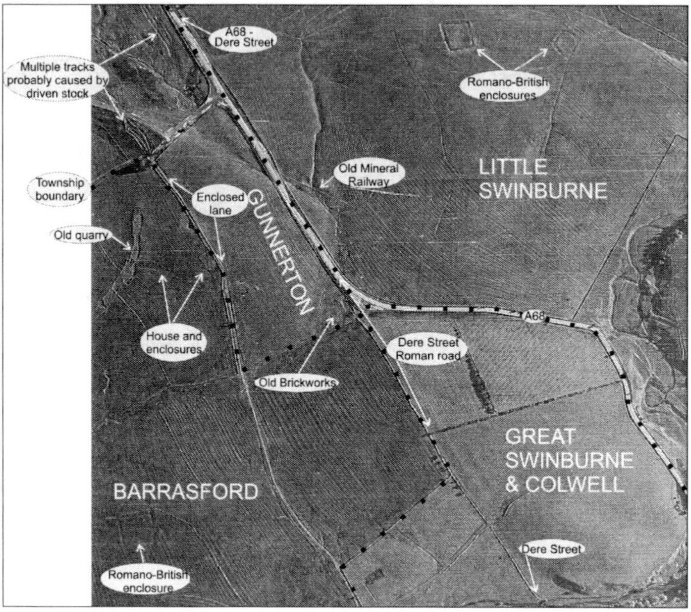

Left: Annotated aerial photograph of the course of Dere Street around Coulson's Close, Chollerton Parish.

Below: Looking southwards from Dere Street down the western approach road to West Woodburn Old Bridge.

removed by droving, excavations on more isolated sections of the road have identified a metalled surface between two metres and three metres wide.

This section of the route (i.e. southwards from Chew Green to the last of the Golden Pots, from which Featherwood is just visible in the south), although least well-defined, is the earliest and most frequently mentioned in historic documents, where it is known by a number of variations upon the name Gamelspath. The earliest documentary reference, as Kenmylispet, occurs in 1249 when it was a recognised place of trial for the inhabitants of Redesdale and Coquetdale; thereafter, the frequent occurrence of Gamelspath in the sources was directly related to its role in Border conflict and mediation.

At Chew Green the remains of medieval and later settlements are also attested by documentary sources as well as surviving remains. Perhaps the most interesting of the latter are the remains of a building – still visible on a small haugh across the Chew Sike east of the Roman site – containing whisky bottles and other drink-related parapher-

View of West Woodburn Old Bridge from the same perspective as Swinburne's view published by Hodgson in 1827.

Sketch of Woodburn Old Bridge (East Woodburn) 'on the drift way for Black cattle from Scotland', by Edward Swinburne, published by Hodgson (1827).

nalia, interpreted as the site of a whisky house similar to that recorded further down the valley in the eighteenth century at Slyme Foot. This suggests that Chew Green served as an overnight lairage for stock and a meeting place for drovers, served perhaps by a small resident population of farmers who may also have dabbled in other businesses close to the heart of drovers, such as the blacksmithing and the procurement and sale of whisky.

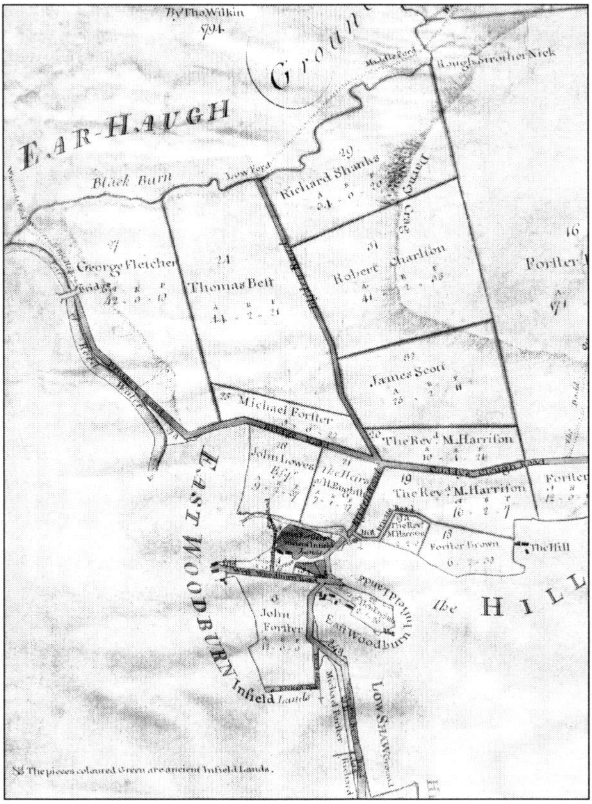

Left: Woodburn Old Bridge shown on the East Woodburn Inclosure Map of 1794. The main road has been diverted off the original course of Dere Street to cross the bridge and continues south via East Woodburn Village.

Below: Dere Street and Woodburn Old Bridge (bottom right corner), shown on the Corsenside Inclosure Map of 1794.

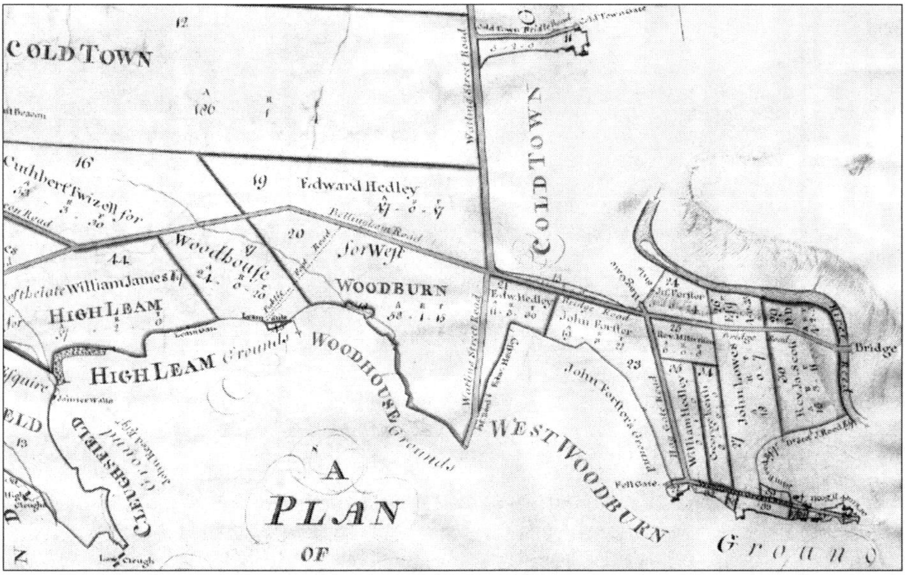

Above: Dere Street case study – ruined sheep stall next to Dere Street at High Rochester.

Left: The course of Dere Street running south from Featherwood.

The course of the road is clearer as it passes Chew Green and continues to the Border ridge, a crest of the Cheviot Hills which it follows northwards from the earthwork remains of a Roman signal station. It is confined to a narrow terrace on the west side of the ridge as it approaches Blackhall Hill, which the road splits to avoid. Blackhall Hill itself is capped by two prominent cairns, probably burial mounds, and there are a number of earthworks, perhaps the remains of cross-dykes upon the road as it turns north-westwards from the north side of the hill and descends as a clearly defined green way towards the dramatic earthworks of Woden Law hill fort. This part of the route, by now heading decisively north-west into Scotland, is particularly rich in prehistoric remains, with settlement and other remains particularly abundant within a kilometre or so of the road south-east of Buchtrig.[1]

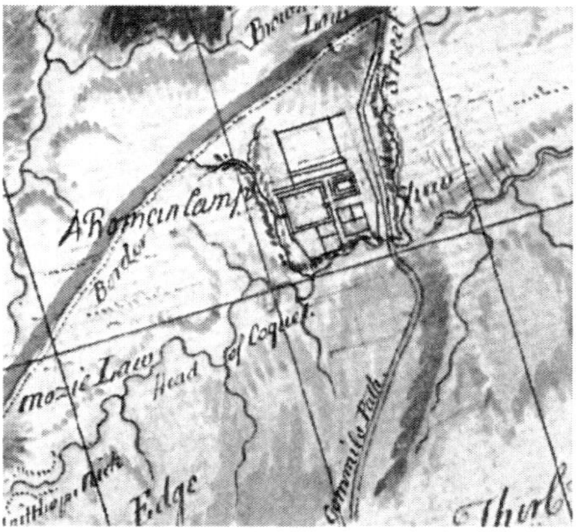

Above: A view of Chew Green Roman military complex from the south, with Dere Street and various medieval and later earthworks to right of view.

Left: Chew Green shown on Roy's Atlas of Scotland 1747–55.

Below: The Chew Green whisky house on Dere Street.

The course of Dere Street as it crosses into Scotland just north of Chew Green.

Langleeford

Information from Mr Walter Brown, shepherd of Langleeford for over forty years until his retirement in 2010, whose interest in and knowledge of the landscape of his working life is unbounded, suggests that Langleeford was the hub of a road network passing along and across the Harthope Burn, connecting Wooler and the A697 route to the east with border crossings to the north-west, via Broadstruther, Commonburn House and the College and Bowmont Valleys. Central to this hub of roads was Langleeford itself, where, downstream of the present farmstead, are the remains of an apparent long-house associated with large paddocks on the line of a north–south road which crosses the valley here. Various other enclosures are apparent on the north side of the valley at the point where the cross-valley track takes the course of a tributary stream, running northwards upslope past a natural hummock known locally as Gospel Knowe before flattening out at, or a little before, a gate known as the Postgate (marked by an inscribed estate boundary stone), which allowed access by horse to the shepherd's cottage of Broadstruther, another mile or so to the north.

The track to Broadstruther from Langleeford is narrow and, in places, overgrown, and may never have been suitable for any form of transport other than foot and horse. It contains few features of interest other than those already mentioned, but at one point the judicious placement of stones across a tributary burn has created a combined ford and drinking pool. Broadstruther, now converted to a hunting lodge, is associated with another series of enclosures and stells related to the management of sheep, but which may also have provided seasonal lairage for drovers. Hereabouts the track divides, one

Looking south towards Langleeford from a north–south track which crosses the Harthope burn at Langleeford.

Track from Langleeford to Broadstruther as it crosses a small stream where a ford has been constructed to serve as a drinking pool.

branch turning north-east towards Wooler, the other north-west towards Kirknewton – from where the border can be reached via the College Valley and Thompson's Walls – and the River Bowmont, which meanders around the Cheviot massif within a wide valley from Yetholm on the Scottish side of the Border. The Harthope Valley route upstream from Langleeford becomes narrow and difficult, eventually running up against the slopes

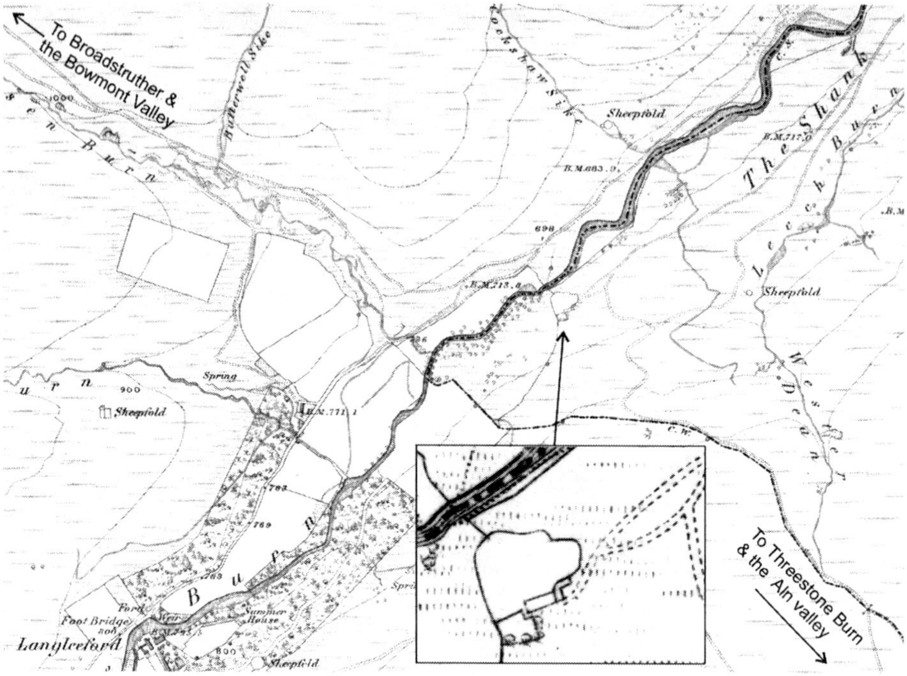

The remains of a house and attached enclosures (inset) north-east of Langleeford (bottom left of view) shown on the first edition Ordnance Survey plan, *c.*1860. Note its position on a track leading from the Bowmont Valley towards the Aln Valley and south-east Northumberland.

of the Cheviots and petering out before the steep ascent to the Border line. However, the cross-valley route south-east from Langleeford snakes uphill from Old Langleeford towards Threestone Burn and Scrainwood, the former providing easy access to the A697 route, the latter linking with the long-distance Salter's Road near Prendwick in the Aln Valley.

NOTES

1 The name Buchtrig is probably derived from 'bucht', a mainly Scottish word for a sheep (milking) pen.

SEVEN
Conclusions and Topics for Further Research

Conclusions

It is clear that people have been driving livestock over significant distances in the Northumbrian hills for at least a millennium and probably much longer. Indeed, such practices were an integral part of pastoralist activity in the uplands. Over the centuries this has taken a variety of forms. Several distinctive practices were employed during the medieval period. The most comprehensively studied of these to date, partly as a result of the of the work of the Royal Commission on Historic Monuments (Ramm et al., 1970), is the seasonal transhumance, known as shieling or summering, undertaken by entire communities, which moved up onto the high pastures in April and returned to their wintersteeds in the valleys during August. Less well investigated, in the area of Northumberland National Park at any rate, are the demesne farming systems adopted by both feudal lords and monastic institutions on their upland estates, which involved the establishment of directly managed cattle farms (vaccaries) and sheep farms (bercaries). The heyday of this kind of demesne farming lasted up until the mid-fourteenth century. Thereafter, the fall in population levels and other socio-economic changes resulting from the Black Death rendered such direct seigniorial stock management less and less economic. Instead, landowners predominantly rented out the upland pastures to their manorial tenants, for use as summering grounds, during the late medieval and early modern periods, which probably ensured that seasonal transhumance was even more prevalent during these centuries.

Transhumance finally ceased in the mid- to late seventeenth century as permanent settlement extended throughout the upper dales. However, the numbers of livestock and the proportion of cattle to sheep kept on these upland farms during the mid to late seventeenth and the early to mid-eighteenth centuries remained remarkably similar to that prevailing in the sixteenth and early seventeenth centuries, with numerous small herds of cattle (generally under twenty head). Sheep may have been present in equal numbers, overall, but were less widely distributed amongst the tenant smallholders. Cattle generally accounted for about half the value of the goods on the farm, as in the period before 1640.

The growth of the long-distance cattle droving trade from Scotland to England took place against this background. Although it originated much earlier, with recorded activity stretching back to the late medieval period, cross-border droving was vulnerable to the continual vicissitudes in relations between the two countries up until the beginning of the eighteenth century. It was only after Anglo–Scottish economic relations had been placed on a permanently stable and peaceful footing, with the Union of the Parliaments in 1707, that the droving trade could fully develop to meet the growing demand for meat from the expanding urban centres of England, most notably London itself. As a result, by the end of the eighteenth century, 100,000 cattle were being driven south across the Border each year.

A multiplicity of routes through the Northumbrian hills were accessible as drove-ways for this traffic. The pattern of usage probably significantly shifted over time, as the progress of turnpiking and enclosure restricted movement and access to pasture and increased the costs of droving along some of the routes. Notable examples include Clennell Street, which led from Windy Gyle to Alwinton in Upper Coquetdale and was already an important highway by the early thirteenth century. Other routes following the North Tyne where none of the routes had been turnpiked and contemporary maps show the drift roads skirting the enclosed ground. Particularly important was the Great Drift Road which crossed the Border at Brownhart Law, following the moorland course of Dere Street (there known as Gamelspeth), before branching off at Featherwood along the high ridgeway which follows the Rede/Coquet watershed before eventually descending to approach Elsdon from the north-west. This route kept the drift road largely clear of the enclosed land in the valley. From Elsdon it headed directly south across Ottercops towards Stagshaw Bank, again following a course which kept it largely clear of enclosed ground.

By contrast, the use of Dere Street south of Featherwood may have declined after the end of the eighteenth century, when much of its course was turnpiked, although the old bridge at East Woodburn, first erected between 1715–1718, remained a sufficiently important link in the droving network to be illustrated by Hodgson (1827, facing p.167; cf. Plackett 1997, 49–50). The crucial hubs in the network were annual fairs held at places like Elsdon, Haltwhistle, Newcastle and most important of all, Stagshaw Bank north of Corbridge. Here all manner of exchange might take place, including the purchase of local cattle to augment the drovers' herds, the sale of cattle to the local meat market, or the onward sale to drovers who would take the livestock further south.

By the end of the eighteenth century, sheep had become more important in the droving trade than previously, as it was realised that they too could be herded over long distances. This in turn reflected changes in the local economy, as landowners amalgamated several holdings to form larger, more viable tenancies, resulting in the creation of huge sheep farms in Redesdale, North Tynedale and Upper Coquetdale. These farms typically covered several thousand acres apiece, with stock numbering between 1,500 and 3,000 sheep, but only miniscule herds of cattle by comparison (generally no more than forty head, often less).

By the mid-nineteenth century the long-distance cross-border droving was being supplanted by the growth of the railways, which provided a more economic service and delivered livestock to their destination in better condition. In parallel with this shift to rail transport, the longstanding historic fairs were gradually replaced by auction marts located beside railway stations such as Bellingham, Rothbury, Hexham or Scots Gap. However, neither droving nor drovers disappeared. The drovers themselves became intermediaries between railhead, auction mart and fair, little diminished in numbers but employed in very different patterns of work and, increasingly, in an urban rather than rural setting. Droving still occurred in the countryside, mainly from farm to railhead, but this was carried out by the farmers, their families and employees, not professional drovers. The distances involved were generally relatively short, but longer droves were obviously necessary in cases where the farms were remote from the nearest railhead, as was true of those in Upper Coquetdale for example (Rothbury being the nearest railway station and mart).

This pattern continued into the early twentieth century. From the 1920s or 1930s, road haulage gradually began to replace rail transport, although the latter remained important right up until the closure of Northumberland's rural branch lines to freight traffic in the 1950s and '60s. It is the motor lorry, with its great flexibility, which has finally put an end to droving over all but the very shortest distances.

Possible Subjects for Further Research

There is an abundance of historic documentation, archaeological evidence and illustrative material, much of which it has only been possible to touch upon briefly in the present study. The following represent some areas which could be explored further.

The archaeological identification of Umfraville vaccaries in Redesdale and the equivalent monastic installations in Kidland, for example, should be considered a priority within the overall study of the region's medieval upland settlement to illuminate a site category hitherto known locally only from the documentary sources.

There is abundant source material for the sixteenth and early seventeenth centuries including probate inventories, rentals, some surviving manor court records for Redesdale and North Tynedale in the Duke of Northumberland's archives, as well as watch schedules and official Border surveys sponsored by the Elizabethan and Stuart Governments. Much related correspondence and other documentation has been assembled and summarised in the Calendar of Border Papers and the State Papers (Cal. SP; LP Hen VIII). Extensive use of this material has been made by the Royal Commission on the Historic Monuments of England (Ramm et al., 1970), by Watts (1971; 1975) and most recently by Winchester (2000), for example, but it still has considerable potential to further inform our understanding of the upland farming communities in this period, their agricultural economy and distinctive practices, notably seasonal transhumance. For instance, the figures relating to livestock losses as a result of Scottish reiving recorded in the Calendar of Border Papers may give some impression of total herd sizes in particular communities (although the reliability of such unverified 'quasi-insurance claims' is not without question and will require careful assessment).

Further research is required on the development of upland farming systems in the period 1640–1750, when permanent settlement extended throughout the upland dales, replacing the former pastoralist regime of summering grounds occupied by transhumant communities. A valuable contribution using the historical documentation has been made by Brassley (1985) and important studies focussed on more localised areas, using both historical and archaeological evidence, have been made by Harbottle and Newman (1973 – Upper North Tynedale), Charlton and Day (1979 – Redesdale/Upper Coquetdale) and by Woodside and Crow (1999, 63–70 – Hadrian's Wall central sector), but more remains to be done.

Relatively little study has been devoted to the infrastructure of droving, not only the drove roads themselves but also the inns and fairgrounds, the crosses which served as waymarkers from the medieval period onwards, the paddocks and pens used to hold the drovers' herds overnight, and the cross-dykes which channelled or blocked the passage of livestock along the moorland droveways. Significant work has been accomplished by Plackett (1997, 46–51), and in particular by Beryl Charlton and John Day in the

Otterburn Training Area (Charlton and Day, 1979, 225–9; Charlton 1996, 122, 125–30), but the potential exists to extend this over a much wider area and study the multiplicity of known routes in much greater detail.

Further research on the conveyence of livestock by rail, in particular to identify and collect information regarding the numbers of stock carried, would provide a clearer understanding of the upland economy between the mid-nineteenth and mid-twentieth centuries. Specifically, this would shed light on the gradual replacement of rail transport by road haulage, and with it the final demise of droving. It is possible that ledgers relating to the North British Railway company and its successor, the Scottish division of the LNER, which contain such information, may survive in railway archives in Edinburgh.

APPENDIX 1

Inquisitions Post Mortem relating to the Redesdale Liberty

Includes important references in the Inquisitions Post Mortem relating to Umfraville holdings in the liberty of Redesdale and the ten towns of Coquetdale. These are based on the extensive transcripts reproduced by Hodgson (1827, 31, 107–10) and the generally more summarised extracts published in the Calendar of Inquisitions Post Mortem (Cal. IPM).[1] These inquisitions contain much information regarding settlement and land use in Redesdale and Coquetdale.

1. Sir Gilbert de Umfraville, Earl of Angus. 30 April 29 Henry III (1245); Cal. IPM vol.I, no.49; the fuller text in Cal. Doc. Scot. i, no.1667 is reproduced here; see also Hodgson 1827, 107–8.

There are in the manors of Hyrbottle, 408 acres of land and 3 roods, whereof each is worth yearly 5*d*; total, £10 3*s* 7*d*.

Also there are 80 acres of meadow [and] 18½ acres, whereof each of 20 is worth yearly 6*d*, and of 78½, each is worth yearly 2*d*; total thereof, 23*s* 1*d*.

Also there are two mills there, worth yearly £17 11*s* 4*d*.

Also a burgus (borough, at Harbottle) returning by the year with grazing, £4 12*s*.

Also the jurors say there are within the manor of Otterburne in demesne, 168½ acres and 1 rood, whereof each is worth yearly 5*d*; total, 70*s* 3½*d*.

Also there are 43½ acres of meadow, each worth yearly 4*d*; total, 14*s* 6*d*.

Also a mill worth yearly £8.

And the advowson of the church at Ellesden.

(Marginal note) That church is worth 80 marks, and Vincencius Cornwalais holds it.

And they say that in Alwenton there are 9 'bondi', each of whom holds one 'bondagium' worth yearly 10*s*; total £4 10*s*.

(Marginal note) There is the advowson of the church there, worth yearly 80 marks, and the vicarage 20 marks, besides the portion of Halistan (the portion of Alwenton rectory's revenue accruing to Holystone Priory). And William de Lexington holds that church.

Also they say that in Otterburne, a member of Hyrbotle, there are ten 'bondi', holding ten bondagia' each worth 8*s* 8½*d*; total, £4 7*s* 1*d*. Also there are in the said Otterburne and Alwenton thirty-eight cottars, whose services and labours ('opera') are worth 48*s* 11*d*.

Also they say there are in the said vills (of Otterburn and Alwinton) 2 'bracinagia' (brewhouses) worth yearly 25*s*.

Also there are in the said vills rents of 'liberorum' (freemen) the total whereof is £12 15*s* 8*d*.

Also there are 'gresmanni' (or cresmanni – Hodgson translates as 'assart-men'), whose services and rents are worth £13 10*s* 7*d*.

Also (in the manors of Redesdale and Coquetdale) there is pasture for 1,140 sheep, worth 111*s* 8*d*.

Also the pasture for mares is worth £12.

Also they say regarding the cow pastures, 1400 [acres?], 900 of which are worth 4*d* and 500 worth 2*d* – that the total is £23; besides Hollesden (the valley of the Hosedon Burn N of Alwinton), worth 2 marks.

Also the forges there render iron, worth yearly £4 2*s*.

Also the wards there are worth yearly, 18*s* 4*d*.

Also there are six entire knights' fees, and one sixth of a knight.

Also they say that the monks of Novi Monasterii (Newminster) hold three granges (in the liberty of Redesdale and the barony of Prudhoe) viz., Tolland, Fyleton and Ruhehope (Rowhope) and pay yearly £12.

2. Gilbert de Umframvill alias Dunfranvyl, Earl of Angus, alias Denegus. Whelpington, 13 Oct., 1 Edward II (1308); Hodgson, 1827, 107–8; cf. Cal. IPM, V; no.47.

Gilbert de Umfraville held of the king in chief (capite) the valley of the Rede, with the liberty, in which is a certain castle at Hirbotell, called the Castle of Hirbotell, which is worth nothing annually within the enclosed ground, because there are great and lofty buildings there which take much to support them.

Also, there is there a certain park, containing in circuit about one league, in which are wild beasts; the sale of the underwood of which yields nothing, but the agistment of it is worth 6*s* 8*d*.

Also, there is there, a certain borough called Hirbotell, the rent of which is worth £2.

Also, there is a capital messuage at Oterburn, the herbage attached to which, with the inclosure, is worth 2*s*.

There are also four score acres of arable land in demesne, each acre of which is worth 4*d*, in all £1 6*s* 8*d*.

Also, at the same place, there are 40 acres of meadow, each at 12*d* an acre, worth £2.

There is also there, a park, containing nearly a league in circuit, in which are certain wild animals: the agistment of which park is worth 10*s*.

Also, there are 9 bondages there, each of which contains 18 acres, and each worth 5*s* a year, in all £2 5*s*.

Also, there are 9 cottages (i.e. cottage smallholdings) there, each annually worth 3*s* and altogether £1 7*s*.

Also, from the rent of free tenants there, the sum of £5 9*s* 2*d*.

Also, in the same place, there are 24 vaccaries or cow pastures, which are worth £141 18*s*.

There are also there, in the village of Ellesden, free tenants, which pay £2.

Also, there are four wastes there, the agistment of which is worth £2.

Also, there are two ponds (stagna) there, the fishing of which is worth 2*s*.

Also, there are 4 water mills there, worth £17 6*s* 8*d*.

Also, the pleas and perquisites of the court are worth £2.

Also, the said Gilbert, on the day of his death, held the said valley of Rede in franchise, by the service of defending the said lands from wolves and robbers.

Gilbert de Umfraville also held:

Alwenton, 200 acres arable and 10 acres meadow, the lordship of the ten towns of Alwenton, Clonhill, Bydellesden, Angreham, Faudon, Ryhill, Scharberton, Nodirton, Boroudon, and Thirnum, which rendered nothing to the earl but knight's service and suit at his court of Hirbotell, and two water-mills, all held of the heirs of Vesci in chief of the barony of Alnewyck by service of 2 knight's fees, and doing suit at the court of Alnewyck.

Robert his son, aged thirty and more, is his next heir

3. Robert de Umframvill, alias de Umfraunvill, Dumframvill, late Earl of Angus. 10 May, 18 Edward II (1325); vol.VI, no.607; cf. Hodgson 1827, 30–1 for a fuller transcription.

Redesdale Liberty (extent given), including the site of the castle of Hirbotil and lands woods and rents therin, viz:

200 acres of waste and 200 acres of moor in [Redesheved]; 300 acres of moor at [Herlessyde]; 20 acres of wood and 200 acres of moor at Spithope [Nuthope]; 100 acres of wood and 200 of waste in Cotynghopp; 100 acres of moor in Suleshop [Fulhope]; 300 acres of wood in [Kyneshope] (i.e. Grasslees Burn); 100 acres of wood in Yerdhopp; 80 acres of arable land and 20 of meadow in Carwyk; 300 acres of moor and 300 of waste in Coketmore, with a messuage and 12 acres of land in a place called Mickelwanges; 24 acres of land at Little Wodbourn; 12 acres of land at Wolrych; a rent of 16*s* 7*d*, and a messuage and a carucate of land (96–120 acres) in Helvesdon (Elsdon); and 6*d* and 3 pounds of cumin in le Leme.

Helvesden [alias Ellesden]. A messuage and a carucate of land, held by John son of William by service of one 20th of a knight's fee and 1*d* yearly; a messuage and a carucate of land, held by William de Sok ...(?) by service of one fortieth of a knight's fee and suit of court; and a messuage and a carucate of land, held by Gilbert de Caprewyk (?) by service of one 20th of a knight's fee, 5*s* 2*d* rent, and suit of court.

All held of the king in chief by service of keeping the liberty of Redesdale from robbers and wolves.

Schirmundesdene [alias Shirmunden]. The manor [extent given in the original but not in Cal. IPM, VI, 607].

Alwenton. Four bondages and 4 cottages, all wasted by the Scots.

Faudon. The manor [extent given in the original].

Clenyl. The manor held by Thomas Clenyl by service of half a knight's fee, 6*s* 8*d* for guard of the castle of Alnewyk and 15*d* for cornage.

Bedilsden [alias Bitelsden]. A moiety of the manor held by Robert de la Vale by service of half a knight's fee, 6*s* 8*d* [alias 3*s* 4*d*] for guard of the said castle, 40*d* [alias 15*d*] for cornage, and suit at the court of Schirmundesden.

Borouden. The manor, held by John de Borouden by service of a knight's fee, 13*s* 4*d* for guard of the said castle, and 15d cornage.

Nedderton. A moiety of the manor held by Henry son of John by service of ½ knight's fee, and 15*d* for cornage.

Thirnom. A moiety of the manor held by John de Horseley by service of 7½*d*; and the other moiety held by Hugh de Raymyngton and Joan his wife by service of 7½*d* and 1lb pepper, price 18*d*, yearly.

Angram [alias Angraham] (Ingram). The manor held by John de Laybourn by service of half a knight's fee, and 15*d* for cornage.

[Foxden and] Scharperton. Four messuages and a carucate of land, held by Gilbert de Borouden by service of a quarter of a knight's fee

All held as of the barony of Alnewyk by service of ... yearly.

Extent: 8 June, 18 Edward II (1325); vol. VI, no. 607.

The knight's fees mentioned above with the variations there given within square brackets and the following:

Thirnhom. Certain tenements held by Alice de Sadlingestan by service of one tenth of a knight's fee, now worth nothing by the devastation of the Scots.

Aldenscheles. The manor held by John de Horsley by service of a fifth of a knight's fee, now worth nothing by the devastation of the Scots.

Linsheles. Certain tenements held by Thomas Shert by service of one fortieth of a knight's fee, now worth nothing by the devastation of the Scots.

Alwenton. The advowson of the church.

4. Elizabeth, widow of Gilbert de Umfraville, Earl of Angus. Bywell , 23 March, 3 Edward III (1330).

At the time of her death Elizabeth held in dower:

The manor of Otterburn, in herbage, worth 2*s*.
Four score acres of arable demesne land, at 4*d* per acre.
40 acres of demesne land, in meadow, at 6*d* an acre.
A park, which, because it is not enclosed, is in agistment worth no more than 2*s*.
A water mill, of the value of £1 10*s*.
9 bondages, each containing one toft, and 12 acres of ground, and each paying 2*s* 6*d*.
9 cottages, each at 12*d* 9*s*.
Rents of free tenants, payable at different times £2 10*s*.
Ten vaccaries or cow pastures, appertaining to the said manor.

5. Robert de Umframvill, alias de Umfraunvill, Dumframvill, late Earl of Angus. Monday the feast of St Oswald, 5 Edward III (1331); vol.VII, no.390; cf. Hodgson 1827, 109–10.

This represents a revision of the 1325 inquisition (no.3 above) following a petition by the Umfraville heir, Gilbert III, to correct errors in the original extent and reduce an overgenerous assignment of lands to Robert's widow, Eleanor, as her dower. Among other lands in Northumberland Robert held on his death:

The site of the castle of Herbotel, including 6 acres of land called 'Ramshalgh', which is worth nothing.
A certain borough there (Harbottle), in which are divers free tenants rendering £2 13*s* 10*d* yearly for the said borough.

The divers lands and tenements underwritten, held with the castle and borough of Herbotel within the liberty of Redesdale, viz.:

A certain plot of ground at Hoperesfeld valued at 6*d*.

Diverse plots of waste and wood at Rodeshevede (Redeshead) held by tenants at will and valued at £20.

Diverse plots of moor at Herleside in the hands of tenants at will and valued at £5 6*s* 8*d*.

Diverse plots of wood and moor at Spithope in the hands of tenants at will and valued at £10.

Diverse plots of wood and waste at Cotynshope in the hands of tenants at will and valued at £3 3*s* 4*d*.

Diverse plots of moor at Fulhope, 'erroneously called Suleshope,' in the hands of tenants at will and valued at £3 6*s* 8*d*.

Diverse plots of wood, with 100 acres of land within the bounds of the said wood, at Kyngehope (Grasslees Burn), 'erroneously called Kynesope,' in the hands of tenants at will and valued at £10 13*s* 0*d*.

Diverse plots of wood at Yerdhope, which are in common of all the towns adjacent, and are valued at nothing.

Diverse plots of moor and waste at Koketmore (or Cokemore) in the hands of tenants at will and valued at £11 15*s* 2*d*.

One messuage at Mikelwanges and 9 acres of land there; in times of peace valued at £1 10*s*, but worth nothing now for lack of tenants

12*d* yearly from the rents of free tenants at Little Cairewik.

And a cottar (unfree smallholder tenancy) there (Little Cairewik), rendering 3*s* yearly

24 acres of (arable) land at Little Wodeburn (Wodeburn Parva) in the hands of tenants at will and valued at £1.

12 acres of (arable) land at Wulrich (or Wolrich) in the hands of tenants at will and valued at £1.

18*s* 2*d* and 1lb pepper yearly from the rents of free tenants at Helvesden (Elsdon).

80 acres of (arable) land and 20 acres of meadow at Kayrwik in the hands of tenants at will, which, in peaceable times, are worth £10, and now £5 (not to be counted amongst the Eleanor's dower lands).

6d yearly rents of free tenants at Le Leme.

A messuage and 30 acres of (arable) land and meadow at Grenesonesfeld (i.e. Girsonsfield), with common of pasture, in the hands of tenants at will and valued at £1 14*s* 0*d*.

10*s* 6*d* and 1lb pepper. yearly from the rents of free tenants at Hatherwik (or Hayherwiyk, i.e Heatherwick).

One messuage and 30 acres of (arable) land and meadow at Smalburn (mod. Dargues), with common of pasture, valued at 18*s*.

8*d* yearly from the rents of free tenants at Caldeton (Coldtown).

1½ lb pepper yearly in rent from free tenants at Troghwenn (Troughend).

12*d* and 1lb pepper yearly from the rents of free tenants at Blakhelme (Blakehope).

Divers lands and tenements in Helvesden, Clenill, Bedelsden, Boroudon, Nedderton, Thyrnom, Angreham [Ingram] and Sharperston, held freely of the said Robert (names of tenants given), by homage and fealty, and by service of rendering 13*s* yearly, and 30*s* yearly for the ward of the castle of Alnewike, as is more fully contained in the extent taken after the death of the said Robert [see no.3].

6. Eleanor, widow of Robert de Umfraville, Earl of Angus. Tuesday after (?) St Mary Magdalene, 42 Edward III (18 July 1363); vol.XII, no.250; reproduced in Hodgson 1827, 110.

At the time of her death, the lands Eleanor held in dower in respect of her late first husband, Robert, included the following in Redesdale:

A pasture, called Erleside, in Redesdale, the rent of which was 10*s*.

20 acres of wood, called Akenside, valued at 10*s*.

Four messuages and four bovates (48 acres) of (arable) land at the W...de (Whisker Shield?), by Ellesden, in the hands of tenants at will rendering £2 yearly, held in dower.

100 acres of wood at Kynghope (Grasslees Burn), valued at £1.

Two messuages and two bovates (24 acres) of (arable) land at Little Wodburne, in the hands of tenants at will rendering 10*s* yearly.

One messuage and one bovate (12 acres) of (arable) land in Wolrig, by Herbotill, worth 5*s*.

A pasture in Redesdale, called Fulhope, worth £1.

A parcel of land called Greneson Heseles, held in dower and worth 10*s*.

Two parts of the pasture of the Smalburne, in Redesdale worth 3*s* 4*d*.

A yearly free rent of 10*s* plus 1lb pepper from the Ladyland in Hatherwyk.

An annual free rent of 5*s* from lands formerly belonging to Gilbert de Kayrewyk, in Ellesden.

An annual free rent of 2*s* from lands formerly belonging to Nicholas Don, in Ellesden.

An annual free rent of 13*d* from lands formerly belonging to Thomas Shert, in Lynsheles.

7. Maud, wife of Henry Earl of Northumberland. 10 March, 22 Richard II (1398); XVII; no.1246. She died seised of various places, including:

A third part of the lordship of Redesdale. Oterburn. The manor with divers places, shielings (scalinga) and wastes, to wit, Over Redesheved, Erlsyde, Shetilhop and lands called the Abbotesland of Jedworth in Troughwen, Baxsterland, Boversland, Garareschele, Smalbourne, Byschopland, Kirkestilland (Birkhill?), Lytell Wodbourne, Hatherwyk, Oderdesfeld, Grenesonhesils, Over Monkryge, Wellestrother, Nether Monkryge, Farneclogh, Middilwanges, Chapyngtonfeld, Hirnhousfeld, Mekilhyresfeld, Shotilhough, Shotilhough park and 21*s* 2*d* rent from Herbotle, 3lb pepper, 3lb cummin, 32*s* 4½*d* from £4 17*s* 1½*d* from divers free tenants of the manor.

All the lands etc in Redesdale are held of the king in chief by knight's service.

Shirmondesden in Cokdale. A third part of the demesne lands of the manor, to wit, 100 acres land (i.e. ploughland) towards the east and 26½ acres meadow, a third part of the park and of 2 water-mills,

3*s* 11½*d* rent of assize, 2*s* 4*d* castle ward, 1½lb pepper and 1lb cummin from three husbandlands in Alwenton, three cottages there and a third part of a pasture called Butterland, held of Henry earl of Northumberland by knight's service. Fawdon. A third part of the town held of Henry earl of Northumberland in socage, for 3*s* 4*d* yearly.

8. Robert Tailbois, Knight. 30 May, 10 Henry VII (1495), Cal. IPM Hen VII, vol.I; no.971. Properties inherited by George Tailboys from his father include:

The castle of Herbotell, which is worth nothing yearly.

Also details the Manor of Oterburn, also worth nothing, and various pastures, messuages, tofts, Ellesdon church, Halistane abbey, etc, most of which are worth little or nothing due to their situation in the Marches.

'All the lands and tenements which are within the bounds of the said castle and manor are said to be and are within the liberty of Riddisdale'.

Various obligations are also inherited, including:
(5) a fair at Herbotell within Ridesdale on the feast of the Nativity of the Blessed Virgin Yearly, with court of piepowder, and (6) a market on Tuesdays weekly there...

The summer grounds comprise:

Redeshed	200 acres
Lomesden	500 acres
le Rampeshop (Ramshope)	500 acres
Spythop	1,000 acres
Cotenshop	1,000 acres
Akynsyd	300 acres
Byrdhop	2,000 acres
Thillez (Sills Burn)	2,000 acres
Kellyburn	5,000 acres
Gylsyde (Earlside)	300 acres
Chetelhop & Baythamhop	5,000 acres
Redles, Wyllyward (Wilkwood) & Wharlemore (i.e. Thirl Moor?)	6,000 acres
Dulez (Dudlees)	500 acres

all of which pastures are in the march of Scotland and are worth clear yearly 20*s*.

9. 1604 Border Survey and 1618 Redesdale Rental.
For comparison, the 1604 survey of Debateable and Border lands and the 1618 Redesdale Rental list the following 'high lands called summer grounds' or 'Ellsden Sheylding grounds consisting of 16 parts' [see opposite; variant spellings are given in brackets; modern spelling in italics]:

1604 Survey, 83, 104,

Summer or Sheyding ground	Rent	1618 Rental, 333–7	Rent	Principal Tenants
Caverleye (Caverlee, i.e *Collierlee*)	1*s*	–		Dunns
Coomesden	1*s*	Batenhope & Comesden	2*s*	Reads
Whitleie (Whitlie)	1*s*	Whitlee & Reedshawe	1*s*	Reads
Lounsden (Lumsden)	5*s*	Lunsden	5*s*	Reads
Ravenshoulme (Ramshope)	5*s*	Rameshope	5*s*	Fosters
Catlope (Shatloape)	5*s*	Chetelhope	5*s*	Brownes
Cat Clough (Cat Cloughe)	3*s* 4*d*	Catclewghe	3*s* 4*d*	Halls; Reads; Hedleys
Earle Side	10*s*	Earlsyde	10*s*	Halls
Spiddopp Haughe (Spitop Haugh)	7*s*	Spithope & Burnies (i.e. *Byrness*)	7*s*	Halls
Blakeupp Borne Haugh (Blackburne Haugh)	3*s*	Blackburne Haughe	3*s*	Hedleys; Reads
Dead Wood	3*s* 4*d*	Deedwood	3*s*	Hedleys
Roukin (Rookin)	4*s*	Rooken	4*s*	Fletchers; Coxons
Ikenside & Sevensikes (Ekinside& Sevensides)	6*s* 4*d*	Akenside, Cragg Shields	6*s* 4*d*	Potts, Bentes & Seavin Sykes
Cottens Hope (High & Lowe Cottensop)	10*s*	Cottenshope Head	3*s* 4*d*	Halls; Spores
Middle Quarter	3*s* 4*d*	" "		
Hollingburne Foot	3*s* 4*d*	" "		
The Phillippe (Phillipe, i.e. *Fulhope*?)	2*s*	Filhaupe (*Fee Farm*)	1*s*	William Wanles
Parker Side & Windie Haughe	3*s* 4*d*			
Dunhope Borne	3*s* 4*d*			
Soppeth	3*s* 4*d*	Soppothaughe	3*s* 4*d*	Tenants of Harbottle

NOTES

1 Calendar of Inquisitions Post Mortem and other analagous documents preserved in the PRO, covering the reigns of Henry III to Henry VII, (HMSO, London, 1898–).

APPENDIX 2
The Newminster Charters relating to Kidland

These documents have been extracted from Newminster Abbey's chartulary (NC 73–81; cf.NCH XV (1940), 449–50). The boundaries of the various grants given below are simply those considered most likely. Many of the names given in the charters cannot be firmly identified with modern features and toponyms, so other interpretations are possible.

1181

Odinel de Umfraville II leased to Newminster Abbey the grazing in his forest of Alwent and Kidland 'with all its hills and valleys', for a term of twenty-nine years, for which the monks payed 220 marks to Odinel, 3 marks to his wife, Alice, and 5 marks to his eldest son, Robert (NC 73–4). The monks' rights were tightly circumscribed. They had no power to lease grazing rights themselves. They could take what wanted from forest by order of the lord's foresters, but their dogs were to have one foot cut off to prevent them chasing the lord's game.

Bounder 1 – by the boundary of Bitlesden [Biddlestone township] as far as the boundary of Clenil [Clennell township], and thence by stream [*rivulum*] of Kidland [Kidlandlee Dean] southward as far as the great road [*magnam viam*] of Ernespeth [Yarnspeth stretch of Clennell Street], and by that road as far as the river/burn [*rivum*] of Ernespeth [West Burn?], and by that burn to its very source, and eastward to the boundary of William de Vesci [Baron of Alnwick – i.e. the boundary of his manor of Alnham], and so as far as the aforesaid boundary of Bitlesden.

1184

Robert de Umfraville confirmed the lease for 40 marks, following the death of Odinel [also confirmed by Richard and Gilbert, Robert's brothers] (NC 74).

Pre-1195

William de Umfraville – a third brother – gave the abbey his land on the Cheviot moor called Witetowes (NC 75):

Bounder 2 – from the stream [Well Clough?] nearer the Hangande-scauhe [Yarnspeth Law?] towards the north just as that same stream falls into the Osweiburne [Usway Burn], and thus directly west as far as the cross which the aforesaid monks set up in the sight of my knights [*per visum militum meorum*] there; and from there across to the nearest stream bed from the southern part of Hetherdes Rode [Ward Law?], from there straight on beyond Hardrode as far as the great quarry [*ad petariam magnam*] lying on the slope and from that slope between the 'rastres of Scrothope' [Shorthope], and there by that Gruin [?] as far as the river bank of Rohope [Rowhope] and so in crossing just at the point the stream of Elyn [Wardlaw Burn or perhaps

Trows Burn?] flows into the aforesaid river of Rohope and by that same stream of Elyn as far as the road of Hinclesheued [Clennell Street approaching the Border], and by that same road up to Wyndihege [Windy Gyle], and by Wyndihege as much as I have there [i.e along the Scottish Border] as far as the source of the Osweiburne and by that same river as far as the road of Hernespeth [Yarnspeth – Clennell Street] and by that same road as far as the first-named stream closer to Hangandescawe.

1195/1216

Richard de Umfraville gave Kidland and Alwenthopes to Newminster (NC 76). This represents the same area as covered by Odinell's lease:

Bounder 3 – from the cross which I made the aforesaid monks set as a boundary at the head of Halrehopeburne [Allerhope Burn] down that same Halrehope burne southwards into the Alewent [Alwin], as far as the point where Kidlandburne [Kidlandlee Dean] flows into the Alewent, and so westwards up that same Kidlandburne as far as the ditch (*fossatum*) which the monks made as boundary between themselves and Thomas of Clenill, and so by that ditch as far 'in Redepeth' onto the great road of Ernespeth [Yarnspeth – Clennell Street], and so by that same road of Ernespeth as far as the river of Ernespeth [West Burn?], and so by the river itself as far as the head itself of the river of Ernespeth [Yarnspeth Law?], and so eastwards to the boundaries of Eustace de Vesci [Baron of Alnwick], and by those same boundaries as far as Cousthotelau [Cushat Law] and so as far as Steng [Sting Head], and so midway between Holhopcriwes [Wholehope Hill?] and Blakedenhed [Black Butt?], and so across Frodesmor [Wether Cairn/Wholehope Hill] as far as the afrorenamed cross at Halrehopeheued.

1195/1226

Richard de Umfraville granted the abbey Scorthope, Fastside and Alribarns (NC 76):

Bounder 4 – from that spot where the near stream bed [Murder Cleugh?] from the southern part of Hetheredrode [Ward Law?] flows into Heppdenburne [Hepden Burn/Barrow Burn], and so descending by the Hepdenburne as far as that place where the streambed from middle Alribarnclou [Barrow Cleugh?] falls into Hepdenburne, and thus ascending by the same clough as far as the cross which I caused to be set up in Hardrode [Barrow Law?] on the boundary between between the aforesaid monks and Henry the crossbowman (*balistarius*) and so towards the south as far as the cross placed above the Swire of Fastside [?], and so southwards by crosses as far as the Koket, where the cross is placed above the bank, and so ascending by the Koket as far as Ruhopeburne [Rowhope Burn] and so up the Ruhopeburne as far as that point where the stream of Slyn [Wardlaw Burn/Trows Burn?] flows into the aforesaid Ruhopeburne, and thence eastwards by the boundaries of Ruhoppe to the aforesaid nearer streambed from the southern part of Hetherederode.

Pre-1226

Richard de Umfraville grants to the abbey all the land in Hepden [mod. Barrowburn] which was formerly held by Henry the crossbowman (NC 77), and which Richard had bought from Henry (NC 77–78):

Bounder 5 – from that place where the stream of Hepden flows into the Koket [Barrowburn] up as far as the most northerly Altriclou [Barrow Cleugh?] and from there across as far as Hardrode [Barrow Law?] and thence as far as the saddle beneath the Cundos [?] and from there descending by the hanging willows on Fastesyde [?] as far as the Koket.

Post-1226

Henry the crossbowman (*balistarius*) confirmed grant by Gilbert de Umfraville I of all land in

Hepden which Henry had sold to his former lord Richard de Umfraville for 54 marks – the sum was actually paid by the monastery – and which Richard had transferred to Newminster (NC 77-78).

1226/44

Gilbert de Umfraville I gave Turfhill or Tursill – the hill now called Shillhope Law – to Newminster (NC 55, 66, 78; cf. NCH XV (1940), 437):

Bounder 6 – By the stream of Hepden [mod. Hepden Burn/Barrow Burn] northwards as far across as Wndinfald [?], and so from Wndinfald across by the boundary of Fairhaluh [Fairhaugh township] to the Oswaiburne [Usway Burn] and so by the Oswaiburne to the shieling/lodge (*logia*) formerly belonging to William Bataille, now to John of Letelwell [Batailshiel], and thence by the Thestirclou [Lee Cleugh?] southwards to Koket [Coquet] and so by the Coket ascending to Hepdenburne mouth.

1226/44

Gilbert de Umfraville I also granted the monastery a licence to build a fulling mill with associated mill-pond (*stagnum*) on his land on the south side of the Coquet at Hepden [Barrowburn], between Hepden Burn mouth and Rowhope burn – *licenciam faciendi et firmandi stagnum molendini sui fullonici apud Hepden super terram meum ex australi parte de Coket, inter Hepdenburnemuth et Ruthopeburn* (NC 78).

Gilbert de Umfraville I and wife, Theophania, quitclaimed hunting rights on Cheviot and Coquetdale moors, which previous grants had retained, for sake of his father's and his ancestor's souls. Henceforth it was not lawful for anyone except the monks to hunt wolves and foxes on this land (NC 79).

1270

Gilbert de Umfraville II confirmed all his predecessors' charters and remitted 18 marks/annum rent which monks had paid. Since his accession the monks had paid a total of £160 in rent to Gilbert (NC 79–80).

Late twelfth century?

Monks entered into agreement with neighbouring lords over the return of straying horses (Robert de Muschamp) and boundary lines (Geoffrey de Lucy) (NC 80).

1233

The abbey made an agreement with Thomas, rector of Alwinton, over payment of tithes from Upper Kidland [mod. Kidlandlee], Holehope [Wholehope], Apetreley, Elfenseth, Whiteburne [White Burn], Ruhope [Rowhope] and their members Hernispeth [mod. Yarnspeth], Heppeden [mod. Barrowburn] and Turfhil [Shillhope Law] (NC 81).

(Various dates)

Newminster obtained grants of way-leave for their servants, flocks and herds on road to Kidland from all neighbouring landowners (NC, passim; NCH XV (1940), 450).

APPENDIX 3
NORTHUMBERLAND FAIRS

TABLE 1: FAIRS IN NORTHUMBERLAND IN 1794[1]

May

4th, Wooler – for a few cattle, sheep, horses, hiring servants etc.
10th, Allendale – for cattle.
12th, Alnwick – a large show of both fat and lean cattle, hiring servants etc.
14th, Haltwhistle – for cattle, chiefly cows for grazing.

June

Tuesday before Whitsuntide, Belford – a few cattle and sheep.
Wednesday before Whitsuntide, Morpeth – for cattle, sheep etc.
Whitsun Eve, Stagshaw Bank (near Corbridge) – for cattle, sheep, horses etc.
Whitsun Tuesday, Whitsun Bank (near Wooler) – a large fair for cattle, horses and great numbers of sheep, principally long-woolled hogs and ewes and lambs, and a hiring for servants.
Friday in Trinity week, Berwick – for a few lean and fat cattle.

July

4th, Stagshaw Bank (near Corbridge) – This is one of the largest sheep fairs in the north of England at which above 100,000 sheep are shown; principally of the black-faced heath sheep, which mostly come from south-west Scotland. There are also great numbers of cattle, horses, and swine.
Wednesday before the 22nd, Morpeth – for fat cattle, sheep etc.
Last Monday, Alnwick – fat and lean cattle.

August

5th, Hexham – cattle, horses and sheep, chiefly lambs, both of the Cheviot and heath kind; from the vicinity of Langholm, in Scotland.
12th, Newcastle – holds nine days for horses; and for fat and lean cattle, on the last or 12th.
23rd, Belford – a few cattle and sheep.
24th, Whittingham – for fat and lean cattle, and a few horses. The best show of fat cattle of any fair in the county.
26th, Elsdon – a few cattle.

September

Saturday after the 15th, Bellingham – a few cattle, chiefly small cows.
19th, Harbottle – for a few cattle, mostly steers and heifers.
27th, St Ninians (near Wooler) – a very large show of sheep and cattle, with a few horses. The sheep are mostly draught or cast ewes, and shearling wethers.

October
First Tuesday, Alnwick – for fat and lean cattle.
2nd, Rothbury – for cattle, mostly steers and heifers.
17th, Wooler – for very great numbers of sheep, of the Cheviot and long-woolled kinds: a few cattle and horses.
29th, Newcastle – for horses, cattle, and swine.

This is one of the largest fairs in the north of England. The horse fair begins nine or ten days before the 29th, and continues every day in the town, where great numbers of remarkably fine horses for the field, the road, and the carriage, are sold daily. The abundant choice of every kind brings great numbers of dealers from London and various other distant places: its celebrity has increased very much of late years, and we believe it may be justly classed among the first horse fairs in the kingdom.

The show of cattle is also very great, not only for the breed of the country, but also for large droves of kyloes (Scotch cattle), which are purposely driven from the Highlands to sell at this fair. The fair on the 29th is held on the town moor, and is called the Cow-hill fair.

November
1st, Rothbury – for young cattle.
8th, Hexham – cattle.
14th, Allendale – mostly small cows.
22nd, Newcastle – fat cattle, chiefly cows. This fair is held in the town, and is called the Stones fair.
22nd, Haltwhistle – a few fat cows, and lean cattle for wintering.

TABLE 2: FAIRS IN NORTHUMBERLAND IN 1841[2]

March
25th, Hexham.
26th, Newcastle.
27th, Morpeth.

April
26th, Ovingham.
2nd Thursday, Stamfordham.
Last Friday, North Shields.
Last Friday, Allendale.
Friday in Easter week, Rothbury.

May
4th, Wooler.
12th, Alnwick.
14th, Haltwhistle.
First Monday, Felton.
Third Thursday after 1st, Warkworth,
Third Tuesday, Norham, Weetwood Bank.
Wednesday before Holy Thursday and two following days, Morpeth.
Tuesday before Whitsunday, Belford.
Whitsun eve, Stagshaw Bank.
Whit Monday, Rothbury.

June
Third Tuesday, Norham.
Trinity Monday, Rothbury.
Friday in Trinity week, Berwick.

July
2nd, Belford, Hexham (wool fair).
4th, Stagshaw Bank.
8th, Harbottle.
First Saturday after the 5th, Alnwick, wool fair.
Second Tuesday, Long Framlington.
Wednesday before 22nd, Morpeth.
Last Monday, Alnwick.

August
5th, Stagshaw Bank, lamb fair.
6th, Hexham.
12th, Newcastle.
14th, Stamfordham.
22nd, Allendale.
23rd, Belford.
24th, Blanchland, Whittingham.
26th, Elsdon.
Thursday nearest 18th, Warkworth.
Wednesday before 26th, Berwick.

September
4th, Whittingham.
19th, Harbottle.
29th, St. Ninian's.
Saturday after 15th, Bellingham.

October
2nd, Rothbury.
17th, Wooler.
24th, Stagshaw Bank.
25th, Morpeth, Longframlington.
26th, Ovingham.
28th, Newcastle.
First Tuesday, Alnwick.
Third Thursday, Norham.
Thursday before 23rd, Warkworth.
Friday after 29th, Allendale.

November
1st, Rothbury.
9th, Hexham.
22nd, Newcastle, Haltwhistle.
First Monday, Felton.
First Friday, North Shields.
Thursday before 23rd, Warkworth.

December
First Wednesday, Berwick.
Christmas Eve (but if Christmas day falls on a Monday, then on the Saturday before), Alnwick.

Table 3: Market Days in Northumberland in 1960[3]

The following are the regular market days in the county:
Monday – Alnwick and Wooler (alternate Mondays).
Tuesday – Hexham and Wooler.
Wednesday – Morpeth and Scots Gap (fatstock).
Thursday – Acklington, Rothbury, Bellingham and Belford.
Friday – Alnwick and Berwick.
Saturday – Berwick Corn Exchange.

Special livestock sales are held at various times in the year, but mention may be made of those for lambs held from July to September, for ewes in September and October, and for store cattle in October and November.

NOTES
1 From Bailey & Culley 1805, 171-74.
2 T. and J. Hodgson 1840, 5-27.
3 Pawson 1961, 164.

APPENDIX 4

Selected Stock Returns for Five Northumberland Parishes

Parochial Returns 1870

	1	2	3	4	5	6	7	8	9
A	139	106	32	1204	249	377	482	38,158	18,952
E	95	46	42	2093	405	611	753	36,474	17,285
F	27	22	3	398	118	144	131	24,454	11,406
G	21	17	4	290	96	65	120	8,138	4,895
T	26	14	12	434	110	71	157	8,757	4,216

Parochial Returns 1891

	1	2	3	4	5	6	7	8	9
A	92	N/A	N/A	1,495	354	305	425	38,059	19,488
E	129	N/A	N/A	2,667	560	614	768	42,633	23,093
F	37	N/A	N/A	617	157	147	211	24,228	13,520
G	28	N/A	N/A	471	112	79	196	8,099	4,920
T	26	N/A	N/A	441	105	81	143	9,705	9,705

Parochial Returns 1911

	1	2	3	4	5	6	7	8	9
A	84	51	33	2,027	286	371	654	37,701	25,838
E	115	54	61	2,635	505	627	745	43,020	30,239
F	31	18	13	887	266	162	220	23,761	15,340
G	28	19	9	478	160	53	253	8,200	5,446
T	25	13	12	557	106	61	216	9,652	6,895

Parochial Returns 1931

	1	2	3	4	5	6	7	8	9
A	79	43	36	1,782	350	387	759	34,009	21,168
E	125	71	55	2,719	650	622	951	41,613	26,122
F	30	21	9	751	265	97	287	20,618	10,541
G	24	17	7	410	167	60	211	8,300	5,040
T	25	16	9	602	145	60	177	9,438	6,363

Key to letters for parish names:
A – Alwinton;
E – Elsdon;
F – Falstone;
G – Greystead;
T – Thorneyburn.

Key to numbered columns:
1 – Number of returns from parish to Government survey.
2 – Number of returns from farms of less than 50 acres excluding mountain and heath land.
3 - Number of returns from farms of more than 50 acres excluding mountain and heath land.
4 – Number of acres of hay grown in parish.
5 – Number of cows and heifers of all ages in milk and in calf.
6 – Number of other cattle two years of age and above.
7 – Number of cattle under two years of age including calves.
8 – Number of sheep one year of age and above.
9 – Number of lambs under one year of age.

APPENDIX 5
THE ORAL HISTORY PROJECT – BACKGROUND INFORMATION

The oral history interviews were all conducted by Ian Roberts. Interviews were recorded with the following:

William Bolton, Fourstones
Laurence Dagg, North Tynedale
Mrs Margaret Davy, Thropton
Geoff Logan, Fenton Hill
Mr Iain Hedley, Overacres, Redesdale
James Johnson, Cambo
Hubert Robinson, Stagshaw
W. (Bill) Robson, Redesdale
W.A. (Willie) Robson, North Tynedale
Mr Tommy Simpson, West Woodburn

The following provided oral information which was noted:
Mrs D. Bell, North Tynedale
W. Brown, Langleeford
A. Cowen, Scots Gap
L.I. Hedley, Redesdale
A.D. McCracken, North Tynedale
Mrs M. Robinson, West Cocklaw Farm
G.W. M. Sewell, Stannington
R.M. Tindall, Fourstones
Mrs M. Walton, Elsdon

The interviews are lodged with, and can be consulted through, the Northumberland National Park Authority, the Heritage Centre in Bellingham and at the Northumberland County Record Collections at Woodhorn.

APPENDIX 6
Source Material in the Northumberland County Record Office

The selection of documentary material listed below is arranged according to the subject area in the card index catalogue. All material is held at Melton Park, Gosforth, unless otherwise specified.

Droving

ZAN M16/B11, pp47–9, *Memories of a Morpeth Drover, c.*1880s.

EP 46/85, Alston Moor Drift Roll, 1597 (delineating a drift road to the fells). (Held at The Kylins, Morpeth.)

Markets and Fairs

ZHE 34/1d, Misc. info on Alnwick, Morpeth, Newcastle and Stagshaw Bank Fairs, including tolls.

ZMD 115, Stagshaw Bank fair purchases, 1298, Photostat of Duchy of Lancaster MSS in the PRO (transcript in Archaeologia Aeliana 3rd ser. 2, 1–9).

NRO 4804/2, Engraving of Morpeth Market Place, 1836.

ZHE 43/15, Plan of Bellingham Fairground, 1836.

NRO 2114, Instructions for accounting for tolls and tollage at Corbridge and Stagshaw Bank Fairs, 1806.

NRO, Proclamation of Belligham Fair, nineteenth century.

ZSI/39, Minute Book with information on fairs, 1782–99.

ZAD 16, Haltwhistle Market, 1855.

NRO 2815, Notice regarding Haltwhistle and Stagshaw Bank Fairs, 1785. The date of Haltwhistle Fair was to be altered from 14 May to 12 May for this year only to avoid a clash with the larger Stagshaw Bank Fair.

ZAD 1, Haltwhistle Market and Fair. eighteenth- and nineteenth-century records of the market; and records of the fair between 1672 and the nineteenth century, including a proclamation, regulations and tolls.

NRO 306/1, Hexham Goods Station Register, 1837–39.

ZBU B5/8/23, Tabulated Calendar of Fairs for horses, black cattle and sheep within reasonable range of Ewart in north Northumberland, extending from St Boswells (Roxburghshire) to Stockton (Co. Durham) (undated, but can be assigned to the late eighteenth or very early nineteenth century on the basis of internal evidence).

ZBU B6/4/11, Includes a calendar for Northumberland and the northern counties, giving dates of fairs etc., 1788.

Farming (selection only)

ZTR XII 2, Orders of the Manor Court of Netherwitton, re grazing and other farming matters, 1662–6, 1671, 1686.

ZMD 169/1-28, Papers and photographs, re agriculture and farms, 1707–*c.*1964.

NRO 752/1-2, Two pocket diaries of JCT (Tynedale), 1839, 1841, refer to farming.

NRO 851, Diary of farming Lilburn Grange Farm (West Lilburn), M.T. Harvey, 1842–3.

NRO 2803, Farm account books of the Robsons of Birtley, Kielder & Newton, and the Phillips of Flotterton, 1788–1930.

NRO 1706, An account of farming life in the early twentieth century around Wooler.

NRO 1992, Farming account books of the Stephenson family of Chollerton, North Tynedale and Redesdale, 1830–80.

NCRO 414/11a, Ridley of Park End Papers.

Bibliography

Published Documentary Sources

Agricultural Returns of Great Britain with abstract returns for the United Kingdom, British Possessions and Foreign Countries (London, 1884)

Anderson, J. (ed.), Calendar of the Laing Charters (Edinburgh, 1889)

Bain, J.A. (ed.), Calendar of Documents relating to Scotland, preserved in Her Majesty's Public Record Office, London, I: AD 1108–1272 (Edinburgh, 1881). (Cal. Doc. Scot.)

Bain, J.A. (ed.), Calendar of Letters and Papers relating to the affairs of the Borders of England and Scotland, 2 vols, preserved in Her Majesty's Public Record Office, London (HM General Register House, Edinburgh, 1894 & 1896). (CBP)

Calender of the Close Rolls, preserved in the Public Record Office, covering the period 1272–1509 (London, 1900–63) (Cal. Close R.)

Calendar of Inquisitions Post Mortem and other analogous documents, preserved in the Public Record Office. Multiple vols covering the reigns of Henry III – Henry VII (London, 1898--). (Cal IPM)

Calendar of State Papers, Domestic Series, preserved in the Public Record Office. Multiple vols with addenda covering the reigns of Edward VI – George III (London, 1856--). (CalSP)

Fowler, J.T. (ed.), *Chartularium Abbathiae de Novo Monasterio*, Ordinis Cisterciensis, fundatae anno mcxxxvii, Surtees Society 66, 1876 (Durham, London & Edinburgh, 1878)

Hartshorne, C.H. (ed.), *Iter of Wark, 1279*, Memoirs illustrative of the history and antiquities of Northumberland – Proceedings of the Archaeological Institute at Newcastle, 1852, Vol II, *Feudal and Military Antiquities of Northumberland and the Scottish Borders*, Appendix III, ix–LXviii (London, 1858)

Hodgson, J., *History of Northumberland*, Part 3, vols I, II & III: Containing Ancient Records and Historical Papers (Newcastle upon Tyne, 1820, 1828, 1835)

Hodgson, R.W and J. Hodsgon, (eds), 'A rental of the ancient principality of Redesdale 1618', copied from an original roll in the possession of William John Charleton, of Hesleyside, esq., AA1, 2 (1832), pp326–338

Innes, C. (ed.), Liber S. Marie de Calchou, 2 vols (Edinburgh, 1846)

Letters and Papers, Foreign and Domestic, of the reign of Henry VIII, preserved in the Public Record Office, 21 vols (London, 1862–1932)

Macdonald, A., Calendar of Deeds in the Laing Charters relating to Northumberland, AA4, 28, 105–31 (1950)

Maxwell Lyte, H.C. (ed.), *Liber Feodorum, The Book of Fees* (commonly called the *Testa de Nevill*), 2 vols, Part I: AD 1198–1242; Part II: AD 1242–1293 and Appendix, Public Record Office (London, 1920, 1923)

Nicolson, W. (ed.), Leges Marchiarum (London, 1747)

Sanderson, R.P. (ed.), Survey of the Debateable and Border Lands adjoining the Realm of Scotland and belonging to the Crown of England taken AD 1604 (Alnwick, 1891)

Stephens T. (ed.), The Register of Baptisms, Marriages and Burials solemnized in the Ancient Parish Church of Elsdon in the County of Northumberland from AD 1672 to AD 1812 Society of Antiquaries of Newcastle upon Tyne (Newcastle upon Tyne, 1912) (EPR)

Journal Abbreviations

AA1 *Archaeologia Aeliana*, First Series etc.

References

ADDISON, SIR WILLIAM, 1980, *The Old Roads of England*, London

BAILEY, J., and CULLEY, G., *General View of the Agriculture of the County of Northumberland*, 3rd edition, London, 1805

BAILEY, M., *The English Manor* c. *1200*-c. *1500*, Selected Sources translated and annotated, Manchester, 2002

BARROW, G.W. S., 'The Anglo-Scottish Border', *Northern History 1*, pp21–42, 1966

BARROW, G.W. S., 'Pre-feudal Scotland: shires and thanes', *The Kingdom of the Scots: Government, Church and Society from the Eleventh to the Fourteenth Century*, pp1–68, London, 1973

BATES, C.J., *The Border Holds of Northumberland*, AA2, 1891, 14

BONSER, K.J., *The Drover*, 1970

BRASSLEY, P.W., *The Agricultural Economy of Northumberland and Durham in the period 1640–1750*, 1985

BURNETT, J., *Plenty and Want*, 1979 (first published in 1966)

BUTLIN, R.A., 'Field systems of Northumberland and Durham', A.R.H. Baker and R.A. Butlin (eds), *Studies of Field Systems in the British Isles*, 1973

CAMDEN, W., in E. Gibson (ed.), *Britannia*, London, 1722

CATHCART KING, D.J., *Castellarium Anglicanum*, 2 vols, New York, 1983

CHARLTON, D.B., *Upper North Tynedale: A Northumbrian Valley and its People*, Northumbrian Water, Newcastle upon Tyne, 1987

CHARLTON, D.B., *Fifty Centuries of Peace and War: An Archaeological Survey of the Otterburn Training Area*, The Ministry of Defence Otterburn Training Area, 2nd edition, 1996

CHARLTON, D.B., and DAY, J.C., 'Upper Redesdale, Northumberland: An Archaeological Survey', in P.A.G. Clack and P.F. Gosling (eds) *Archaeology in the North*, pp228–242, 1976

CHARLTON, D.B. and DAY, J.C., 'Excavation and Field Survey in Upper Redesdale', *AA5* 6, pp61–86, 1978

CHARLTON, D.B., and DAY, J.C., 1979, 'Excavation and Field Survey in Upper Redesdale: Part II', *AA5* 7, pp207–233

CHARLTON, E., 'Notes on North Tynedale in 1279', *AA2* 3, pp147–157, 1859a

CHARLTON, E., 'The inquisition after the death of Adam de Charlton of Tyndale', *AA2* 3, pp261–262, 1859b

CLARK, B., 1973, 'Memories of Redewater', *Redewetter*, 1, p34

COCHRAN, L.E., *Scottish Trade with Ireland in the 18th Century*, Edinburgh, 1985

COGGINS, D., FAIRLESS, K.J. and BATEY, C., 'Simy Folds: An early medieval settlement site in Upper Teesdale', *Medieval Archaeology*, 27, pp1–26, 1983

COLLINS, E.J.T. (ed.), *The Agrarian History of England and Wales*, vol.VII: 1850–1914, Part II, Cambridge, 2000

COWPER, R.A.S., 'Northumbrian drove roads', *Journal of the University of Newcastle upon Tyne Agricultural Society*, 24, pp30–33, 1970–71

CROW J., *Housesteads*, Batsford, London, 1995a

DEVINE, T.M., *Clanship to Crofters' War*, 1993

DEVINE, T.M., *The Transformation of Rural Scotland* (2nd edition), 1999 (first published in 1994)

DIXON, D.D., *Whittingham Vale*, Newcastle upon Tyne, 1895

DIXON, D.D., *Upper Coquetdale*, Newcastle upon Tyne, 1903

DODGSHON, R.A., *Land and Society in Early Scotland*, Oxford, 1981

DONALDSON, G., Scotland, 'James V–James VII', *The Edinburgh History of Scotland*, vol.3, Edinburgh, 1978

FAULL, M., and WOODHOUSE, S. A., *West Yorkshire: An Archaaeological Survey to AD 1500*, 3 vols, Wakefield, 1981

FOREMAN, S., *Loaves and Fishes*, 1989

FORSTER, F.S., 'The snowball effect of Redewetter', *Redewetter*, 2, pp16–17, 1974

GATES, T.M., *The Hadrian's Wall Landscape from Chesters to Greenhead: An Air Photographic Survey*, unpublished report, Northumberland National Park, 1999

GATES, T.M., 'Flying on the frontier. Recent archaeological air photography in the Hadrian's Wall corridor', P. Frodsham (ed.) *Archaeology in Northumberland National Park*, CBA Research Report RR 136, Council for British Archaeology, York, 2004

GRADY, K., 'The Cattle and Meat Trades in Leeds, 1780–1900', in *Northern History*, vol. XXXVII, December, Leeds, 2000

GRAY, M., *The Highland Economy 1750–1850*, 1957

HAIGH, D., and SAVAGE, M., 'Sewingshields', *AA5*, 12, pp33–147, 1984

HALDANE, A.R.B., *The Drove Roads of Scotland*, Edinburgh, 3rd edition, 1971 (first published in 1952)

HANSON, T. W., 'Cattle ranches of Sowerbyshire', *Transactions of the Halifax Antiquarian Society*, pp50–5, 1949

HARBOTTLE, B., and NEWMAN, T.G., 'Excavation and Survey on the Starsley Burn, North Tynedale, 1972', *AA5*, 1, pp137–75, 1973

HARTSHORNE, C.H., 'Memoirs illustrative of the history and antiquities of Northumberland – Proceedings of the Archaeological Institute at Newcastle, 1852', *Feudal and Military Antiquities of Northumberland and the Scottish Borders*, vol.II, London, 1858

HEDLEY, W. P., 'The Medieval Forests of Northumberland', *AA4*, 28, pp96–104, 1950

HEY, D., *Yorkshire from AD 1000*, London and New York, 1986

HIGHAM, N., *The Northern Counties to AD 1000*, London and New York, 1986

HINDLE, B.P., *Roads, Tracks and their Interpretation*, Batsford, London, 1993

HODGSON, J., *History of Northumberland*, Part 3 vols I-III, containing ancient records and historical papers, Newcastle upon Tyne, 1820; 1828; 1835

HODGSON, J., *History of Northumberland*, Part 2, vol.I, containing the history of the franchise of Redesdale, and the Umfraville family; Also, of the parishes of Elsden, Newcastle upon Tyne, 1827

HODGSON, J., *History of Northumberland*, Part 2, vol.III, Newcastle upon Tyne, 1840

HODGSON, T. and J., *The Newcastle Memorandum Book and Register of the Northern Counties for 1841*, Newcastle upon Tyne, 1840
HODGSON, J.C., 1916, Notices of ruined towers, chapels, etc., *AA*3, 13, pp1–16
HOLDERNESS, B.A., *British Agriculture since 1945*, 1985
HONEYMAN, H.L., 'The Golden Pots', *AA*4, 4, pp90–103, 1927
HOPE DODDS, M. (ed.), *A History of Northumberland XV: The Parishes of Simonburn, Rothbury and Alwinton, with the Chapelry of Holystone and the Lordship of Kidland*, Newcastle upon Tyne and London, 1940
HOSKINS, W.G., *One Man's England*, London, 1978
HUNT C.J., *The Lead Miners of the Northern Pennines in the 18th and 19th centuries, Newcastle upon Tyne*, 1970, (1984 edition)
JOBEY, G., 'Some rectilinear farmsteads of the Roman period in Northumberland', *AA*4, 38, pp1–38, 1960
JOBEY, G., 'A note on scooped enclosures in Northumberland', *AA*4, 40, pp47–58, 1962
JOBEY, G., 'Enclosed stone-built settlements in north Northumberland', *AA*4, 42, 41-64, 1964
JOBEY, G., 'A Romano-British settlement at Tower Knowe, Wellhaugh, Northumberland', *AA*5 1, pp55–79, 1973
JOBEY, G., *A Field-Guide to Prehistoric Northumberland, Part 2*, Newcastle upon Tyne, 1974
JOBEY, G., 'Iron Age and later farmsteads on Belling Law, Northumberland', *AA*5 5, pp1–38, 1977
JOBEY, G., 'Iron Age and Romano-British settlements on Kennel Hall Knowe, North Tynedale, Northumberland, 1976', *AA*5, 6, pp1–28, 1978
JOBEY, G., 'The settlement at Doubstead and Romano-British settlement on the coastal plain between Tyne and Forth', *AA*5, 10, pp1–23, 1982
JOBEY, G., 'A note on some northern palisaded sites', A. Connor and D.V. Clarke (eds) *From the Stone Age to the Forty Five*, Edinburgh, pp197–205, 1983a
JOBEY, G., 'A settlement on Boggle Hill, Thorneyburn (NY 783862)', *AA*5, 12, pp241–242, 1984
JOLLIFFE, J.E.A., 'Northumbrian institutions', *The English Historical Review*, 41, pp1–42, 1926
JONES, G.R. J., Multiple estates and early settlement, Sawyer P. H. (ed.) *Medieval Settlement, Continuity and Change*, London, pp15–40, 1976
KAPELLE, W.E., *The Norman Conquest of the North: The Region and its Transformation, 1000–1135*, London, 1979
KING, A., 'Gauber High Pasture, Ribblehead – an interim report', R.A. Hall (ed.) *Viking Age York and the North*, CBA Research Report No.27, The Council for British Archaeology, London, pp21–25, 1978
LOMAS R., *County of Conflict: Northumberland from Conquest to Civil War*, East Linton, 1996
McCORD, N. and THOMPSON, R., *The Northern Counties from AD 1000*, Essex, 1988
McDONNELL, J., 'The role of transhumance in northern England', *Northern History* 24, pp1–17, 1988
McDONNELL, J., 'Upland Pennine hamlets', *Northern History*, 26, pp20–39, 1990
MACKENZIE, E., *A Historical and Descriptive View of the County of Northumberland*, Newcastle upon Tyne, 1811 (2nd edition, 1825)
MILLER, E., 'Farming in northern England during the twelfth and thirteenth centuries', *Northern History*, 11, pp1–16, 1976 for 1975
MINGAY, G.E. (ed.), *The Agrarian History of England and Wales vol. VI: 1750-1850*, Cambridge, 1989
MITCHELL, B.R. and DEANE, P., *Abstract of British Historical Statistics*, 1962
MOORE, M., *The Lands of the Scottish King in England: The Honour of Huntingdon, the Liberty of of Tyndale and the Honour of Penrith*, London, 1915
MOORE-COLYER, R., *Welsh Cattle Drovers*, revised 2nd edition, Ashbourne, 2002 (first published in 1975, University of Wales Press)
NCH IV, Hodgson, J.C. (ed.), *A History of Northumberland XI: Hexhamshire, Part II (Hexham,*

Whitley Chapel, Allendale and St John Lee) and the Parishes of Chollerton, Kirkheaton and Throckrington, Newcastle upon Tyne and London, 1897

NCH XI, Vickers, K.H. (ed.), *A History of Northumberland XI: The Parishes of Carham, Branxton, Kirknewton, Wooler and Ford*, Newcastle upon Tyne and London, 1922

NCH XV, Hope Dodds, M. (ed.), *A History of Northumberland XV: The Parishes of Simonburn, Rothbury and Alwinton, with the Chapelry of Holystone and the Lordship of Kidland*, Newcastle upon Tyne & London, 1940

NICOLSON W., *Leges Marchiarum*, London, 1747

NORTHUMBERLAND NATIONAL PARK, 'The Last Drove', *The Drovers' Post*, Issue 2,2, 2004

O'BRIEN C., 'The early medieval shires of Yeavering, Breamish and Bamburgh', *AA5* 30, pp53–73, 2002

PAWSON, H.C., *Cockle Park Farm*, Durham, 1960

PAWSON, H.C., *A Survey of the Agriculture of Northumberland*, 1961

PERREN, R., *The Meat Trade in Britain 1840–1914*, 1978

PEVSNER, N., GRUNDY, J., McCOMBIE G., RYDER, P., WELFARE, H., and LINSLEY S., *The Buildings of England: Northumberland*, reprinted 2nd edition, Yale University Press, London, 2001

PLACKETT, R.L., 'Roads and Tracks in the English Middle March, Part 1: from Roman Road to New Line', *Tyne and Tweed*, 51, pp45–62, 1977

PLACKETT, R.L., 'Roads and Tracks in the English Middle March, Part 2: Enclosure and coal roads', *Tyne and Tweed*, 52, pp2–20, 1988

PURVES, A., *A Shepherd Remembers*, East Linton, 2001

RAMM, H.G., McDOWELL, R.W., and MERCER, E., *Shielings and Bastles*, Royal Commission on Historical Monuments (England), London, 1970

ROBERTS, I.D., *Upland Farming in Northumberland 1850–1914*, unpublished PhD thesis, University of Newcastle upon Tyne, 1992

ROBERTS, I.D., and WEST, M., Bellingham, *North Tynedale and Redesdale*, Stroud, 1998

ROBSON, R., *The Rise and Fall of the English Highland Clans: Tudor Responses to a Medieval Problem*, Edinburgh, 1989

ROWE, D.J., 'The Culleys, Northumberland Farmers, 1767–1813, *The Agricultural History Review vol. 19*, Part II, 1971

ROWLAND, T.H., *Bygone Morpeth*, Sussex, 1989

RUSHWORTH, A., *High Rochester Fort: A Documentary Assessment of Post-Roman Occupation*, unpublished report, commissioned by The Northumberland National Park Authority, The Archaeological Practice, University of Newcastle upon Tyne, 1996

RUSHWORTH, A. and CARLTON, R.J., *Harbottle Castle: A Documentary Study*, unpublished report prepared for The Northumberland National Park Authority, The Archaeological Practice, University of Newcastle upon Tyne, 1998

SCOLA, R., 1992, Feeding the Victorian City – The Food Supply of Manchester 1770-1870.

SEWELL, G.W. M., *The North British Railway in Northumberland*, Devon, 1992

SIMMONDS, J. and BIDDLE, G., *The Oxford Companion to British Railway History*, Oxford, 1997

SIMPSON, F.G., (ed. SIMPSON, G), *Watermills and Military Works on Hadrian's Wall: Excavations in Northumberland, 1907–1913*, Kendal, 1976

SHEPHERD, M.E., *From Hellgill to Bridge End: aspects of economic and social change in the Upper Eden Valley, 1840–95*, Hatfield, 2003

SMAILES, A.E., *North England*, 1960

SLIGHT, H., 'Old drove roads and drovers', *Tyne and Tweed*, 52, pp38–47, 1997/1998

SLIGHT, H., *The Irish Influence*, 2000

STRACHAN, G.M., *...is that your Last Bid?*, Northumberland, 2002

THIRSK, J. (ed.), *The Agrarian History of England and Wales vol. IV: 1500–1640*, Cambridge, 1967

THIRSK, J. (ed.), *The Agrarian History of England and Wales vol. V: 1640–1750, Part i – regional farming systems*, Cambridge, 1984

THOMPSON, W., 'Cattle droving between England and Scotland', *The Journal of the British Archaeological Association*, n.s. 37, pp172–83, 1932

TOULSON, S., *The Drovers*, Shire Album 45, Princes Risborough, 1980

TROW-SMITH, R., *A History of British Livestock Husbandry 1700–1900*, 1959

TURNER, M.E., *After the Famine: Irish agriculture 1850–1914*, Cambridge, 1996

WATTS, S.J., 'Tenant-right in early 17th-century Northumberland', *Northern History* 6, pp64–87, 1971

WATTS, S.J., *From Border to Middle Shire, Northumberland 1586–1625*, Leicester, 1975

WELFORD, R., Alston manor paine roll, *AA2*, 8, pp264–71, 1912

WHETHAM, E.H., *The Agrarian History of England and Wales vol. VIII 1914–1939*, Cambridge, 1978

WILSON, K., and LEATHART, S., *The Kielder Forests. A Forestry Commission Guide*, Forestry Commission, 1982

WINCHESTER, A.J.L., Landscape and Society in Medieval Cumbria, Edinburgh, 1987

WINCHESTER, A.J.L., *The Harvest of the Hills: Rural Life in Northern England and the Scottish Borders, 1400–1700*, Edinburgh, 2000

WINNIFRITH, Sir J., *The Ministry of Agriculture, Fisheries and Food*, 1962

WOODSIDE, R. and CROW, J.G., *Hadrian's Wall: An Historic Landscape*, The National Trust, 1999

WRATHMELL, S., *Deserted and Shrunken Villages in Southern Northumberland from the Twelfth to the 20th Centuries*, unpublished PhD thesis, University of Cardiff, 1975

YOUNG, A., *Tour Through the North of England*, vol.II, London, 1770

Small-scale droving at Langleeford Hope, as portrayed by the artist Constance Mangone in the 1920s.